Electrical Forensics

Cover Picture: Antenna systems create solar radiation reflections and interference. They also create radio and microwave reflections and interference from other wireless transmission systems in the area. They short circuit the atmospheric layers that they pass through and may increase the rate of lightning strikes in the area if they are taller than the nearby surrounding structures.

Contents

Introduction

Electrical Forensics is developed out of the book "Toxic Electricity". Electrical Forensics presents the technical aspects that were discussed in Toxic Electricity for those who want to diagnose biologically toxic electromagnetic interference exposures. The field of electrical forensics is relatively new and is currently rapidly developing. Toxic Electricity is an expanded version of this book and has additional information in it regarding the biological effects, corporate pressures and political motives regarding the toxicity of the various electrical exposures.

The modern electrical system was invented by Nikola Tesla. While acknowledged as one of his greatest achievements, there is a side of Nikola Tesla that many people do not know. In the first half of his life he was a brilliant man. However, for the second half of his life he was widely acknowledged as being mentally ill. As such, we investigate the problems with the modern electrical system and how it can affect human health.

Electrical systems have been shown time and time again to increase the risk of human illness and disease. Mental illness is one of these diseases and it is not surprising to see the inventor of the alternating current (AC) electricity system develop it. What is surprising is that over one hundred years after the invention of AC electricity that the detrimental health effects of AC electricity are still in denial by many governments, corporations, utilities, and health and safety organizations.

Rather than acknowledge the health issues and develop research into the toxic effects of AC electricity, the opposite has happened. AC electricity health research is almost none existent and the development of the AC electrical power system is rampant around the world. Billions of dollars pour into the development of AC electricity annually in the USA alone.

"There is a cult of ignorance in the United States, and there has always been. The strain of anti-intellectualism has been a constant thread winding its way through our political and cultural life, nurtured by the false notion that democracy means

that "my ignorance is just as good as your knowledge." - Isaac Asimov

The electrical system has been changing since the days of Nikola Tesla. It is a system that has been significantly altered by the advent of the electronics industry. Electronic power generation and electronic devices are in the process of changing the way the electrical system works. Harmonics is a poorly understood aspect of electrical engineering and is a characteristic feature of electronics. Harmonics greatly increases the electromagnetic radiation emissions from the electrical system and my research is indicating that it causes biological damage and mutations.

If you own electronic products, then your home and work place may be filled with harmonic energy fields!

The effects of harmonic energy are added to by the development of wireless communications. Today, there are fields of energy in your environment that have never existed in the history of the human and we will investigate the impacts on human health. Did you know that there are human sickness "Hot Zones" around cell phone towers? If you are feeling tired, it may be the cell phone tower near your home that is interfering with your energy levels.

Electrical lighting products seem harmless, but may actually be inducing a myriad of illnesses into the human, and that includes cancer! The lighting products that are available today vary widely. We will review them and advise on the safest forms of these products for the human environment. This is particularly important if you have babies and developing children in your home.

A concerning development is that approximately 300,000 people in Sweden have registered as having Electromagnetic Hypersensitivity (EHS). EHS is caused by exposure to electrical, electronic and wireless products and Sweden is the only country that currently recognizes it as a health condition. This new epidemic in the population is predicted to keep on increasing as the use of technology gains momentum.

We will discuss the various aspects of the electrical system throughout the book and take a look at how the march of electronics into the electrical system has caused it to change. Electricity has been known to be a factor in many illnesses and diseases and we are now in an era of the modern electrical system that this rate and range of illness and disease is increasing.

Diagrams and photographs are used to illustrate many of the concepts of the book. If you are reading this in black and white, then descriptions of the pictures accompany them to explain the concepts. The concepts of the book should be accessible to most people through the visual explanations of subjects discussed in the book. Key points will be in bold font.

This book is aimed at the general public, the medical profession and the engineering profession. Extensive mathematics is avoided and the book presents the health concepts of the modern electrical system in a readable format to the general public.

This book contains the very latest research on the human environment. It should be viewed as the current ideas on the subject and the contents are subject to review by the scientific community.

The author and publisher accept no liability whatsoever for any of the contents and the book is published in the spirit of unrestricted access to the latest ideas and scientific theories in a changing world.

You should always consult with a licensed and certified medical professional on any aspects of health, illness or disease.

"It's a rare person who wants to hear what he doesn't want to hear."

Dick Cavett

Electricity

This quote is a good summary of what has happened in the last 100 years: *"All life on Earth has adapted to survive in an environment of weak, natural low-frequency electromagnetic fields (in addition to the Earth's static geomagnetic field). Natural low-frequency EM fields come from 2 main sources: the Sun and thunderstorm activity. But in the last one hundred years, man-made fields at much higher intensities and with a very different spectral distribution have altered this natural EM background in ways that aren't yet fully understood."* - *Unknown.*

We have all been born into an electrical society. Today, there is no place on Earth that is free of man-made electromagnetic radiation with the advent of ground based radio and microwave transmissions and later, Space satellites that are routinely beaming electromagnetic energy to the surface of the Earth.

I was born in 1970 in Europe and I have never experienced life free from electricity. Electricity has always been close by wherever I have traveled in life. Like most people, I never really thought about the detrimental health aspects of it. It is the same with light. The presence of electric lighting has just been a normal part of life for me. No one ever told me it was harmful.

It is also the same with the Sun. No one really educated me about it. My behavior around sunlight revolved around not getting burned and enjoying sunny days.

Sunlight, artificial light, and electricity are all part of the electromagnetic radiation spectrum and this is shown on the next page.

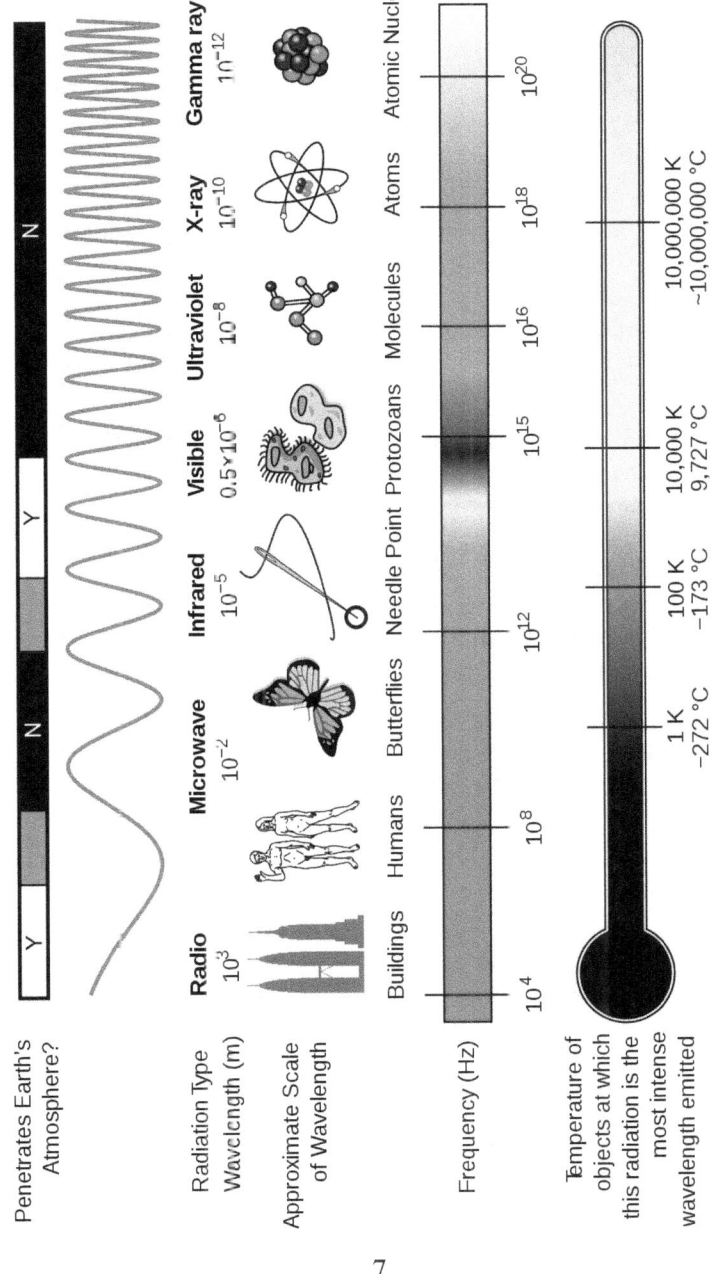

With the advent of radio and microwave communication technologies, our environment is now filled with electrical energy. You are now subjected to a wide range of man-made electromagnetic frequencies that were not there just a few decades ago. Indeed the man-made electromagnetic spectrum is increasing on a daily basis as the human addiction to modern technologies continues to gain momentum.

As the use of technology is increasing, we are witnessing the rise of childhood development problems, human illness, cancer, and the shortening of the human lifespan. They are all connected and it would be foolish to ignore this fact. Indeed, in 2011 the link between cancer and cellphones has become established. Cellphones in the future may be viewed the same way that asbestos and cigarettes are today.

Aside from the soup of man-made electromagnetic radiation that we now find ourselves immersed into, we have changed the atmospheric gas composition drastically over the last few hundred years of the Industrial Revolution. This is commonly referred to by many as the carbon levels rising in the atmosphere. They are currently at double the recorded levels in the historical records and there are no doubts that the use of energy to fuel the Industrial Revolution caused this to occur.

This is changing the natural electromagnetic environment that nature produces. Human actions are changing the energy fields that we are walking around in. The most unnatural electromagnetic environments are found in the home and workplace. It is quite possible that your home may actually be the most toxic place that you spend time in.

It is hard to believe that your home may be toxic to you, but it is true. While the toxicity of homes is extensive, we will stay in the area of electromagnetic radiation exposures in this book.

Homes started to get really toxic with electromagnetic radiation exposures when the building codes required an electrical socket to be installed every ten feet in the home. Take a look around you, you are never far from an electrical outlet.

That also means that you are never far from an AC electrical cable.

When you are in a room in your home, you have an AC voltage waveform riding on your body. I first noticed this effect when I was sixteen and working with oscilloscopes at the engineering training center. It looks just like the AC waveform on the electrical cables, just a lower voltage. This is shown in the next picture.

The human body has a voltage waveform riding on it when near to AC electricity. This waveform reduces the further away you get from the electrical system.

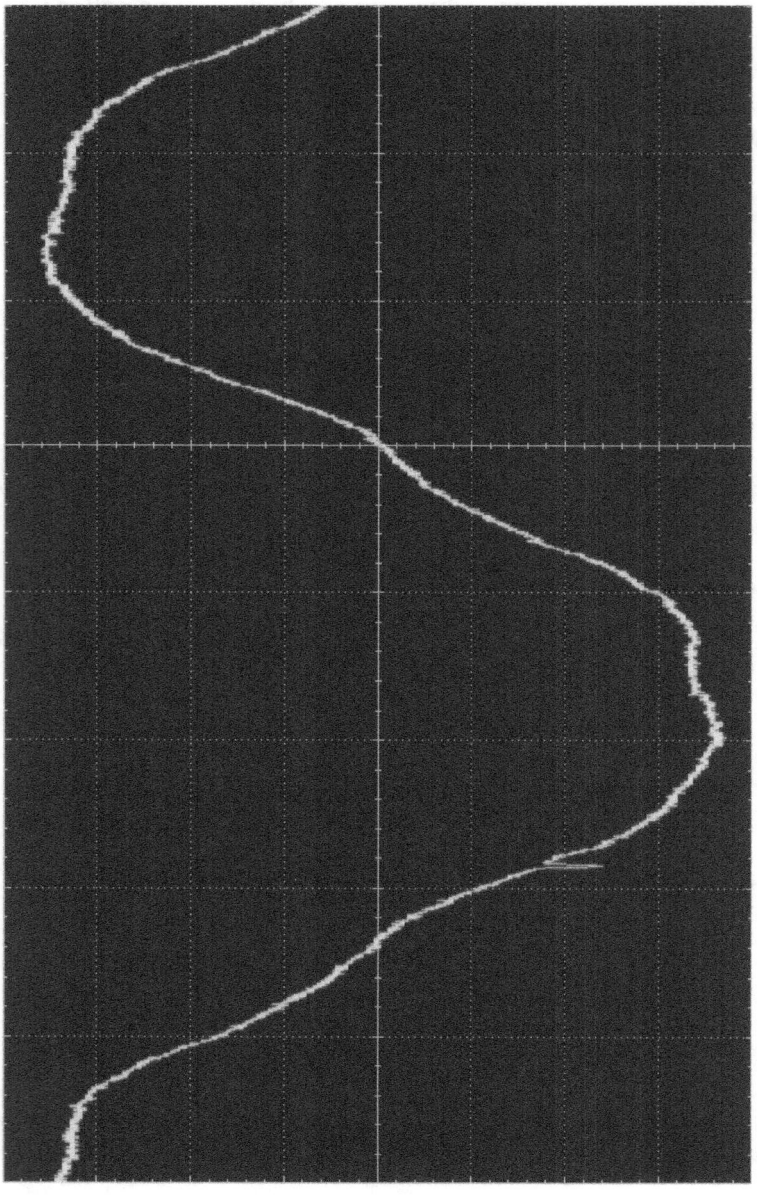

Everyone told me that it was harmless when I noticed it when I was sixteen. The problem is, it is not harmless!

To understand some of the things that the book talks about, we need to introduce some terms that are used in electrical engineering:

- Most electrical research has been done on pure 50Hz and 60Hz electrical sine waves. Hertz (Hz) is a measurement of frequency. It basically is the number of sine waves per second. The American electricity system is 60Hz and that means that there are 60 sine waves per second on the electrical cables.

- It is called an alternating current (AC) system due to the first half of the sine wave being positive polarity and the second half of the sine wave being negative. So the AC electrical current is constantly reversing many times per second, hence the term "alternating".

- Electrical current (I) on the system only flows when you plug something in or turn something on. This is called the "impedance" (load) and the current that flows on the system will be dependent on the impedance. Electrical current is analogous to the speed of a flowing river.

- The voltage (V) is the potential difference between two points. The higher the voltage is, the more energy you can send through an electrical cable. Contact with voltage is considered dangerous to a dry human at above 50 volts and may cause electrocution to occur. Electrical voltage is analogous to the width of a river.

- Watts (W) is a measurement of electrical energy and is obtained simply by multiplying the voltage with the current. It is analogous to the surface area of water flowing in a river.

- Impedance (Ohm) is used to control the flow of electrical current. It is analogous to the slope of the river. High impedance would be similar to a level river that has a very slow flow. Low impedance would be akin to a fast flowing river on a steep slope.

- An electrical short circuit would be comparable to the fastest flow of water that occurs. Short circuits are what blow the fuse or trip the circuit breaker. This is akin to a dam bursting and creating a very high flow of water in the river. This high flow is prevented by using fuses or circuit breakers that stop the flow a short time after the dam busts.

- Electromagnetic fields are produced by the various forms of electricity and they have two components to them. These are electric and magnetic fields. The electric field is a result of the voltage and the magnetic field is produce by the current flow. The higher the current and voltage are, the higher the electromagnetic fields become.

- Electromagnetic interference (EMI) is caused by the presence of man-made electromagnetic fields that expose the human to unnatural electromagnetic radiation that it has no genetic adaptation to.

There is a problem with performing research on a pure AC sine wave because that is not how the system works in real life. In the real world of AC electricity there are many higher frequencies of energy on the system. This has become especially apparent with the adoption of electronics because the loads on the system add frequencies of energy to the system.

This real world AC electricity is termed "Dirty Electricity" and it is very harmful to the human. Dirty electricity puts very large fields onto cables and may completely fill your home with electromagnetic radiation fields. The people who are most vulnerable to the effects of this are babies and young children. Attention Deficit Disorder (ADD) and Autism are on the rise and may well be connected to the effects of dirty electricity.

Samuel Milham, MD, MPH, has researched this area and has found from census data that many illnesses and diseases were born with the adoption of electricity into the home and workplace. His book "Dirty Electricity" extensively documents his findings in this area.

It is not just the electricity that is causing health problems in the general population, it is also the products that the electricity powers. You may be purchasing products that are making your family sick and not even realize it! Certain combinations of products when connected to your electrical system can make it start to radiate large electromagnetic fields into your environment.

The human mind and body cannot sense most forms of electromagnetic radiation. It shows up as general sickness that may move onto disease and perhaps premature death. As such, it is important to be aware of your electromagnetic environment.

We will start by looking into the most common application of electricity and that is light.

"Natural electromagnetic relationships form the basis of all cycles in nature. The construction and preservation of these relationships is only possible due to natural energy and their destruction takes place because of energy emanating from the technological unnatural energy"

Hertel

Electric Light

Electric light presents a hazard to human health. There are many sources of electric light and you should learn to recognize these sources. Electric light is almost everywhere in modern society:

- Artificial street lighting.
- Artificial home lighting.
- Artificial office lighting.
- Car headlights.
- Traffic lights.
- Signs.
- Emergency vehicle lights.
- Security lights.
- Televisions of every type.
- Computer monitors of every type.

So what may electric light be shown to do in the future? In the future the following conditions may be proven to be related to electric light:

- Cancer.
- Depression.
- Heart attacks.
- Circulation issues.
- Diabetes.
- Brain and nerve issues.
- Disruption of circadian rhythm.
- General aches and pains.

- Aggression.
- Psychiatric problems.
- Gender changing.
- Triggering of the mating cycle.
- Increased fertility.
- Conception issues.
- Sexual dysfunction.
- Almost any of the current medical problems in society may be related to electric light.

Dr. John Nash Ott was the leading researcher in this field and he had extensively proven that he could induce cancer, brain disease, sleep problems, aggression, and gender changing into plants and animals by the end of the 1980's. He did this simply by exposing them to electrical lighting products!

The problems with the particular types of electric light are as follows:

- Artificial light:
  - Artificial lighting is not full spectrum daylight and may cause illness in the human body.
- Office lighting:
  - This tends to be florescent lighting and is produced by just a few colors of light. It has a very spiked spectrum which does not occur in nature. The electronics that control them may emit electromagnetic interference (EMI).
- TV and computer monitors:
  - These tend to produce their light by mixing red, green and blue colors and it is an unusual spectrum which does not occur in nature. The light is similar to florescent lights. The electronics that control them may emit electromagnetic interference (EMI).

- Street lights:

  ○ Street lights are predominantly gas discharge lighting and this is one of the most toxic forms of lighting to the human mind and body. The light tends to be monochromatic and they have problems with emitting electromagnetic interference (EMI).

- Neon signs:

  ○ These tend to have similar problems as streetlights.

You should be careful when choosing a home to live in and pay close attention to the location of streetlights. Streetlights can emit large amounts of electromagnetic radiation, especially so when they switch on and also when they start to fail. The light also tends to be monochromatic or have a spiked spectrum of light and this type of light was shown by Dr. John Nash Ott to be harmful to the human mind and body. Indeed, I have noticed a trend in people who have died prematurely young and the presence of streetlights outside of their properties.

Regarding the toxic effects of lighting, I found during a Dieffenbachia plant growth experiment in my home that I started to get ill with fatigue, headaches, and insomnia. The experiment was performed by growing plants under the following light sources: Light emitting diode (LED), compact florescent (CFL), and a high pressure sodium street light (SOX).

After two weeks I decided to discontinue the experiment and within a day I had noticed withdrawal symptoms showing up that cleared up within the space of three days. This comprised of aches and pains in my feet, legs, chest, intestines, and head. On the second day of withdrawal a large headache appeared that would not respond to medication and this lasted for two days. There were no doubts that this combination of products was the cause of the problems.

I had very little exposure to the light as they were in rooms that had their doors closed. Most of the time I was generally between 30 to 60 feet away from the products. The products were switched on at 07:00 and turned off at 19:00 daily by automatic timers. I would check the experiment in the morning to ensure that the lights had turned on and in the evening to ensure that the lights had turned off.

My conclusion is that extended exposure to the electromagnetic radiation that this combination of lighting products produced was sufficient to produce depression symptoms into the human.

The streetlight exposed plant died several months later. The CFL and LED plants went on to show strange stunted growth patterns with very small glossy dark green leaves.

The diagrams on the following pages show the various electric lighting effects. Electromagnetic interference, harmonics and stray voltage/current/frequency will be looked into later in the book.

Streetlight Emissions

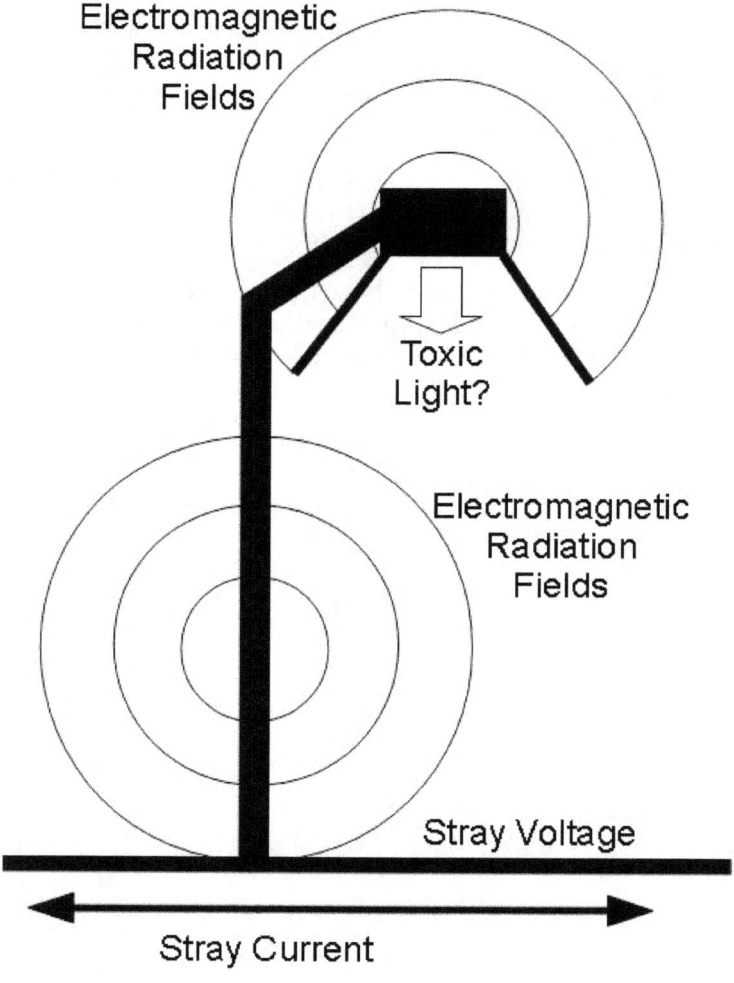

Three light bulbs are shown. At the top is the high pressure sodium light (SOX), the middle shows the compact florescent light (CFL), and the bottom shows the light emitting diode (LED) light.

This is the current waveform for the three products combined.
Note the distortion in the sine wave.

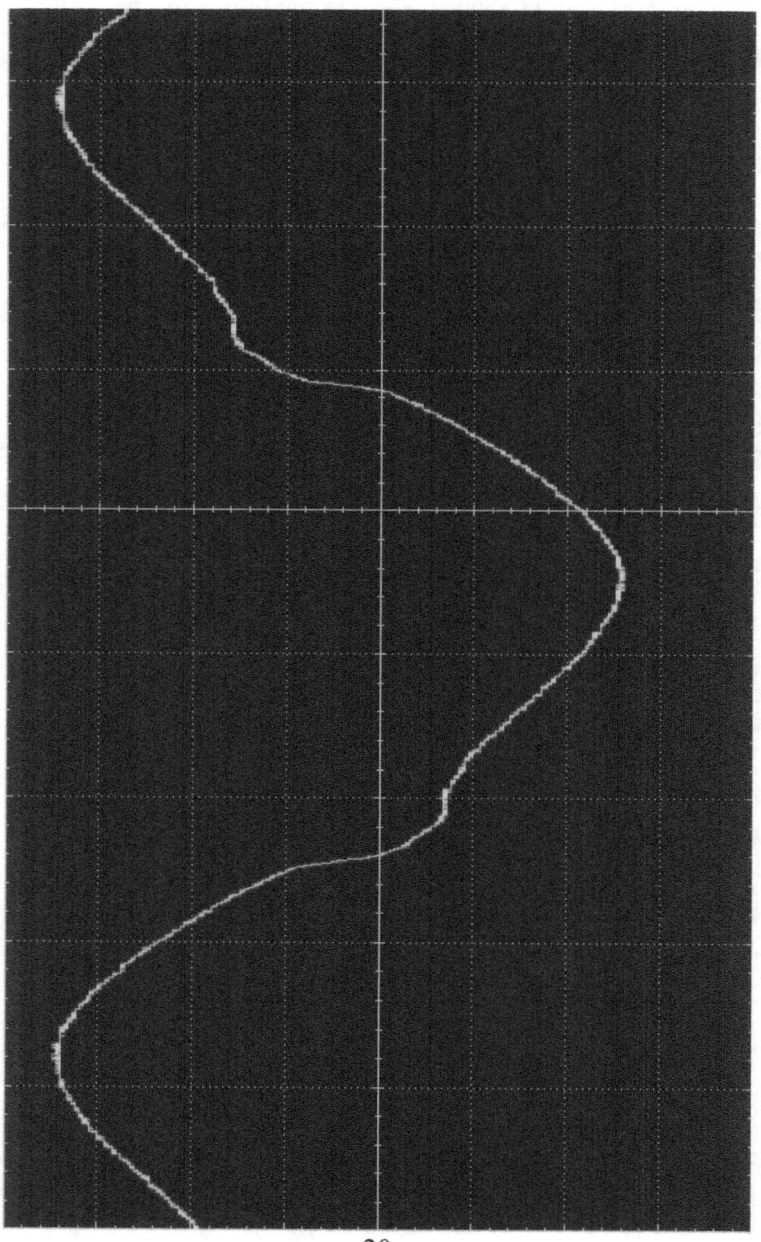

This is the frequency content of the current waveform for the combined three products. The repeating spikes are known as the "Harmonics". Note that zero Hertz is at the bottom of the page and the highest frequency is at the top of the page for these frequency graphs.

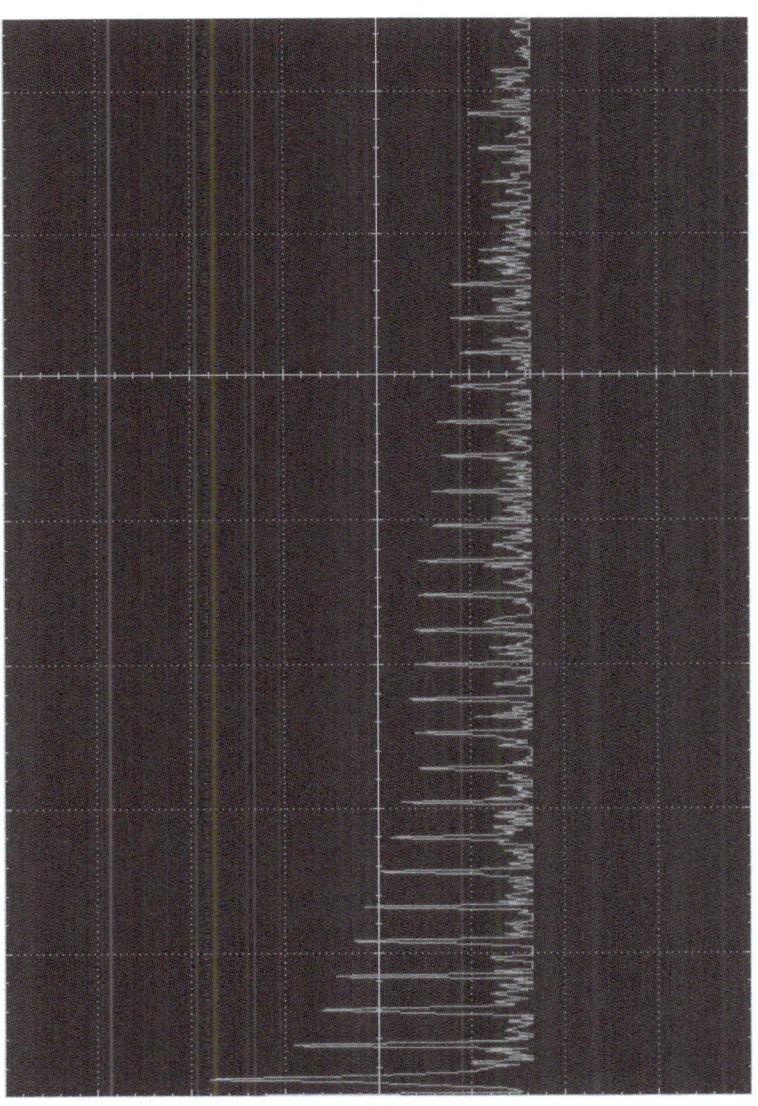

Dr. John Nash Ott called streetlights "Crime Lights" as he had noticed that in areas with them that the people would be subjected to higher rates of crime. This effect has been repeatedly shown to be true by other researchers in the field.

All types of artificial lighting have the possibility of making you ill. Artificial lighting should be avoided if your health is important to you.

I would recommend that you avoid the use of the new lighting that has been developed, such as gas discharge (florescent, sodium, mercury, neon, and so on) and light emitting diode (LED) lighting. These have been developed in order to use less energy at the expense of the quality of the light. They appear to create dirty electricity on your electrical system and large electromagnetic fields in your environment. They may turn your home wiring into a wide band radio transmitter!

In the case of the LED light, long term exposure to the semiconductor spectrum of light is currently unknown. The LED lights can be very bright and you may need to be careful that it does not damage your eyes in the long term. Certain types of LED lights are already acknowledged to be causing insomnia in people due to the large amount of blue light in their spectrum. Indeed, I noticed this effect when working with one. My sleep patterns were off for about two weeks after working with it.

When reviewing thestranger.com article *"Kill the Lights",* we find: *"The beams from the high-intensity, light-emitting diodes are striking. The rays turned my skin the color of white taffy and cast crisp shadows on the pavement. "Zombie blue" is exactly right: Like a day-for-night special effect in a vampire movie, the test streetlights create the sort of atmosphere where you almost expect the undead to emerge from the flower beds and begin eating your face."*

A major problem with electronic lighting products such as florescent lights, compact florescent lights (CFL), and light emitting diode (LED) lights is that they use an electronic inverter system to control the lamp. The inverter system is built into electronic light bulbs. Inverter systems inject strange frequencies of energy back into the electrical system that they are connected to. So instead of having a 60 Hz electrical system, you actually have an electrical system that contains many far higher frequencies of energy. This significantly changes the electrical system and may have the ability to make you ill.

The electronic products also have what is known as a non-linear current draw. This means that they do not have a sinusoidal current draw, but rather a distorted current draw. This creates harmonics on the electrical system.

There are many people reporting health issues around compact florescent lights and it is probably linked to the high frequencies of electrical energies coupling into the human body. This is called "Biological Coupling" and we will look into this later in the book.

LED lights have not been around as long as CFL lights, so there are currently less reports of problems with these light bulbs. However, they are starting to emerge. The biological coupling effects of the LED light bulbs appear to be quite similar to the CFL.

My recommendation is to avoid these electronic forms of lighting products until more is known about their problems and how they can affect human health.

These effects can be seen in the following pictures.

This compact florescent light (CFL) draws current from the electrical system in spikes. It will put harmonics onto the electrical system.

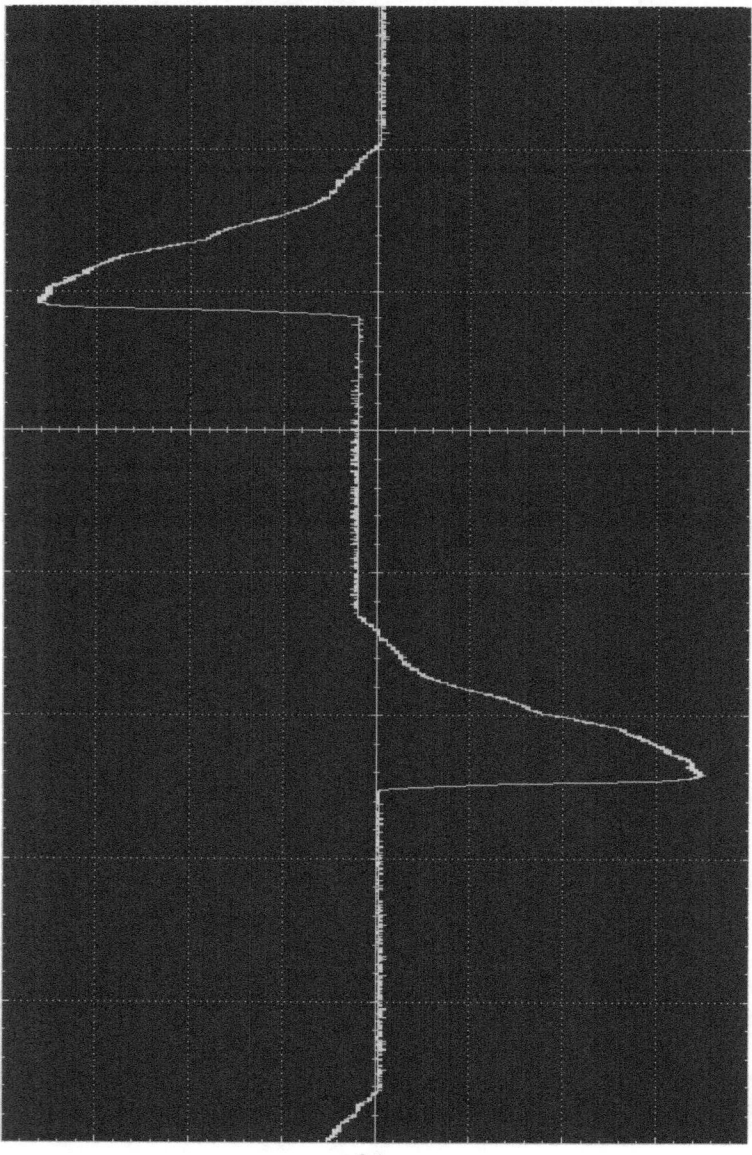

This is what the human body voltage looks like when near to it. There are a wide range of electrical energies on it.

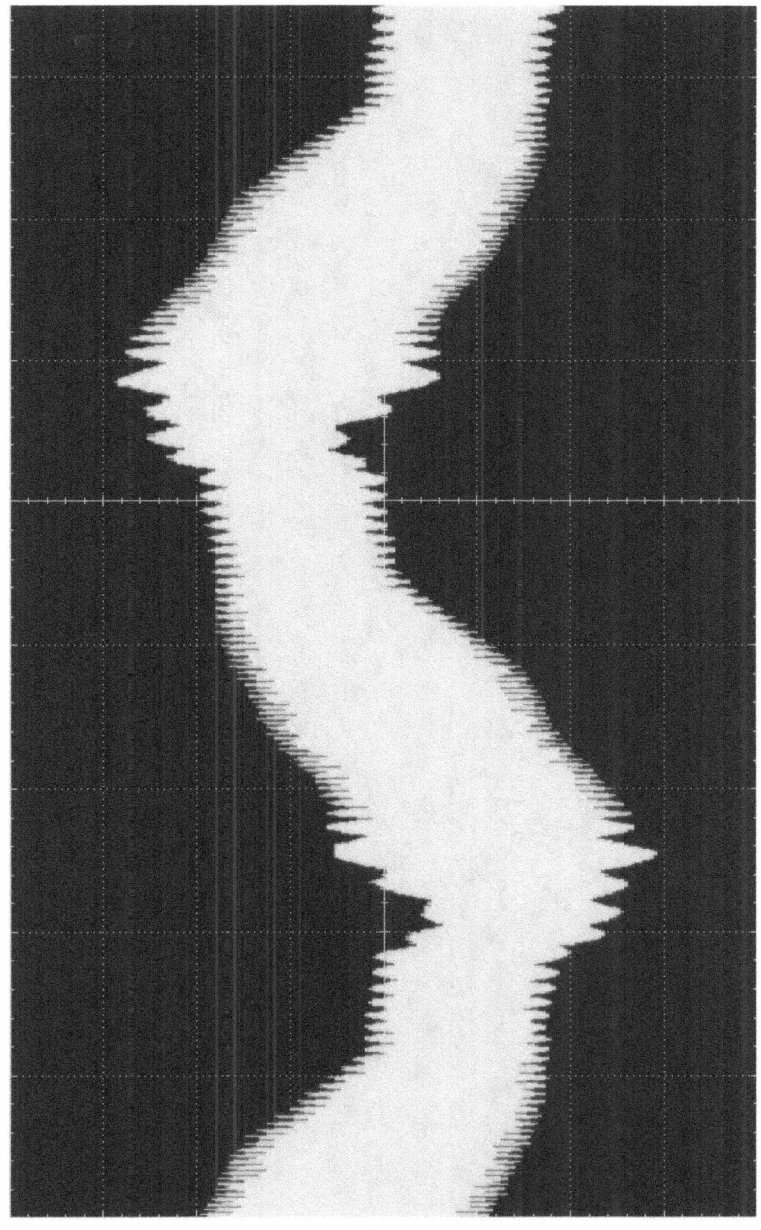

It has put a wide range of frequencies of electrical energy onto the human body, including a very large spike at 60,000 hertz.

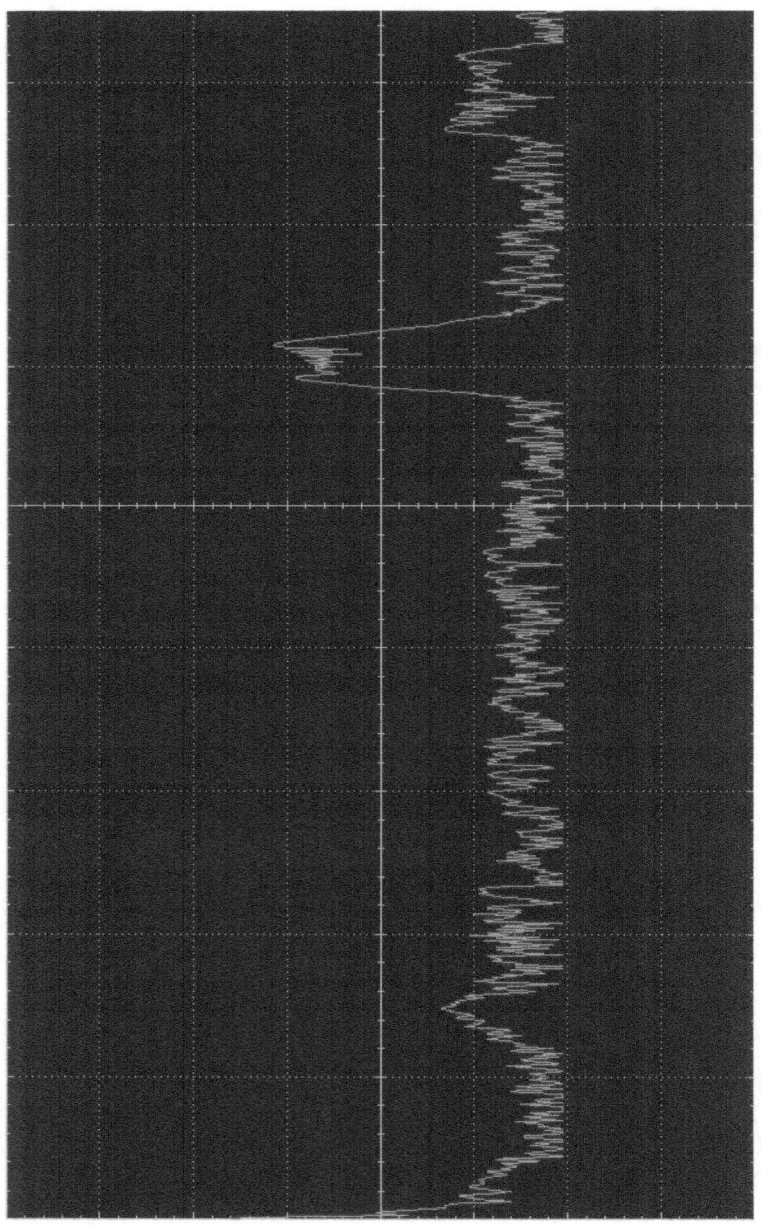

This is the current waveform for the light emitting diode (LED) light. It has a lot of distortion on it and this will create harmonics.

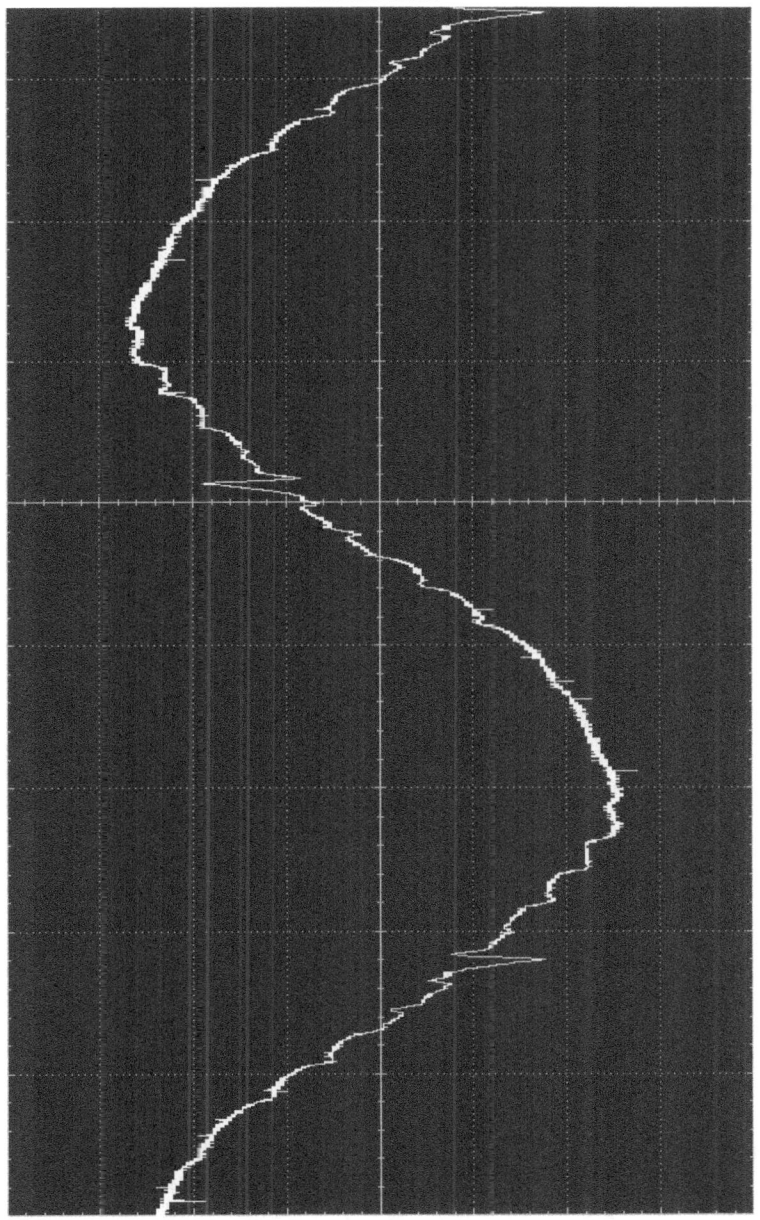

This is what the human body voltage looks like when near to it.
There are many types of electrical energy.

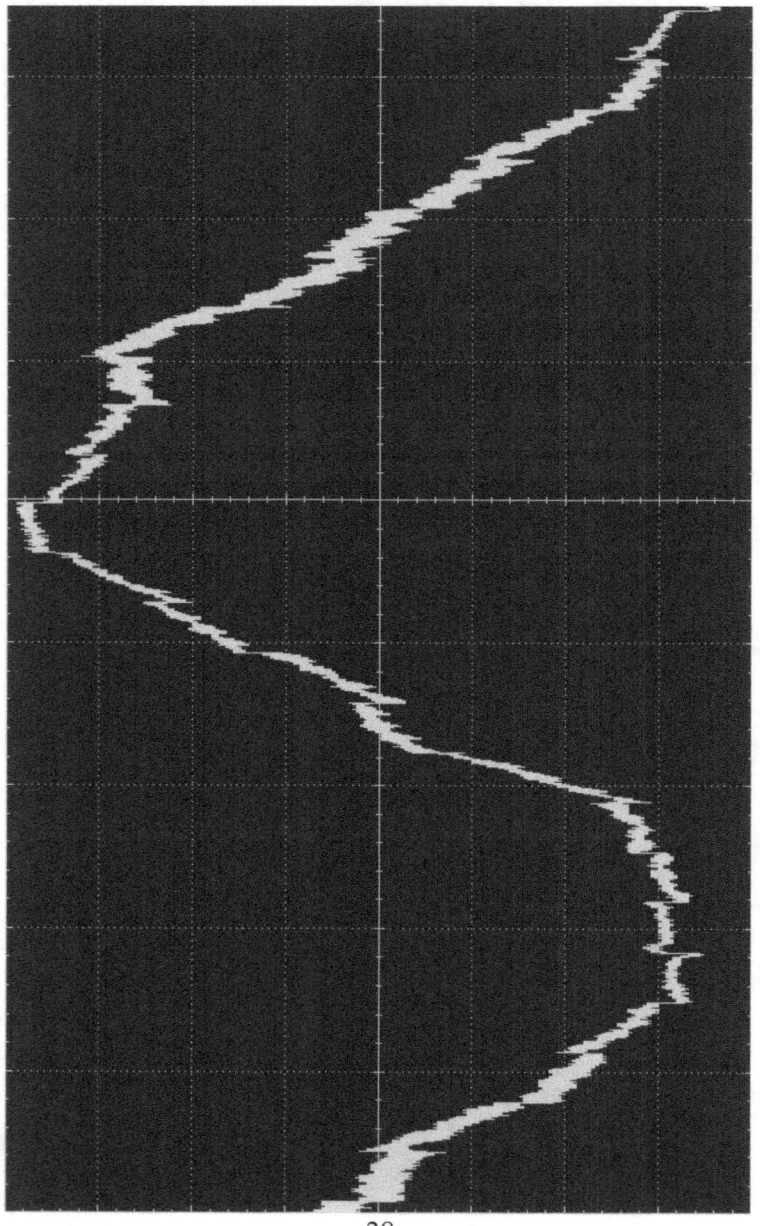

The human body voltage has a range of frequencies on it,
including spikes at 62,500Hz, 125,000Hz and 187,500Hz.

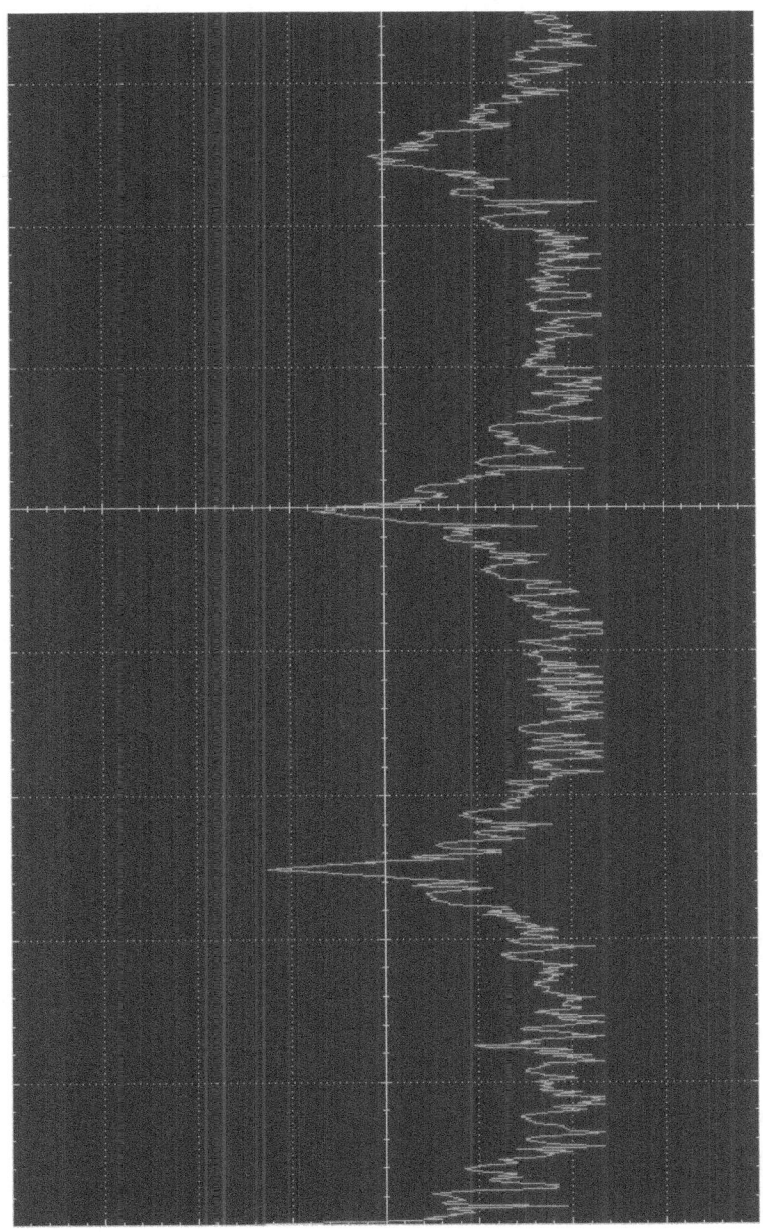

The newer LED lights may have a problem with longevity, particularly if installed into hot areas or enclosed light fittings. These are relatively new products and do not have a proven history of reliability yet.

People have formed a very unnatural habit of staring at computer screens for eight hours per day. This may have long term consequences for both your mental and physical health. You should avoid doing this and if your job requires it, then you should consider changing your job to one that does not require so much time in front of a computer. Computer generated light may changing how the mind works and there is much research being performed in this area currently. The long term health consequences of the latest generation of computer displays have yet to emerge. "Computer Vision Syndrome" is the medical term for the health effects that may occur from computer systems and some of the symptoms can be:

- Headaches.
- Blurred vision.
- Neck pain.
- Redness in the eyes.
- Fatigue.
- Eye strain.
- Dry eyes.
- Irritated eyes.
- Double vision.
- Polyopia.
- Difficulty refocusing the eyes.

The first edition of this book took me two weeks to write and had me working on a laptop computer with a 17 inch LED display for twelve hours per day. My previous exposure was about an hour per day. I had symptoms of tired eyes, irritated eyes, difficulty concentrating, and a withdrawal headache after I finished that was followed by tiredness. The week of proof reading the printed book and minor editing that followed was marked by dry, cracked and chapped lips that took weeks to clear up. There are no doubts that extended exposure to computer monitors can affect your health.

After having this experience, I later realized that it was preventable. Simply by moving the computer in front of a shady "full spectrum" window prevents the conditions from occurring. This is due to significantly diluting the artificial light from the computer monitor with outdoor light that the human is genetically adapted to. This is shown in the next picture.

It is likely that daytime office environments would be healthier if the ceiling was painted sky blue and the walls had green nature landscape scenes on them. Clearly, the office staff sitting facing shady full spectrum windows is already proven for its beneficial health effects and has been so for many decades. You should be aiming to keep your environment as natural as possible for good human health. Natural potted plants can assist in this process in the office environment.

Computer Screen Alignment

The correct alignment of a computer screen to the shaded full spectrum ultraviolet transmitting acrylic window.

When reviewing the BBC News article *"Web addicts 'have brain changes'"*, we find: *"There was evidence of disruption to connections in nerve fibres linking brain areas involved in emotions, decision making, and self-control."*

The recent adoption of large screen televisions may bring with it an increase in human health problems in the future. Large screen TV's consume a large amount of power and emit a corresponding amount of artificial light. Sitting too close to a large screen television may actually damage your health in the long term due to the excessive artificial light exposure from it. It is especially important to not let children sit close to the television for this reason.

Incorrect radiation levels may be able to affect your sex drive and it may be proven in the future that human sex drive is governed more by radiation types and levels than any other factor, even more so than hormones! Generally, a feeling of contentment replaces sexual desire in natural radiation environments.

There are many differences in the colors and spectrums of lighting products and each type of light may be able to affect you in a certain way. After much experimentation I have found that I prefer the light quality of soft white filament light bulbs for nighttime use.

You will only realize that the quality of light is bad when you contrast it to a known good light source. The standard to judge light by is outdoor daylight. There are no light bulbs that can match this standard and the closest thing that appears to do so is the halogen filament light bulb.

Most types of indoor lighting are known to be devoid of ultraviolet light (UV). This is a concern when used for daytime applications, as natural daytime UV light is essential to correct human development and good health. When reviewing the BBC News article *"Sun 'stops chickenpox spreading'"*, we find:

"UV light has long been known to inactivate viruses, and Dr Phil Rice, from St George's, University of London, who led the research, believes that this holds the key why chickenpox

is less common and less easily passed from person to person in tropical countries."

The following photograph shows the difference between natural outdoor light and indoor light. The difference is striking!

Indoor light filtered by four panes of coated low-E glass on the left as contrasted to natural sunlight through an open window on the right. The center line is shade from the frame.

If you work in a daytime indoor environment, then the lighting should mimic what nature does. It should have a natural daytime spectrum of light that matches outdoor daylight. This would be achieved with full spectrum filament lights that have the correct amount of blue and ultraviolet light in their spectrums to mimic outdoor daylight. Your indoor lighting level should be approximately 1,000 lux (Lux is a measurement of brightness of light).

From 10:00 to 14:00 there should be an additional set of lights that is turned on that increases the brightness of the office environment, to mimic the peak in daylight that occurs outdoors. The indoor environment during this time should have an illumination level of approximately 2,000 lux. You can easily achieve this in your office environment by simply having a desk lamp that you switch on during that time to increase the light illumination that you are exposed to. You should be using full spectrum filament light bulbs of the correct spectral emissions for this exposure.

You should make sure that you go outdoors for an hour at solar noon and sit in the shade of trees. Do not wear any sunglasses, glasses, contacts, make-up nor sunscreen for this exposure. You need this exposure daily to keep up the solar cycle in the human mind and body. Without it, you may start to get fatigued as the day goes on. Daily outdoor exposure to sunlight is very important if you have an indoor occupation.

If you do not get the correct light exposures in the day, then your sleep cycle may kick in. The human body when kept in an indoor environment of low lux light will not realize that it is daytime, as it cannot sense the increasing levels of daylight that the genetics are accustomed to. As such, by late morning your body may start sending a signal for you to sleep!

If you can, during any of your daily breaks, you should try and go outdoors to get natural daylight. You will also be getting fresh air and pollen exposure, which are also necessary for good health. The recommended cycle for indoor daytime lighting is shown on the next page.

Indoor Daytime Lighting Cycle for Human Health

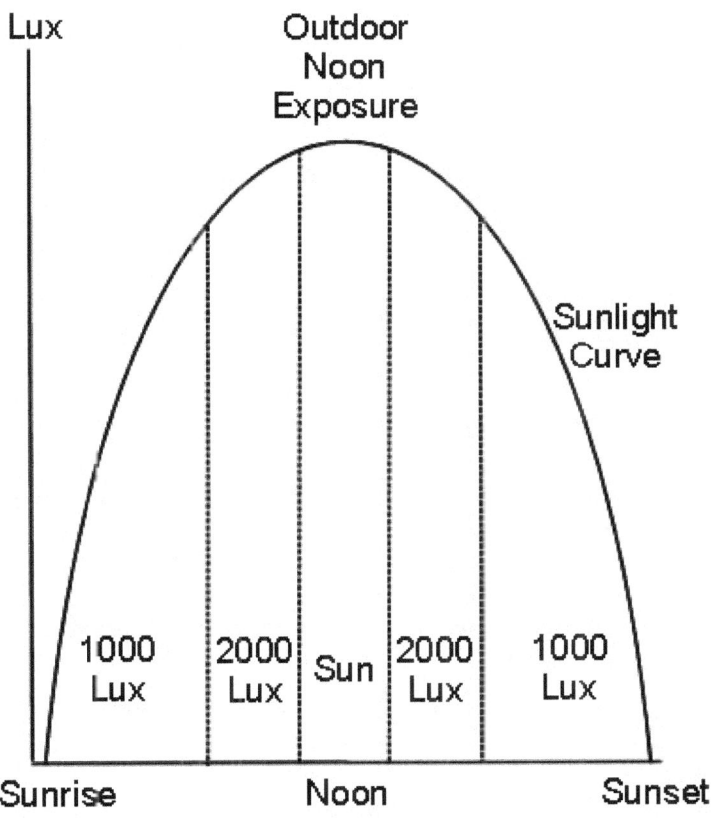

Nighttime lighting is very different from daytime lighting. You want to be using products that have minimal blue light in them. Blue light exposure is well known to cause insomnia. If you install lighting products that have too much blue light in their spectrums, then you may enter into a life of insomnia and not realize that it is your light bulbs that are causing it! Insomnia rapidly leads to fatigue and onto depression. These daytime lighting products are commonly sold as "Daylight" or "Full Spectrum" light bulbs and should not be used in nighttime applications.

You should stick to the tried and tested filament light bulbs for your nighttime exposures. Avoid the compact florescent and LED bulbs as some of these are well known for their excessive blue light content. Keep your lights low, as bright light can also trigger insomnia.

All electric lighting is unnatural and you should limit your exposure to it. Keep to lighting products that generate their light through heat and avoid products with unnaturally high amounts of blue light in them. These will appear excessively white to the eye and may induce insomnia into you. Filament lighting is the only lighting product that I advise people to use and keep the lighting levels low during the evening.

Low voltage halogen lighting products should be avoided due to the emissions from them. They may have high amounts of man-made ultraviolet light, some create dirty electricity, electric and magnetic fields. Man-made ultraviolet light is known for its ability to cause skin and eye problems and ultraviolet light is not present during the nighttime in nature. You will not find any electronic lamp dimmers in my home, as they are a product that you should avoid using. Lamp dimmers can create dirty electricity, electric and magnetic fields.

You should be using the correct voltage light bulb. In the USA these are sold as either 120 volt or 130 volt light bulbs. You should be using the 120 volt versions, as they are far more efficient at producing light. The 130 volt versions should only be used if your light bulbs are frequently breaking within a few days of installing them. If you use 130

volt light bulbs when they are not needed, your light bulbs will last a very long time, but will give out a poor quality of light.

You should be aware that the many sources of artificial lighting can affect your mental and physical health. You should be choosing your daytime artificial lighting products based on the proven health benefits of "Full Spectrum" light bulbs that are comparable to outdoor daylight. Health benefits have been reported by many gardeners who use these products to grow their plants indoors during the winter months. Nighttime artificial lighting products are different to daytime products and should be used in your home for good sleep patterns.

Nighttime over-illumination is a problem in the modern world and it may be able to affect your health. Keep it as low as possible during the nighttime and only increase lighting levels if you feel that you need more light in your environment. You should think candles, not necessarily use candles, but rather the illumination level that candles create. There is a reason why candles are considered romantic and it is likely related to the low level of light that they create.

If you have your environment too bright during the nighttime, then you may upset the circadian rhythm that governs your sleep cycles. Keep lighting as low as possible during the nighttime. You should also keep your skin covered as much as possible to prevent it from absorbing the artificial light.

Some lighting products suffer from flicker that is not noticeable to the eye. The newer LED lights and gas discharge lights appear to suffer from this effect. Indeed, most streetlights are actually flashing at 120 times per second. It is simply too fast for your eyes to detect it.

Flicker can do a lot of very strange things to the human mind and body. Commonly reported effects are:

- Epilepsy.
- Headaches.
- Disorientation.

- Anxiety.

- Seizures.

- Motion sickness.

- Eyestrain.

The health problems of flicker generally peak in the 5 to 30 times per second range. As such, you should not spend time in environments that have flashing or flickering lights. This may a problem for emergency service workers who work in environments that have these strobe lighting products in them. When multiple emergency vehicles are together, then their light flash rate will be much higher and may cause these problems to occur. The electromagnetic pulses from strobe lights may lead to electromagnetic hypersensitivity to occur in people who are close to them.

If you were to grow plants under strobe lighting products, you would notice a changed growth pattern. People have noticed that plants grow larger under them when compared to plants grown in a window. This is probably the plant reacting to the electromagnetic pulses and the high intensity light from the strobe. In nature, fast moving broken clouds can mimic the strobe lighting effect.

Many people say to mimic nighttime lighting by flame, as that is what we evolved in before the adoption of electricity. Both Dr. John Nash Ott and myself believe that it is healthier to go to bed when it goes dark and to avoid nighttime lighting of any kind. When reviewing the msnbc.com article *"Nighttime lights linked to depression"* we find: *"Exposure to a dim light at night, such as the glow of a TV screen, may prompt changes in the brain that lead to mood disorders, including depression, according to a new study in hamsters."*

What lighting products do I have? I have conventional filament light bulbs at my home. You will not find any florescent, compact florescent (CFL), light emitting diode (LED), or any other types of lighting products within my home.

I use filament lighting products because they do not create dirty electricity effects on my home electrical system. I do not have any lamp dimmers. If I want the lighting levels lower, then I turn off some lights or use three way light bulbs.

There are extensive human mind and body photosynthesis effects taking place that react to light and for this reason it is important to understand the sensitivity of the human mind and body to light. Light in the human environment is an extensive subject that has many facets. As such, more information on light in the human environment can be found in the book "Toxic Light".

"Health and Light" by Dr. John Nash Ott is also recommended for further reading on this subject.

"Only a full spectrum of natural light could promote full health in plants, animals, and humans."

Dr. John Nash Ott.

Electromagnetic Radiation

"It is clear that radiation produces the electrical current which operates adaptively the organism as a whole, producing memory, reason, imagination, emotion, the special senses, secretions, muscular action, the response to infection, normal growth, and the growth of benign tumors and cancers, all of which are governed adaptively by the electric charges that are generated by the short wave or ionizing radiation in protoplasm."

Dr. George Crile.

Most people associate radiation with nuclear bombs, nuclear power plants, and X-ray machines. This is a very blinkered view and we will show you how extensive radiation in the human environment is and how critical it is for human health.

The modern human has created a radiation environment that has never existed before in all of human history and it keeps on adding to it every year. This is an issue as most of the sources of man-made radiation are not yet fully understood. As a radiation society, we are running before we have even learned to crawl!

The human radiation environment has many aspects to it:

- Solar radiation.
- Cosmic radiation.
- Environmental radiation.

Environmental radiation can come from many sources:

- Electrical storms.
- Static.
- Replacing nature with modern development significantly raises the levels of many types of radiation.

42

- Mining activities bring radioactive minerals to the surface which will increase the background radiation levels.
- Fall out from nuclear bombs and power plant disasters.
- Living close to a nuclear power station.
- Living close to a coal burning chimney.
- Living at altitude.
- Living near large bodies of water.
- Living in snowy climates.
- Living close to a military base.
- Living close to an airport or port.
- Living close to a hospital.
- Living close to any type of broadcast antenna.
- Living close to an amateur radio operator.
- Living close to power poles and lines.
- Living close to tall structures.
- Living close to glass covered buildings.
- Living in an area that is primarily concrete and asphalt.
- Being near to ionizing smoke detectors.
- Using transportation systems.
- Speed traps.
- Transmitting utility meters.
- Electrical products.
- Electronic products.
- Wireless devices.

Man-made electrical and electronic radiation did not exist until the 1800's when scientists started to discover the various forms of it. We have progressed extremely quickly from a new discovery to the many forms of it that are now present in modern society and this seems to have happened with little thought to the consequences to human health.

We now live in a society that is bombarded by electrical and electronic radiation. There is no place in the world that it does not reach with the prolific adoption of satellite and radio communications. Future historians will likely document this as one of the most foolish things that humanity ever did!

The electrical, electronic and wireless interference is commonly called:

- Electromagnetic Interference (EMI).
- Radio Frequency Interference (RFI).
- Microwave Frequency Interference (MFI).

For the purposes of this book we will use the term electromagnetic interference (EMI) for all of the above effects. The health effects of electromagnetic interference are commonly found documented as:

- Electromagnetic Hyper Sensitivity (EHS).
- Electro-Hyper-Sensitivity (EHS).
- Electrical Sensitivity (ES).
- Electro-Sensitivity (ES).
- Radio Wave Sickness (RWS).
- Rapid Aging Syndrome (RAS).
- Electrical Poisoning.
- Electronic Poisoning.
- Wireless Poisoning.
- Radiation Poisoning.
- Radiation Sickness.

For the purpose of this book, we will use the term electromagnetic hypersensitivity (EHS) to cover the above conditions. The strange thing about EHS is that many people have it, but very few of them realize that it is EHS that is causing their problems. EHS has not been publicized well and even many doctors do not appear to be aware of it. Strange, considering the amount of electrical, electronic and wireless equipment that we are now exposed to.

EHS is somewhat of an "Inconvenient Truth" and if it became widely accepted that it was causing human health problems, then many things would have to change. Industry and governments do not like change and in order to avoid it, it is far easier to deny it. For this reason, you should be aware of your environment and of EHS so that you can stay safe until it does become widely acknowledged as being the problem that it is.

The symptoms of it can be:

- Neurological:
  - Headaches.
  - Dizziness.
  - Nausea.
  - Difficulty concentrating.
  - Memory loss.
  - Irritability.
  - Dementia.
  - Depression.
  - Anxiety.
  - Insomnia.
  - Fatigue.
  - Weakness.
  - Tremors.

- o Numbness.
- o Tingling.
- o Seizures.
- o Paralysis.
- o Psychosis.
- o Stroke.
- Cardiac:
  - o Palpitations.
  - o Arrhythmia.
  - o Pain or pressure in the chest.
  - o Low or high blood pressure.
  - o Slow or fast heart rate.
- Respiratory:
  - o Shortness of breath.
  - o Sinusitis.
  - o Bronchitis.
  - o Pneumonia.
  - o Asthma.
  - o Flu-like symptoms.
  - o Fever.
- Dermatological:
  - o Skin rash.
  - o Itching.
  - o Burning.
  - o Facial flushing.
- Opthalmological:

- ○ Pain cr burning in the eyes.
- ○ Pressure in or behind the eyes.
- ○ Deteriorating vision.
- ○ Floaters.
- ○ Cataracts.
- Muscular & Skeletal:
  - ○ Muscle spasms.
  - ○ Altered reflexes.
  - ○ Muscle and joint pain.
  - ○ Leg or foot pain.
  - ○ Arthritis.
  - ○ Swollen joints.
  - ○ Joint irritation.
- Others:
  - ○ Sexual problems.
  - ○ Digestive problems.
  - ○ Abdominal pain.
  - ○ Enlarged thyroid.
  - ○ Testicular or ovarian pain.
  - ○ Dryness of lips, tongue, mouth or eyes.
  - ○ Great thirst.
  - ○ Dehydration.
  - ○ Nose bleeds.
  - ○ Interral bleeding.
  - ○ Altered sugar metabolism.
  - ○ Immune abnormalities.

- ○ Redistribution of metals within the body.
- ○ Hair loss.
- ○ Pain in the teeth.
- ○ Deteriorating fillings.
- ○ Impaired sense of smell.
- ○ Ringing in the ears.
- ○ Mouth ulcers.

Exposure to high frequencies may cause:

- Irregular heartbeat.
- Pains.
- Allergies.
- Miscarriages.
- Birth defects.
- Childhood leukemia.
- Brain tumors.
- Reproductive tumors.
- Cancers.
- Infertility.
- Depression.
- Chronic Fatigue Syndrome (CFS).
- Fibromyalgia.
- Gulf War Syndrome.
- Alzheimer's disease.
- Parkinson's disease.
- Lou Gehrig's disease.
- Behcet's Disease.

- Sexual arousal.
- Aggression.

Dr. Jim Burch PhD of the Cancer Prevention and Control Program at the University of South Carolina, has documented the biological effects of radio frequencies on the human mind and body as:

- **Cell proliferation (Increased ODC activity).**
- **Ion flux across biological membranes (Ca^{++}).**
- **DNA damage (Comet assay is an example).**
- **Gene expression (Oncogenes, stress proteins).**
- **Altered enzyme activity (Radical pairs).**
- **Immune system perturbations.**
- **Endocrine disruption (Melatonin for example).**
- **Altered blood-brain barrier.**
- **Autonomic nerve function (EEG, ECG).**
- **Sleep or circadian rhythm disruption.**
- **Headaches, neurological effects.**
- **Reproduction disorders.**
- **Carcinogenesis (Brain, leukemia).**

EMI can be classed as narrow-band or wide-band. Narrow-band EMI sources can be:

- Smart meters/smart devices/automatic meter readers (AMR)/advanced metering infrastructure (AMI) utility wireless networks.
- Two way radios (transceivers).
- Cordless phones, mobile phones and cell phones.
- Wireless scanners and wireless checkout devices.

- Radio frequency identification devices (RFID).
- Wi-Fi networking.
- Television and radio transmission towers.
- Cell phone towers.
- RADAR systems.
- Rural internet and satellite internet.

Here are some sources of wide-band EMI:

- Computers.
- Cathode ray tube (CRT) TV's.
- Digital flat screen TV's.
- Power lines.
- Electric switches and relays.
- Electric motors.
- Variable frequency drives (VFD).
- Thermostats.
- Bug zappers.
- Inverter systems.
- Florescent lights.
- Compact florescent lights (CFL).
- Light emitting diode (LED) lights.
- Neon signs.
- Stereo systems.
- MP3 players.
- Electronic lamp dimmers.
- Cars.
- Transportation systems.

- Electric and electronic toys.

- Battery powered watches.

- Cordless, cell and smart phones.

- Anti-static devices.

- Electrical grounding systems.

Basically, most digital equipment will have broadband emissions from it. If it is switching a large amount of power, then it may produce large amounts of electromagnetic interference.

The pictures on the following pages show the effects of electromagnetic interference on the human body voltage.

The Human Body Voltage

The human body voltage appears like a capacitor charging and discharging when in contact with conductive flooring that is electrically grounded.

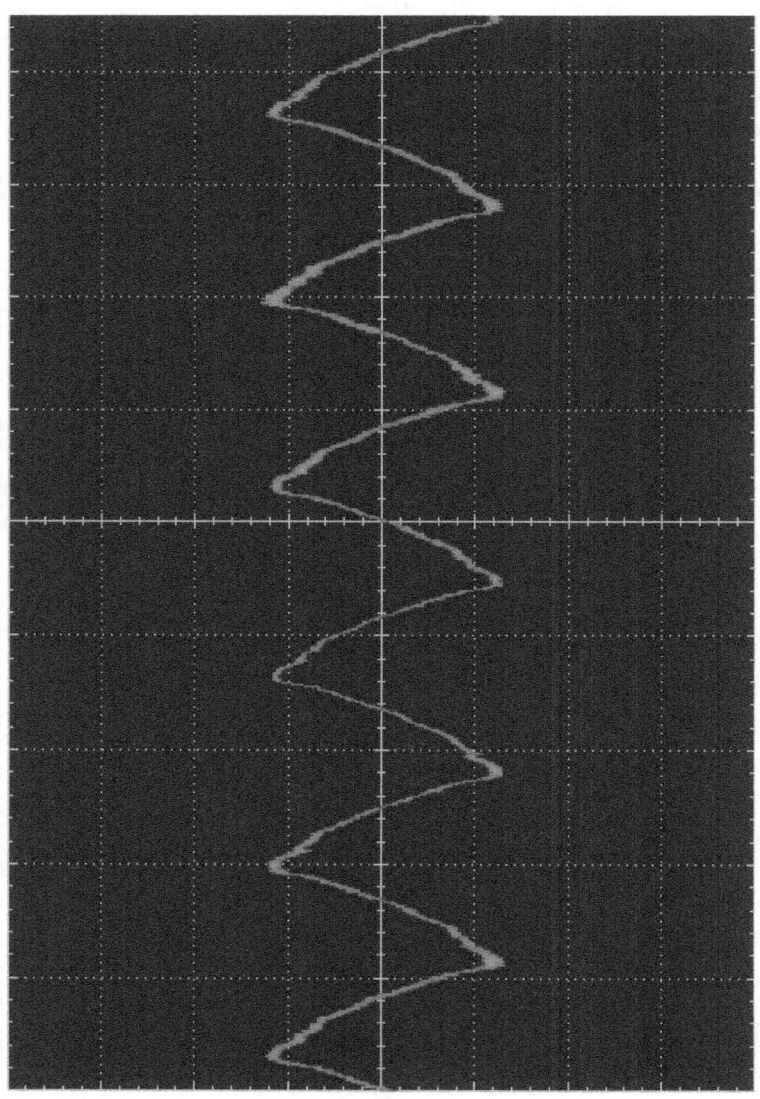

Electrical Forensics © Steven Magee

The Human Body Frequency Spectrum

A fast Fourier transform (FFT) reveals the many frequencies of
electrical energy induced into the human body from contact with
the conductive flooring.

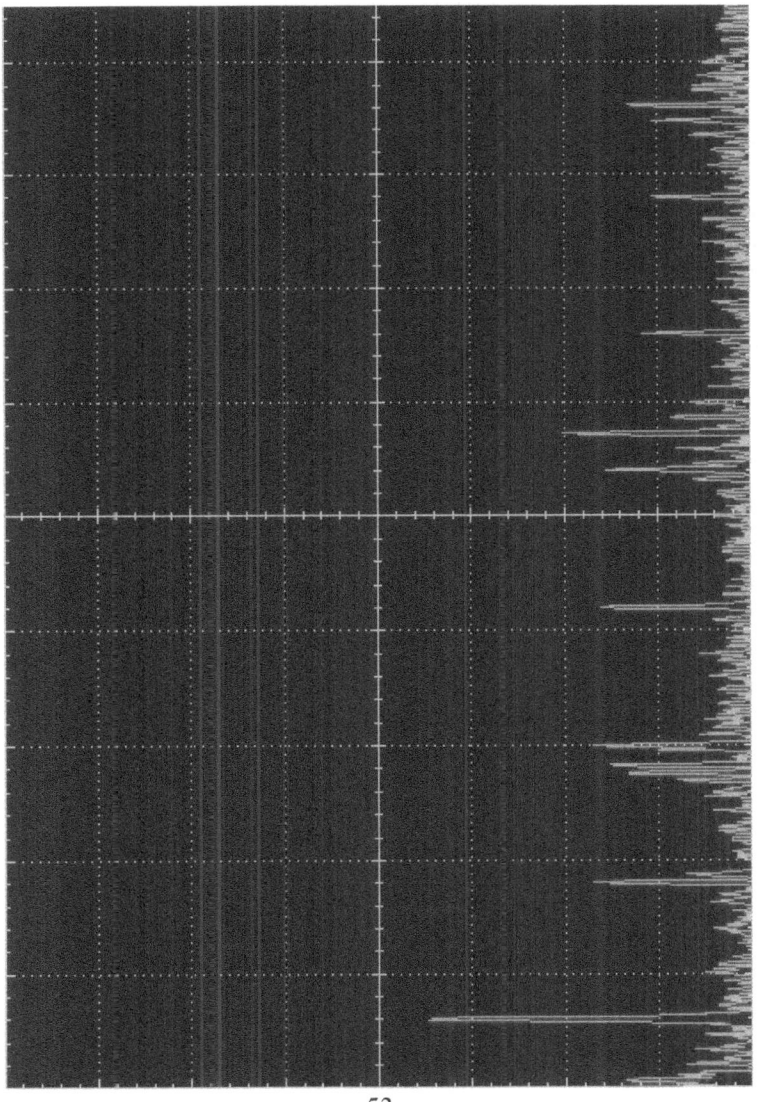

There was a shift that occurred largely in the 1980's from analogue electronics to digital electronics. Analogue electronics did not have a digital microprocessor chip in it and was made out of many basic electronic components. More importantly, it did not have the high speed pulsing that characterizes digital electronics. It is this high speed pulsing that causes digital electronics to be generally very dirty electromagnetic interference producing equipment.

Digital electronics uses electrical square waves to drive it. A square wave is one of the dirtiest electrical waves and as such it has many harmonics associated with it. Harmonics are the many different frequencies of waves that must be added together to produce the square wave. Basically, if you have a 60 Hertz square wave, then it will contain many higher frequencies of waves to produce it. They may be thousands of times higher in frequency than the wave that they are part of. It is for this reason that a standard AM radio when tuned into static can detect electrical noise. It is the harmonics that it is detecting in the square wave.

Computers function on high speed switching of square waves. For this reason you will find some very interesting microwave, radio, electric, and magnetic fields around them. The fields vary with the age of the computer and the different brands of computers. Laptop computers can be a particular problem due to the electronics being located below the keyboard and mouse pad. Some of these areas underneath can have very high levels of EMI producing electronics! It is best with a laptop computer to switch to a large font on the display, push the laptop back, and use a separate keyboard and mouse to control it.

When reviewing the BBC News article "*Scientists question if wi-fi laptops can damage sperm*", we find: "*Scientists are questioning if using wi-fi on a laptop to roam the internet could harm a man's fertility, after lab work suggested ejaculated sperm were significantly damaged after only four hours of exposure.*"

Florescent lights, compact florescent lights (CFL), and light emitting diode (LED) lights appear to produce radio waves from their power switching electronics. These radio emissions appear to vary between the different sizes of light bulbs and also how old they are. It is not a good idea to bring radio frequency producing equipment into your environment and for this reason I advise people against using these products. Testing has shown that these products can couple their electromagnetic fields into water and cause stray voltage effects. This is a concern due to the human body being 70% to 90% water, depending on age.

High electromagnetic interference lighting products are a serious issue when mounted to ceilings that are underneath an upper story. The fields that are coming out of them will make hot zones of electromagnetic radiation in the areas of the flooring above! They may also put harmonics on the electrical cables that run underneath the floor and create extensive electromagnetic interference fields wherever they run.

This is shown in the next picture.

Under-Floor EMI

Electromagnetic fields come up through flooring from electrical products below

Dotted lines represent the edge of the electromagnetic fields emitted by the electrical equipment below the floor

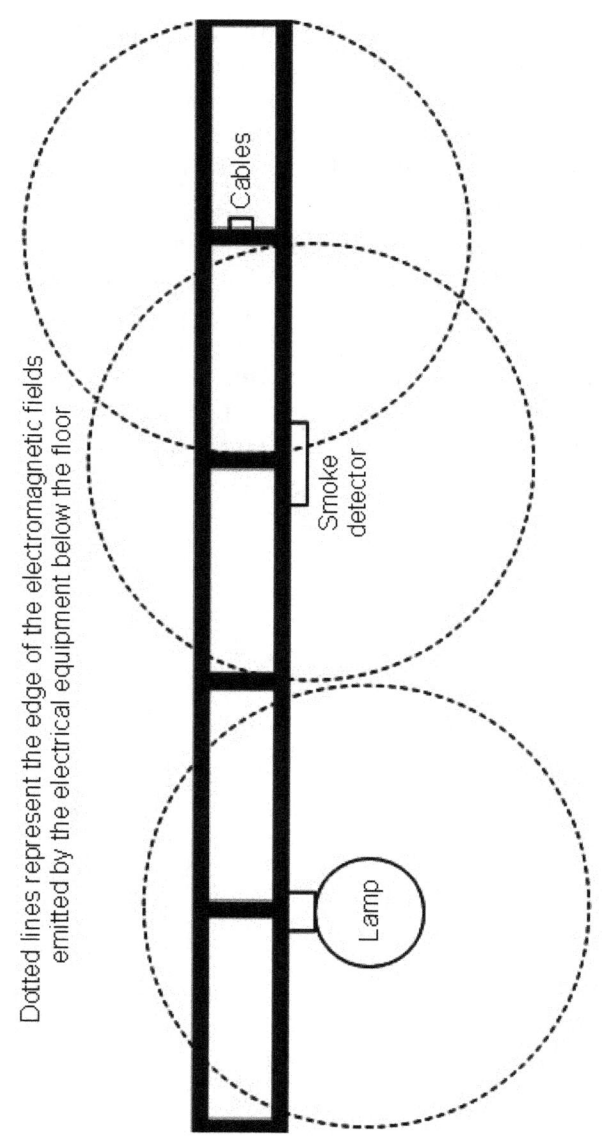

Cables

Smoke detector

Lamp

Hairdressing products have some interesting electromagnetic fields around them and the hairdryer is perhaps one of the worst. The hairdryer consumes a large amount of current and has a brush motor inside it. Brush motors create sparks and this leads to wide band radio wave emissions near to it. It also puts dirty electricity into the electrical system. Hair clippers have large magnetic fields, corded ones put large AC voltages onto the human body, and the cordless ones appear to emit radio waves. It is concerning that these are used near to the head and it is probably a good idea not to expose developing children to these products.

Florescent tanning booths and beds may be an electromagnetic interference hot zone and should probably be avoided. The tanning light spectrum may be an issue as well. Dr. John Nash Ott found that there appears to be a biologically harmful field near the ends of florescent tubes where the cathodes are located. He believed it was a source of X-ray emissions. The florescent tube electronics also produce electromagnetic fields that may be extensive.

Some of the new digital televisions (TV) appear to be producing levels of electromagnetic interference that are affecting peoples health. I measured electromagnetic interference that was produced by my digital TV at a distance of fifty feet away from it! The electromagnetic interference that this particular 32" LCD flat screen TV was producing appeared to be an interference type of radiation. There were pockets of low and high interference AM radio frequencies throughout the home. I had noticed plant deformity and leaf tip problems in the plants in the room of the digital TV which appeared to be caused by the electromagnetic interference. The interesting thing about discontinuing the use of my digital TV was that plants started to grow in my garden that had appeared dormant for years! Plasma TV's appear to be the worst offenders of the new digital TV's with large electromagnetic interference fields around some of them.

Regarding human health, you should ensure that you stay out of the electromagnetic fields of televisions. A good rule of thumb is that the detectable electromagnetic field is

generally three times larger in all directions than the screen size. These fields pass straight though walls and can be very high on the other side of the wall behind the television.

This can be a problem in hotels. The problem that I have with the hotel bed is that literally inches from your head on the other side of the wall may be a very large flat screen TV that is radiating very large electromagnetic radiation fields! The rooms also appear to have energy star lighting products that create a variety of emissions in the room and the light may cause insomnia. When in a hotel, it makes sense to sleep with your head in the center of the room and not against the wall in order to ensure that your brain is not in any strange fields that may be coming through the wall.

You will find emissions of wide band radio waves, X-rays, electrostatic, electric, and magnetic fields around cathode ray tube televisions. In an effort to prevent X-ray emissions, the screen is impregnated with lead. As such, they are an excellent device to study the biological effects of electromagnetic radiation. I call them "the power line within your home" as they emit more powerful fields into the human environment than most utility power lines!

It is quite possible that some of the illness and disease in the population are following the increase in television screen sizes!

Video games have brought children very close to the television. This means that their eyes are absorbing more of the artificial light and they may be spending extended time in the unnatural electromagnetic fields that the television produces. An interesting observation of autistic children is that it occurs 5 times more in boys than girls. Boys do tend to play more on video game systems than girls, and this may be a factor. The testicles are vulnerable to radiation exposures due to being external to the body.

Remote controls may be an issue, as they emit wide band radio wave emissions every time you use them! The transition from infrared to wireless radio frequency controllers is concerning and seems to be happening without any regard to the health symptoms that are being widely reported around wireless transmitting systems. Many video game systems now use transmitting wireless controllers and they may be able to affect the health of developing children and adults.

Solar photovoltaic (PV) power systems on the roofs of residential homes may be an issue. The inverter system that converts the direct current electricity from them into alternating current appears to cause electromagnetic fields to occur on the equipment. The large scale adoption of solar photovoltaic systems in the home has not yet been around long enough to fully understand the health risks that they may present.

Electronic inverter system exposure is shown on the following pages. The higher the power of the system, the larger the electromagnetic interference from them may be.

Inverter Systems and Human Health

Many inverter systems create electromagnetic fields around them. You should be wary about entering these fields. Extended exposure to inverter systems may be harmful to human health.

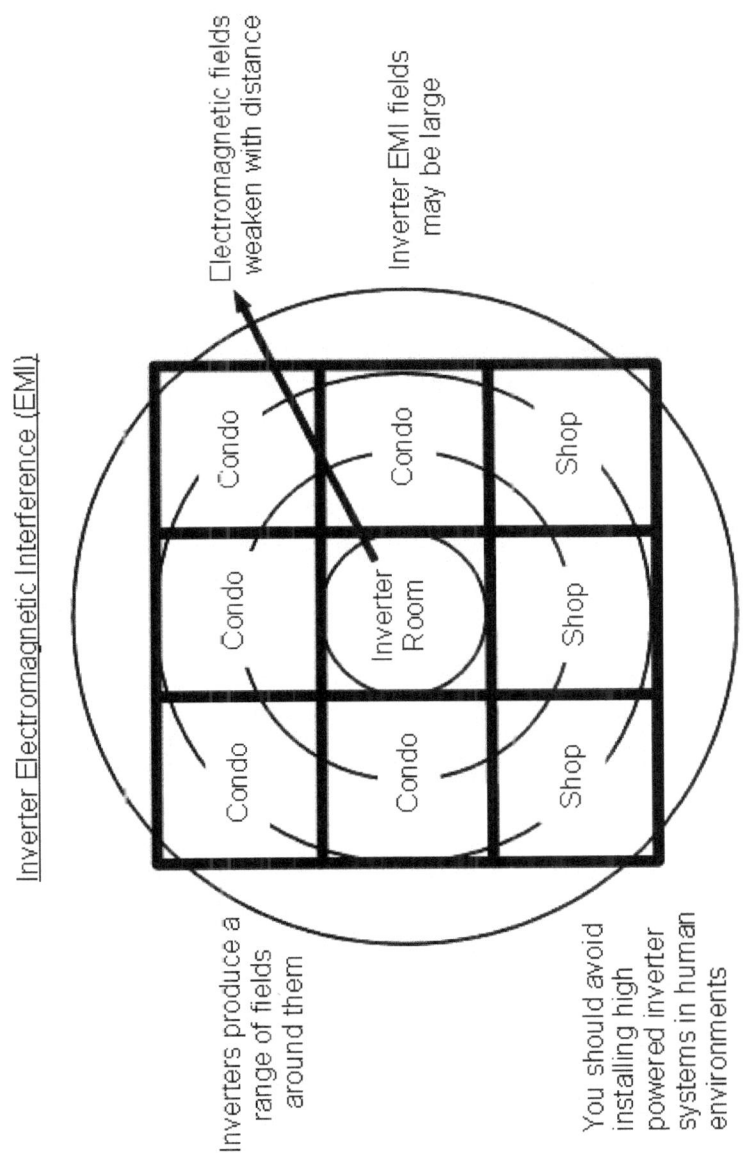

Inverter Electromagnetic Interference (EMI)

Electromagnetic fields weaken with distance

Inverter EMI fields may be large

Condo

Condo

Shop

Condo

Inverter Room

Shop

Condo

Condo

Shop

Inverters produce a range of fields around them

You should avoid installing high powered inverter systems in human environments

Due to the advent of digital equipment, the electrical circuits of the home may need to have line terminators installed in them. Line terminators prevent digital reflections from occurring on the home wiring. Essentially, it is an electrical noise reduction technique that can be used to reduce the home wiring electromagnetic interference emissions.

The radial electrical circuit is shown on the next page. The last socket may now need a line terminator installing into it to terminate the circuit to prevent electronic noise reflections from occurring. A line terminator is generally a small capacitor in parallel with a high impedance bleed resistor. This would be connected across the live and neutral terminals of the final socket in the radial circuit.

Terminating Radial Circuits

Radial electrical circuits may need line terminators installing at the last outlet.

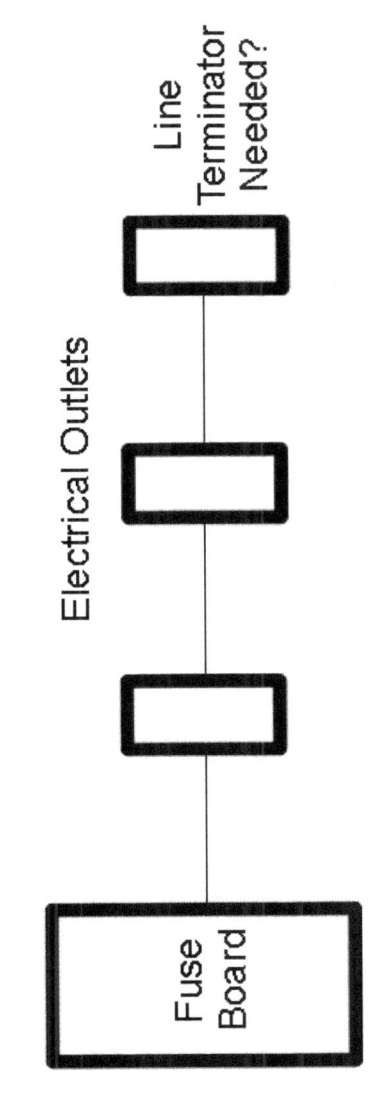

Electrical Outlets

Line terminators prevent frequency reflections from occurring on the circuit. A line terminator is generally a capacitor and a resistor.

Cars and transportation systems can have high amounts of EMI associated with them. In the past this came from their ignition systems and could be heard on the car radio as a buzzing sound that would increase in line with the revolutions per minute (RPM) of the car engine. Today, there is likely to be more electromagnetic interference from the electronic systems of the car and this may include:

- Radio frequency identification devices (RFID).
- Hybrid drive system.
- Electric drive system.
- Engine computer system.
- Global Positioning Systems (GPS).
- Alternating current (AC) inverter system.
- Entertainment systems.
- Cell phone charger.
- Cell phone.

People who have traced their sickness to their cars often change to a basic model of diesel car. They report improved health due to the lack of an ignition system in the diesel engine. I had intense intestinal pains after working with a car ignition system. The risk appears to be greatest when working near to the battery, coil and spark plugs.

When characterizing electromagnetic radiation emissions from transportation systems, they should be measured at various speeds, and also during hard acceleration and hard braking. Dr. Samuel Milham reports that he discovered that the rotating wheels were producing significant magnetic fields in the human occupied areas of the cars he tested at speed.

Using your cell phone in the car is a bad idea due to the radio frequency reflections that may occur. This may raise the radiation environment in the car and may cause interference effects that may be harmful to human health. Not to mention the distraction effect that may lead to a collision!

Electromagnetic interference is occurring with motorbikes and appears to be much stronger due to the compactness of a motorbike. Many motorbikes have their battery and electronic systems mounted under the seat and this area may emit the most electromagnetic interference into the rider. More details on this can be found in the book "Motorcycle Cancer?" by Randall Dale Chipkar.

Electric bicycles are becoming popular and may have similar problems as motorbikes. The dynamo electric lighting system for bicycles may be an issue.

Entertainment systems in cars and planes are an interesting concept. Generally you will find the television mounted into the head rest. As such, there may be a large electromagnetic field around the headrest. Car sickness or jet lag? You may have been excessively exposed to electromagnetic radiation from the television system in the head rest!

The move to hybrid and electric cars appears to be taking place with little concern to the electromagnetic interference environment inside the car. There are reports of people detecting electromagnetic interference fields within these cars that can far exceed the 2 milli-gauss magnetic fields that the International Agency for Research on Cancer (IARC) have set as their limit for constant magnetic field level for safe human health. Other people have noticed that their children appear fatigued on a long drive in a hybrid car as opposed to a normal car. Hybrid cars and electric cars appear to emit high electromagnetic interference during acceleration that may be around 100 milli-gauss and up to 30 milli-gauss when cruising. Constant fields of 2 milli-gauss and above should be avoided due to the elevated cancer risk.

The Prius acceleration problems may have a link to electromagnetic interference in some cases Strange electromagnetic fields can affect the human mind and cause confusion. People may think they are pressing the brake, when they are actually pressing the accelerator! I can recall times when I have been working around electronic equipment and have displayed this type of confused behavior. I have also seen people that I have supervised display it too! Generally, the people that you are with notice your error and correct you.

Cars may be filled various levels of electromagnetic radiation and interference fields that may make you sick. Before buying one of these, you should ask for the following information: Peak values of magnetic field, electrostatic field, electric field, and wide band radio field in the human occupied areas. You should also establish if the fields are pulsating.

It makes sense to be a late adopter of electric car technology. There may be many types of electromagnetic interference fields around them. It will be interesting to see if brings a wave of electromagnetic hypersensitivity (EHS) and disease into the lives of the owners. Riding around in an electric car may be comparable to sitting under utility power lines.

The home electric car charger may be an issue. It will draw a lot of current from the utility system and may cause dirty electricity effects to appear throughout your home. It may also raise the electromagnetic fields around the utility power lines in the area.

Your children may already be driving electric cars! Electric cars for children have been available for quite some time and there may be extensive electromagnetic fields around some of them. You are probably better off staying away from high powered electrical toys like this.

You should establish where the battery(s) is located. I have noticed that on buses that the seat that the driver sits in commonly has the batteries located underneath it! This is an undesirable configuration for human health and the battery(s) should be located with the engine, preferably as far away from the vehicle occupants as is possible.

Electrical, electronic and wireless toys are just a really bad idea around developing children. Some toys will have a wide range of electromagnetic fields around them. If

you are going to have electrical toys around your children, you should assess the electromagnetic interference that it produces before giving it to them.

Electric toothbrushes can have high electromagnetic fields around them and are used near to the brain, so you should consider not using these around developing children.

It is well known that frequent travelers have a high obesity risk. Transportation systems of all types can produce high electromagnetic interference environments. Airplanes, buses, and trains may be filled with electromagnetic interference and it is added to by people using their electronic devices on them.

The recent transition back to electric trams running through the streets is an interesting concept. The overhead power cable has current running through it that is returned through the grounded rails in the road. This will set up electromagnetic fields between them where the people are riding. The harmonics on the current may set up radio frequency emissions. If you ride daily on trams, you should pay attention to your long term health and be aware that you may develop electromagnetic hypersensitivity conditions in the long term. Electric trains may have similar issues. The EMI fields may extend along the route of the tram, even when the tram is not in view. You should avoid driving in the vicinity of electric tram tracks due to the EMI emissions from them. The overhead cables and tram tracks are shown in the next photograph.

Electric Trams and Trains

These may have a wide variety of electromagnetic interference emissions associated with them. An electromagnetic field may be set up in between the overhead power cables and the tram tracks below.

Airplanes have extensive electromagnetic emissions from their RADAR system and jet engines The overhead cable that powers the tram may have dirty electricity emissions on it. The electric train may be emitting extensive EMI in some areas of it, especially near the electric motors and wheels. A ship will have RADAR and communications emissions.

Regarding airplanes, the pilots and air hostesses have high levels of sickness. The airplane has very high sources of electromagnetic radiation and these can be:

- High altitude solar radiation.
- Elevated cosmic radiation levels.
- Close proximity to lightning storms.
- RADAR.
- Communications systems.
- Engines.
- WiFi.
- Entertainment systems.
- Airplane control systems.
- Passenger electronics.
- Artificial lights.

The airport security area is a problem due to the scanners. Extended exposure to these systems has not been effectively studied and may be a long term health risk. It is not a good time to be a frequent air traveler.

Elevators may be an issue. Most elevators are essentially large Faraday cages that go whizzing up and down metal filled elevator shafts. You may find strange electromagnetic fields around elevators. These are added to by the electrical and electronic products within the elevators. Elevators typically have motors, florescent lights and control electronics within them. Regarding the lights, they are generally closer to your head due to the lower ceiling height and the electromagnetic fields will be stronger. You should avoid renting the apartment next to the elevator shaft due to the EMI effects. It is also preferable to use the stairs.

High voltage electric security fences are known for their high levels of EMI. These have similar problems to power lines and earthing and we will look into these problems later in the book. The electronics that power the security fence may have high EMI emissions from them and you should locate the electronic controller far from the human environment. These electric fences are usually found in farms and on top of high security walls.

Electronic lamp dimmers are one of the biggest culprits for producing electromagnetic interference effects within the home. I was quite surprised to find that a large and extensive electromagnetic field that I was detecting throughout a home was coming from a lamp dimmer! Lamp dimmers can completely fill a home with electromagnetic interference. You should avoid these products and instead use the three way filament lights instead.

Lamp dimmer effects are shown in the following pictures.

Lamp dimmers can create a very distorted current waveform.

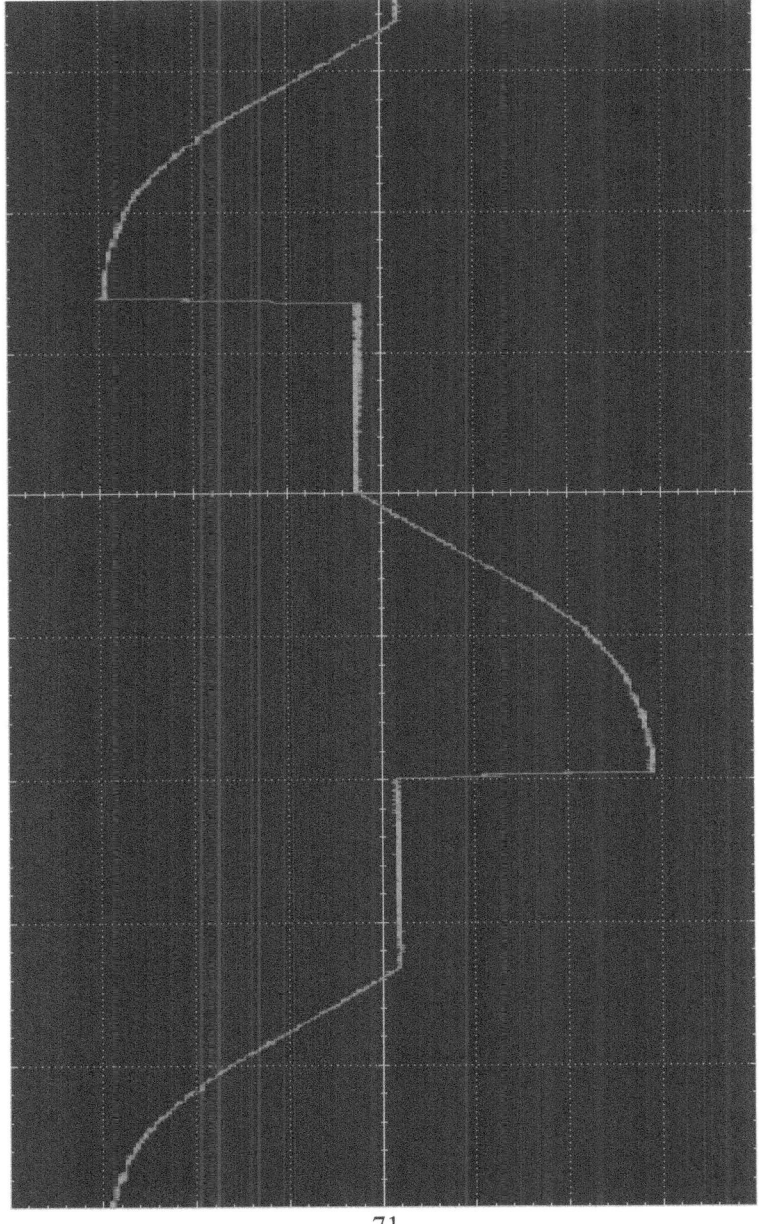

Lamp dimmers put a wide range of frequencies onto the electrical system. These harmonic and electrical noise frequencies can create large fields around the cables that may completely fill the home.

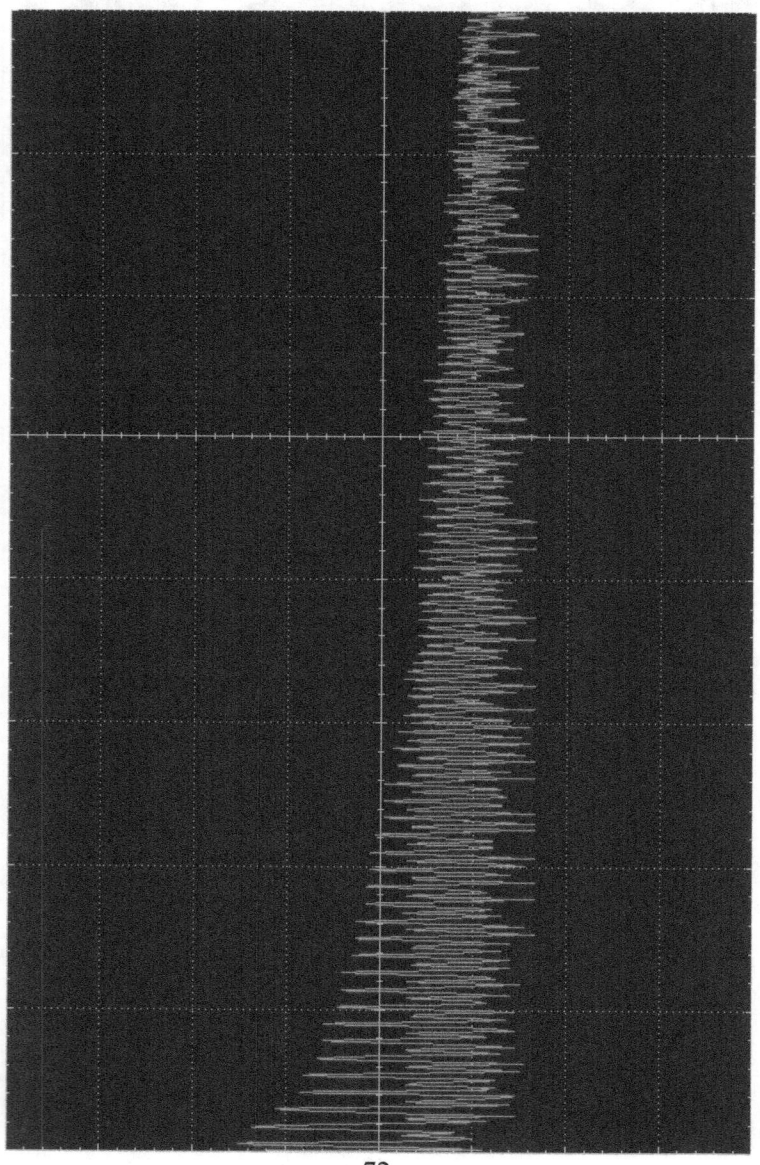

Microwave ovens can produce similar effects. I have detected extensive radio, microwave, and magnetic fields around these and, as such, I no longer use one. They make cell phones look safe!

People have started to realize that computer Wi-Fi networks, cell phone networks, DECT cordless phones, radio frequency identification (RFID) systems and the like are all causing biological problems. Wireless equipment should be avoided where possible. When using wireless equipment, the wireless transmission energy density is at a maximum next to the equipment and fades with distance. You should not place the transmitting equipment next to people or developing children. It is suggested that the wireless router be placed at least twenty feet from where people spend time. RFID security door systems should be avoided and it is preferable to use a standard key.

You are probably inadvertently spending time in these electromagnetic interference fields and do not realize it. The next diagram shows how this may be occurring in your environment.

Home Electromagnetics

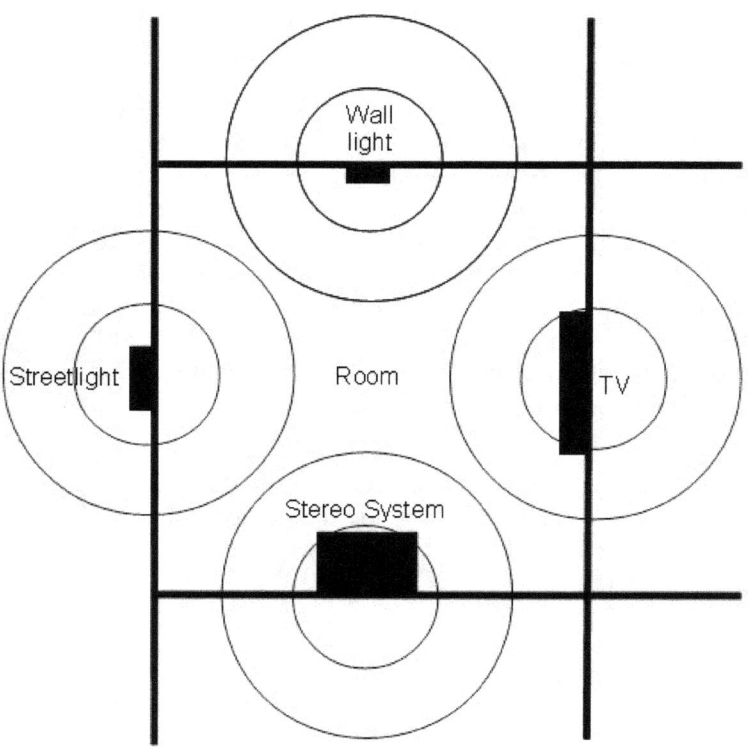

Electromagnetic field size will be dependent on each product
and some will be larger than others

When reviewing the Popular Science article *"The Man Who Was Allergic to Radio Waves"* we find that Per Segerback *"noticed his first symptoms -- dizziness, nausea, headaches, burning sensations and red blotches on his skin -- in the late 1980s, a decade into his telecommunications research work. All but two of the 20 or so other members of his group reported similar symptoms, he says, although his were by far the most severe. His EHS worsened and now, he says, even radar from low-flying aircraft can set it off."*

Electromagnetic hypersensitivity (EHS) has been extensively documented in plants and trees around these electromagnetic fields. The biological effect in plants and trees is not new, it was extensively researched and documented by Dr. John Nash Ott in the 1950's. Indeed, I have grown plants in electromagnetic fields that exhibited the growth defects that he documented.

This is shown in the next photograph. The three plants all looked the same when I bought them. They are all Dieffenbachia's and they all looked like the bushy one on the left. The center plant changed its growth in a Wi-Fi and AC electric field location. The right plant changed its growth in a wide band radio wave field that was produced by a 32" LCD digital television and now has very small and glossy green leaves with no patterning as shown in the following picture. As you can see, they look like completely different species of plants and I call them my "Frankenstein" plants!

Exposure to EMI can cause plant deformity and growth defects. The leafy plant on the left is how the spindly ones to the right used to look before EMI exposure. You can see that there are significant problems with leaf growth, leaf patterning, and stem branching.

On the left is a normal fully grown Dieffenbachia leaf. On the right is a fully grown Dieffenbachia leaf from the plant in the EMI field produced by my 32" LCD TV. As you can see, their leaf growth and patterning is quite different!

This Dieffenbachia plant was grown in a modern office environment that has wireless networking, computers, electronic florescent lighting products, and air conditioning. The leaf growth is very small and it appears to be a stunted version of the original plant.

Babies and children are the most sensitive to the effects of EMI and particular attention should be paid to their environments. In a home with children you should avoid:

- Ionizing smoke detectors.
- Wireless baby monitors.
- Electrical toys.
- Electronic toys.
- Radio controlled and wireless toys.
- Train sets and car race tracks that may produce sparks.
- Battery operated wristwatches.
- Avoid placing the baby to sleep on a party wall with your neighbor as you will not know what EMI producing equipment is on the other side of that wall.
- Avoid placing the baby to sleep near an electrical outlet.
- Avoid having electrical cables running along the floor where the baby may crawl.
- Avoid letting a baby crawl on a floor that may have electrical cables running underneath it. (Upper story of a home).
- Avoid living in apartments, as these present the biggest electromagnetic interference risk from the neighbors around you. A detached house is far better.
- Avoid letting a baby crawl on any type of electrically conductive flooring, such as tile or concrete.
- Keep babies and children away from electrical, electronic and wireless equipment in general.

The next diagram shows some of these concepts with regards to furniture layout. Note that the wall light has been removed in the "good" picture. The streetlight is still shown, as you may not have any control over that. The sofa's are no longer against the walls to move them out of the fields of the electrical cables and any electrical equipment that may be on the other side of the wall. The bed has been moved out of the TV fields.

Electromagnetic Room Layout

Bad

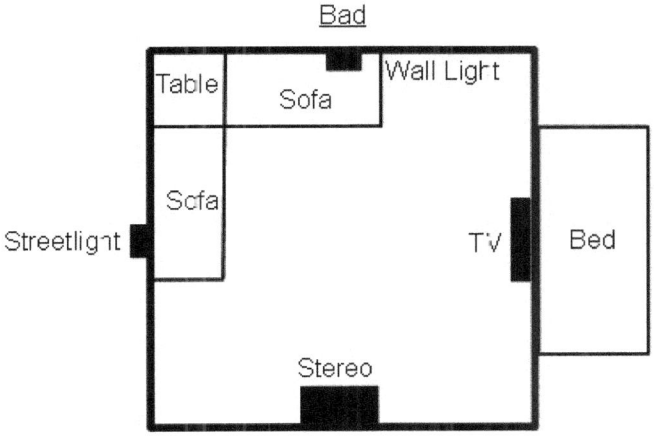

Good

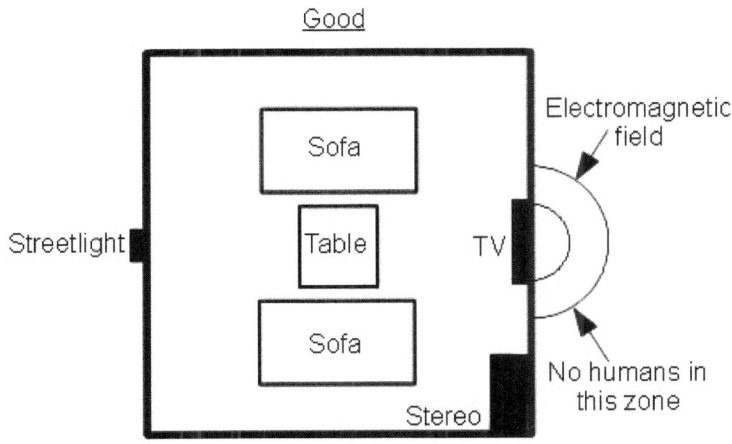

Women may be particularly at risk from the effects of electromagnetic interference exposures from electrical products. They generally wear under wired bra's and metal jewelery. These may couple into the fields through a process known as "induction" and AC voltages and frequencies will appear between the various items of metal on the body. It is easily measured using a digital multimeter or an oscilloscope with a frequency analyzer.

Measuring the AC voltage and frequency of the under wired bra is shown on the next page.

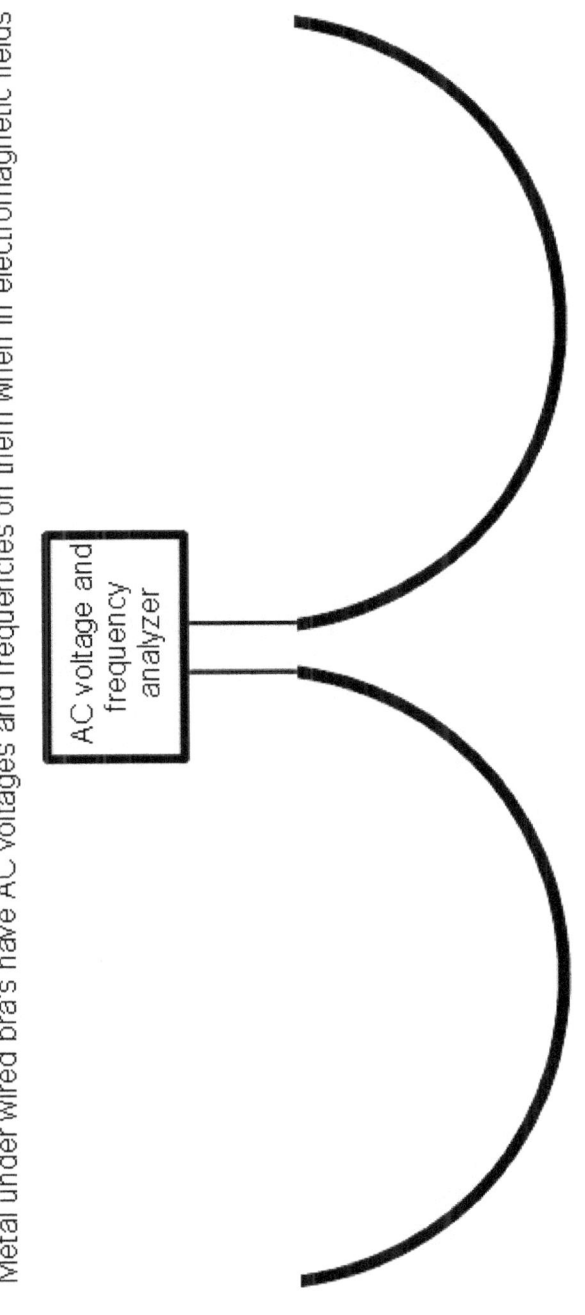

Electromagnetic Under Wired Bra

Metal under wired bra's have AC voltages and frequencies on them when in electromagnetic fields

AC voltage and frequency analyzer

Students are a particularly high risk group, as they tend to live in very small rooms equipped with a microwave oven, refrigerator, television, computer system, cell phone and Wi-Fi. The most concerning product is the refrigerator, as it runs almost continuously. While the motor is running, it will be emitting a large electromagnetic interference field. Students should not sit or sleep next to refrigerators!

Students should also be aware of the products their neighbors have and where they are located on the other side of the wall. They should ensure that there are no electromagnetic interference producing items near to the walls of their beds and their desks.

It is preferable not to have any AC cables near to the bed and to pull the bed out from the wall to move it away from the fields of the electrical cables in the wall. The optimum position for your head is the center of the room when in bed. This will ensure that the field strength is at its lowest for the brain.

If the student room is equipped with a florescent light, then do not use it. Instead, use filament lighting products with stand lamps and desk lamps. If it has a window mounted air conditioner, stay at least ten feet away from it when in use.

Shift workers are a group of people who are much sicker than the general population. Extended exposure to artificial lighting, dirty electricity, radio and microwave transmitters, and computer screens are environmental factors that may be feeding into their illness. Unnaturally overriding the natural wake and sleep cycles of the human body does not help either.

"There are many examples of the failure to use the precautionary principle in the past, which have resulted in serious and often irreversible damage to health and environments. Appropriate, precautionary and proportionate actions taken now to avoid plausible and potentially serious threats to health from EMF are likely to be seen as prudent and wise from future perspectives."

Professor Jacqueline McGlade

Ionizing Radiation

Wikipedia states: *Ionizing (or ionising) radiation is radiation composed of particles that individually can liberate an electron from an atom or molecule, producing ions, which are atoms or molecules with a net electric charge. These tend to be especially chemically reactive, and the reactivity produces the high biological damage caused per unit of energy of ionizing radiation.*

Natural background radiation comes from five primary sources: cosmic radiation, solar radiation, external terrestrial sources, radiation in the human body and radon.

Exposure to ionizing radiation causes damage to living tissue, and can result in mutation, radiation sickness, cancer, and death.

Ionizing radiation is commonly found in smoke detectors through their use of americium. Americium is commonly sourced from reprocessed nuclear fuel out of nuclear reactors. It is radioactive for hundreds of years and is used to ionize the air that passes through the detector to enable the detection of smoke particles.

Ionizing smoke detectors unnaturally raise the background radiation levels in the human environment.

The interesting thing about ionizing smoke detectors is that they are not needed. Photocell smoke detectors have always been available that do not use a radiation source to detect the smoke. After I realized that I had six ionizing smoke detectors installed at my home, I changed them out for photocell detectors instead. You will see them commonly marketed as kitchen smoke detectors, as they are not as sensitive as the ionizing type.

Fall out radiation is also ionizing and the world started to get coated in nuclear fallout radiation from the 1940's onward. Fall out radiation occurs when nuclear bombs are exploded and when nuclear power plants lose control and meltdown. Fallout radiation is spread around the world through the weather systems and as such, there is no place on the surface of the Earth that has not been contaminated. The effects of fallout radiation started to be realized in the 1960's and the nuclear weapons tests were moved underground in an effort to prevent this. Unfortunately, the nuclear surface contamination of the Earth will be emitting ionizing radiation for a few thousand years to come.

It is interesting to note that the USA government has stayed quiet on the issue of radiation fallout over the USA from the Fukushima nuclear power plant disaster in March 2011. The USA has constructed the largest radiation monitoring system in the world and will know exactly how much and where radiation was dropped onto the USA from that accident. Universities and independent researchers have been publishing data and it appears that the fallout was extensive and continuing daily as the Japanese nuclear power plant continues the process of melting down.

When reviewing the Los Angeles Times article *"Radioactive particles from Japan detected in California kelp"*, we find: *"Radioactive particles released in the nuclear reactor meltdown in Fukushima, Japan, following the March 2011 earthquake and tsunami were detected in giant kelp along the California coast, according to a recently published study."*

The Fukushima disaster is going to be remembered by future historians as where humanity gained its knowledge of the effects of widespread nuclear contamination of the ocean, of Japanese nuclear power plant workers and the surrounding population.

Cathode ray tube televisions and florescent tubes may emit X-rays and this is ionizing radiation. For this reason, your cathode ray tube television has lead impregnated into the screen in an effort to prevent this.

The medical and dental field has been routinely performing X-rays of patients for many decades now and this is a source of ionizing radiation for the human mind and body.

Regarding X-Ray machines, occasionally one will be melted down during the recycling of metal and will contaminate the entire batch of metal with ionizing radiation! Some of this radioactive metal does make it back into the marketplace and many people unknowingly have it in their homes. It may even be in your metal coil mattress! It is a good reason to own a Geiger counter so that you can detect these radioactive contaminated metals.

A side effect of ionizing radiation is that it extends the human life span by stressing the body. It is quite possible that exposure to ionizing radiation sources has increased the human life span from an average age of 65 in the 1940's to an average age of 78 today. Age extension by ionizing radiation is extensively documented in the nuclear industry.

The problem of increasing the human life span from 65 to 78 is that there may be 20% more people on the planet than really should naturally be here. With a world population of 7 billion, it is possible that 1.17 billion of them should not be here! This increasing population is raising pollution levels and stressing the world food supplies.

You will also notice it in Japan. Japan had two nuclear bombs dropped on it in 1945. This coated Japan with extensive fallout radiation that raised the background radiation levels. The people of Japan are noted for their longevity. It is quite possible that these longed lived people had just the right amount of radiation exposure from the natural sources and the fallout during their lives to reach the peak of longevity. Unfortunately, too much ionizing radiation will shorten the human lifespan by inducing disease into the body.

Stressing the human body with ionizing radiation is called "Radiation Hormesis". Wikipedia states: *Other analyses have shown persistent depression of peripheral leucocytes and neutrophils, increased eosinophils, altered distributions of lymphocyte subpopulations, increased frequencies of lens opacities, delays in physical development among exposed children, increased risk of thyroid abnormalities, and late consequences in hematopoietic adaptation in children.*

Ionizing radiation exposure is a complex equation and the correct radiation exposure for the human is always found in green environments with tree canopies.

The natural lifespan of humans in green environments is likely to be much shorter due to not having the cellular stresses of ionizing radiation exposure during their lives. Their bodies will live a shorter and healthier lifespan with excellent mental health before dying of natural causes. The correct human lifespan may be as short as fifty years of age away from radiation exposures.

Regarding the energy industry, Wikipedia states: *Nuclear reactors produce large quantities of ionizing radiation as a byproduct of fission during operation. In addition, they produce highly radioactive nuclear waste, which will emit ionizing radiation for thousands of years for some of the fission byproducts. The safe disposal of this waste in a way that protects future generations from radiation exposure is currently imperfect and remains a highly controversial issue.*

Radiation emissions from high level nuclear waste decrease extremely slowly, which requires long term containment and storage for thousands of years before it is considered safe. During normal conditions, radioactive emissions from nuclear power plants are generally lower than coal-burning plants; though several high profile nuclear accidents have released dangerous levels of radioactivity.

There are a number of high radiation exposure occupations and Wikipedia lists them as:

- *Airline crew (the most exposed population).*

- *Industrial radiography.*

- *Medical radiology and nuclear medicine.*

- *Uranium mining.*

- *Nuclear power plant and nuclear fuel reprocessing plant workers.*

- *Research laboratories (government, university and private).*

Solar radiation is a source of ionizing radiation and many health symptoms have been linked to it. Indeed, it is well known that when solar flares erupt, that human health is affected. In particular, disease, suicide, war, aggression and famine has been linked to it. Sunspots can have a similar effect.

When reviewing the amateur-radio-wiki.net article "*Sunspot Cycle*", we find: *"Most shortwave radio users know that there is a correlation between sunspots and propagation conditions. Sunspots are dark regions on the surface of the Sun, which are cooler than surrounding areas. They occur when the lines of the Sun's magnetic field become twisted. There are more sunspots when the Sun is more active, and produces more radiation which can affect the Earth's ionosphere."*

From my experiments, it is clear that various radiation exposures have a poisoning effect on the human mind and body and stress it. It appears that the longer and sicker lifespan has replaced the shorter and healthier natural lifespan for many people.

We can get an estimation of how radiation affects cellular development by growing plants near sources of ionizing radiation. I am currently growing Dieffenbachia's (Dumb Cane) in the ionizing radiation fields of americium smoke detectors to see how this radiation will affect them.

Wikipedia states: *Americium is the only synthetic element to have found its way into the household...Americium is not synthesized directly from uranium – the most common reactor material – but from the plutonium isotope... Most americium is produced by bombarding uranium or plutonium with alpha particles in nuclear reactors – one tonne of spent nuclear fuel contains about 100 grams of americium.*

The following pages show photographs of the experiments that I am currently performing using americium ionizing smoke detectors and plants.

A single ionizing americium smoke detector was used here. This is typical of what a home would have installed in the 1980's.

I found that my home had been constructed in 2004 with six ionizing americium smoke detectors and they were used to perform this experiment.

As can be seen, all of the plants died that were involved in this experiment. The control plant was inadvertently exposed to the radioactive ionizing americium smoke detectors during setting up the experiment and followed the same death process. It appears to be a case of "Delayed Radiation Complications".

I ran the experiment again with cactus, due to cactus being a high radiation plant. I made sure that each cactus was not exposed to the radiation from the other cactus experiment.

I found that the six made in Mexico in 2004 smoke detectors did not harm the cactus but the one made in China in 2010 was particularly biologically harmful. The compliance monitoring group for the University of Arizona tested the two types of smoke detectors used with calibrated professional equipment. China detector figure first and Mexico detector figure is in brackets:

- Victoreen 451B ion chamber: 10-40 microrad per hour for both.

- Ludlum 44-9: 250(60)CPM

- Ludlum 44-3: 10,000(1,500)CPM.

Thank you to the University of Arizona for assisting in this experiment. As you can see, different types of americium smoke detectors can have greatly varying radiation readings. Since there is so much variability with residential americium smoke detectors, it is better not to use them and to use photocell smoke detectors instead. These are commonly sold as kitchen smoke detectors. The radiation stressed cactus is shown in the next photograph.

"My main frustration is the fear of cancer from low dose radiation, even by radiologists."

John Cameron

The single made in China smoke detector cactus was showing stresses that neither the control nor the cactus with six made in Mexico smoke detectors were showing.

Wireless Radiation

T-aditionally, the antenna has been a long piece of straight metal that is energized by electrica. energy to electrify the surrounding environment. The length cf the metal antenna is matched to the frequency of energy that it transmits. The receiving antenna is matched in length and will absorb that frequency of energy from the environment. The electricity that is absorbed by the receiving antenna is then amplified and turned into a useful signal by the system that uses it.

Antenna systems come in many forms and are commonly disguised. The toxicity of anterna systems has long been known. Indeed, the microwave oven was born out of RADAR system development. RADAR was known to heat the engineers who were working with the systems. The engineers who worked with RADAR knew that they could rapidly warm their lunches with the high powered systems!

The microwave oven is the highest power transmitting device in the home. Nothing else comes close to it. Several hundred watts of microwave energy that heats your food by vibrating the water molecules. For the longest time they were banned in Russia as their scientist had deemed the food unfit for human consumption. That is also my assessment of the situation.

If you measure the magnetic, wide band radio wave, and microwave fields around a microwave oven when it is in use, you will find extensive fields in the human environment that extend several feet out from it. These fields are patchy and may pulsate. Most electromagnetic radiation researchers believe the pulsating fields to be the most harmful to human health.

I no longer use my microwave oven. It is a health choice that I made based on research that I conducted on plants in electromagnetic fields. If an electromagnetic field can change the growth patterns in plants, then it probably has the ability to affect human cellular development. You can check to see if your microwave oven is leaking radiation by placing a cell phone inside it and calling it from another phone. If it rings, then your microwave oven is leaking radiation!

The microwave oven is the highest power antenna system in a home, but what is the next highest? It is your cellphone! Many cellphones have the ability to generate approximately 2 watts of transmission energy and they do it right next to your brain! Smart phones can have multiple transmitter systems in them that operate at different frequencies.

When reviewing the Scientific American article *"Mind Control by Cell Phone"*, we find: *"The significance of the research," he explained, is that although the cell phone power is low, "electromagnetic radiation can nevertheless have an effect on mental behavior when transmitting at the proper frequency."*

The interesting thing about this study is that it is talking about exposure to a single cell phone. If you work in a cubicle office with one hundred other people with cell phones and WiFi computers, what would the effect be?

The potential power levels would be 100 times 2 watt cell phones plus 100 times 0.1 watt WiFi. This comes out to 210 watts of radiation emissions!

It is well known that certain plants will deform next to cell phones. When reviewing the emfnews.org article *"Electromagnetic effects on Plant Seeds, Beans and Yeast"*, we find: *"Samples of plant seeds, beans, and yeast microorganisms were located in the close proximity to cellular phones. Cellular phones were operating in stand by mode during this experiment; in other words, experiment provided effects of the 'near' field. The significant difference was observed in the growth cycle of green beans, black beans and black seeds on the twelfth day."*

You should avoid carrying your cellphone in your shirt pocket, as you will be placing the fields of it very close to your heart and lungs. It is a really bad idea to irradiate your organs with radio frequency radiation! You should carry it in a bag to keep it away from your body when not in use. Use the speaker phone feature to keep it away from your head when using it. Avoid the wireless headsets, as they will be irradiating your brain. Even when in standby, cell

phones are communicating with the cell phone tower approximately every ten minutes.

It has taken many years and cellphones are now listed as possible carcinogens and it is likely only a matter of time before they become listed as carcinogenic. Smart people pay attention to "possibly carcinogenic" products and avoid them. After conducting my research on cellphones, I canceled my contract and then watched for withdrawal symptoms. These are the health effects that I saw in the weeks following turning off the cellphone in the order that they occurred:

- Aching bones: Right hand digits, left lower rib, left thigh bone and skull. This was in line with the locations where the phone would be carried or used.

- Fatigue.

- Three days after turning off the phone, I had two nights of insomnia.

- Tiredness in the morning that lasted approximately one month.

- Left thigh muscle was twitching and the nerves were tingling. This was the location where I would carry the phone.

- Rib cage pains.

- Approximately three weeks later, body and intestinal pains for 1 night only.

- Headache that lasted for two days.

- Strange dreams.

It appears that cellphones poison the mind and body with long term exposure. This poisoning effect has been observed in plants near to microwave transmitters and they show stunted and deformed growth patterns. To put this to the test, I devised an experiment to produce withdrawal symptoms in the human mind and body.

The test was very simple. I live very close to three cell phone towers. Each is between 2,000 feet and 2,300 feet from my home. I had identified mylar film as a radiation shielding product, as NASA uses it in spacesuits. Mylar film is commonly sold as thermal "Space" blankets for first aid kits. My experiment consisted of sleeping on top of three sheets of mylar film and under three more sheets of mylar film. I was shocked at how extensive the withdrawal was! Here is what happened:

- Night 1: Withdrawal started the very first night and comprised of general aches and pains. Poor sleep. Feeling of nausea. Low energy in the morning. Spent 8 hours in mylar film.

- Night 2: No aches and pains. Insomnia. Low energy in the morning. 8 hours spent in mylar film.

- Night 3: Mild pain in heart for a fraction of a second. Skull pains for a few hours. Mild insomnia with naps. Tired in the morning. Spent 8 hours in mylar film.

- Night 4: Mild insomnia with naps. Plenty of energy in the morning. Got up early. Spent 6 hours in mylar film. Spent 1 hour hiking outdoors in sunlight to help with the withdrawal.

- Night 5: Slept well. Minor aches and pains. 8 hours under mylar film.

- Night 6: Slept well. Minor pains in intestines and testicles. 8 hours under mylar film.

As you can see, it was an extensive range of symptoms that showed up. I was going to continue for longer, but the Sun had a solar flare, so I stopped the test. I stopped sleeping with the three sheets on top of me but continued to sleep with 3 sheets of mylar film underneath me. I didn't feel quite right, with headaches and fatigue. So after a couple of weeks I took the mylar film off the bed completely and this rectified the situation. I suspect that the mylar film was causing my body to be cycled between low and high radio frequency radiation levels daily and that was causing the problem. I later tested mylar film and found that it acts as an antenna system! So it appears that I was subjected to electromagnetic shielding that had radio frequencies on it.

After seeing this effect, I concluded that the only true solution to eliminate human man-made radiation exposure is to turn off the transmitters that are producing it. It is not realistic nor humane to expect people to move out of the area nor to electromagnetically shield their homes.

The computer WiFi units appear to be the next largest source. They are particularly concerning due to the fact that they are always broadcasting their signals into the human environment. They never switch off. The power level is low at 0.1 watt, but the continual exposure to a digital microwave signal is a bad idea. I no longer use WiFi at home for that reason. When siting your WiFi system, you should consider mounting the unit as far away from the human environment as possible. Distance helps lower the signal strength from the base unit. Many electromagnetic researchers call WiFi *"the cell phone tower within your home"* as higher wireless radiation power levels can be found near to them than what you can find around cell phone towers.

Cordless phones, cordless baby monitors, cordless video systems, cordless alarm systems and cordless weather systems should all be avoided. You should be aiming to keep your environmental electromagnetic radiation levels as natural as possible.

You should avoid transmitting systems in homes that have metal roofs, metal wall studs, metal in their walls (stucco), and metal siding. Metal does the following things in transmission fields:

- Reflects waves.
- Creates interference.
- Absorbs radiation.
- Re-radiates radiation.

- Focuses radiation which creates hot spots.

This is shown in the next diagram.

Metal Homes

EMI
source

Metal homes may be filled with
electromagnetic radiation and interference,
and may be electrified

Structure
stray
voltage

The interesting thing about microwave radiation is that the atmosphere filters it out from the Space radiation. There were only extremely low levels of microwaves in the human environment until the human introduced high powered microwave transmission systems! For this reason you should be concerned. The use of microwaves for communications has raised the human microwave environment thousands of times higher than anything that can be found in nature! You have no genetic adaptation to high powered man-made microwave radiation.

You can replicate the atmospheric filtering effect with a cell phone. Simply put it in a see-through waterproof plastic bag and immerse it in water. About an inch into the water you will see the signal strength go to zero. This is because the water is absorbing the wireless radiation. The same process is occurring in your body when in wireless radiation fields. If there is a signal on your cell phone, then you are absorbing man-made wireless radiation. This may lead to your body becoming toxic and you will get a level of poisoning that could lead to electromagnetic hypersensitivity.

This is a concern with babies and developing children as their bodies are so much smaller. An inch of wireless radiation penetration into them is far deeper than on an adult! Wireless radiation will go very deep into a new born baby.

Regarding cell phone towers, they are generally regarded by electromagnetic researchers as being potentially toxic to the population who live within approximately a quarter of a mile of them. There are a number of studies that have shown that the illness rates spike up significantly in this quarter mile radius from the tower. The studies show that the illness rates are distance related. The closer you live to a cellular transmission tower, then the more likely it is that it will affect you.

Cell phone towers use the "sector antenna" that cover an area of 120 degrees. That is why you generally see a triangular arrangement of antenna systems to give the full 360 degrees coverage of the area. They typically cover a radius of 2 to 3 miles from the tower with good signal strength. This short transmission distance is the reason why you see cell phone towers at regular intervals in populated areas. Many cell phone towers are needed to give complete coverage in a city environment.

Homes near to transmitter systems may have radiation "hot spots" in them that extended time in these areas may lead to electromagnetic hypersensitiivty.

When reviewing the npr.org article *Wi-Fi Refugees' Are Moving To West Virginia To Escape Radio Waves*, we find: *"Dozens of Americans who claim to have been made ill by Wi-Fi and mobile phones have flocked to the town of Green Bank, W.Va.," the BBC reports. They're heading there because of the area's "National Radio Quiet Zone" — 13,000 square miles that surround the National Radio Astronomy Observatory's Robert C. Byrd Green Bank Telescope. The zone, as Wired has reported, is "nearly free of electromagnetic pollution" because of regulations put in place decades ago. Those restrictions aim to keep other electromagnetic signals from interfering with the telescope's work.*

People who live near cell phone towers should consider getting rid of their cell phones, Wi-Fi, and any wireless devices in the home. This action will reduce your radiation environment inside the home.

Directional antenna systems have what is known as "Side Lobe" emissions. The areas that the side lobes extend into are regarded as the most toxic areas for human health. They occur relatively close to the antenna system. Dish antennas are typical of this.

It is becoming common today for communication companies to disguise their antenna systems and you may not be aware of their presence. You should assume that there are transmission antenna systems in the following places:

- Police Stations.
- Fire stations.
- Hospitals.

- Military installations.
- Government buildings.
- Schools.
- Downtown areas.
- Television companies.
- Air and sea ports.
- Anywhere that you can get cellphone signals.
- Anywhere you can get WiFi signals.
- Anywhere that you can see communication towers.
- Anywhere where utility meters are present.

Firemen have gotten wise to the toxicity of cell phone towers and the International Association of Fire Fighters is opposed to them being located near to fire stations. This is their stance: *The International Association of Fire Fighters' position on locating cell towers commercial wireless infrastructure on fire department facilities, as adopted by its membership in August 2004, is that the IAFF oppose the use of fire stations as base stations for towers and/or antennas for the conduction of cell phone transmissions until a study with the highest scientific merit and integrity on health effects of exposure to low-intensity RF/MW radiation is conducted and it is proven that such sitings are not hazardous to the health of our members.*

Further, the IAFF is investigating funding for a U.S. and Canadian study that would characterize exposures from RF/MW radiation in fire houses with and without cellular antennae, and examine the health status of the fire fighters as a function of their assignment in exposed or unexposed fire houses. Specifically, there is concern for the effects of radio frequency radiation on the central nervous system (CNS) and the immune system, as well as other metabolic effects observed in preliminary studies.

It is the belief of some international governments and regulatory bodies and of the wireless telecommunications industry that no consistent increases in health risk exist from exposure to RF/MW radiation unless the intensity of the radiation is sufficient to heat body tissue. However, it is important to note that these positions are based on non-continuous exposures to the general public to low intensity RF/MW radiation emitted from wireless telecommunications base stations. Furthermore, most studies that are the basis of this position are at least five years old and generally look at the safety of the phone itself. IAFF members are concerned about the effects of living directly under these antenna base stations for a considerable stationary period of time and on a daily basis. There are established biological effects from exposure to low-level RF/MW radiation. Such biological effects are recognized as markers of adverse health effects when they arise from exposure to toxic chemicals for example. The IAFF's efforts will attempt to establish whether there is a correlation between such biological effects and a health risk to fire fighters and emergency medical personnel due to the siting of cell phone antennas and base stations at fire stations and facilities where they work.

You can read the full article here:
http://www.iaff.org/hs/Facts/CellTowerFinal.asp

It is well known in the industry that extended exposure close to a transmitter system may be harmful to human health and you should always try to put distance between yourself and transmitting devices.

If you have a job that is located near to a high powered transmitter, then you should consider changing your job. Extended close exposure to a high powered transmitter system should be expected to increase your chances of illness, disease, cancer and premature death.

Pay attention to your hearing, as you may develop "Microwave Auditory Effect". Wikipedia states:

The microwave auditory effect, also known as the microwave hearing effect or the Frey effect, consists of audible clicks (or, with modulation, whole words) induced by pulsed/modulated microwave frequencies. The clicks are generated directly inside the human head without the need of any receiving electronic device. The effect was first reported by persons working in the vicinity of RADAR transponders during World War II. These induced sounds are not audible to other people nearby. The microwave auditory effect was later discovered to be inducible with shorter-wavelength portions of the electromagnetic spectrum. During the Cold War era, the American neuroscientist Allan H. Frey studied this phenomenon and was the first to publish information on the nature of the microwave auditory effect.

If you start to hear strange things that no one else is, start looking into the transmitting devices around you!

The following pictures show building transmitters.

In this building and the surrounding buildings the people may be sick due to the transmissions from these multiple antenna systems. The worst place for human health may be the top floors of the building.

Transmitters on Buildings

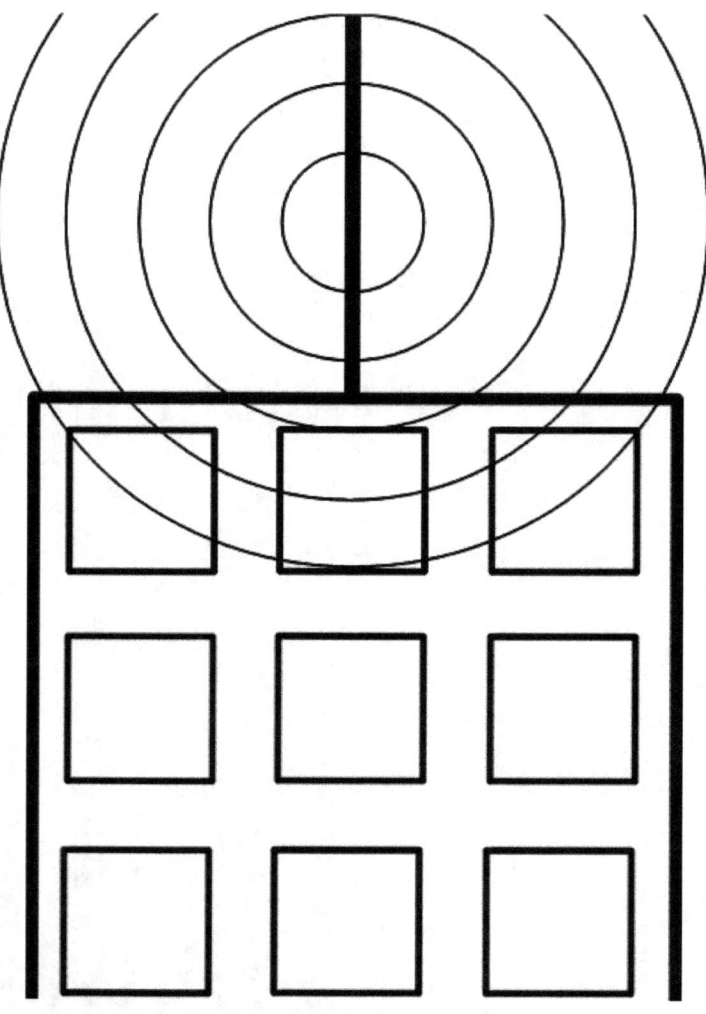

Electrical Forensics © Steven Magee

Can you see the cell phone antenna system?

It is on the top corner of the building. One has to wonder how the people who stay in the hotel must feel? Tall hotels commonly have transmitter systems on their roofs and you should avoid staying in the upper floors.

This cluster of radio frequency antennas, horns and dishes may be making the people in the area sick. Human habitations in the area of transmitting devices is a really bad idea.

Police stations can have high powered transmitter systems and they may be a cause of "Angry Aggression Theory" as applied to police officers.

The military has developed antenna technologies for use against humans and they have known for a long time that they can make people sick with it and damage their long term health. These fall under the class of "electromagnetic weapons".

The utilities are installing wireless transmitting utility meters at homes in number of countries now, including the USA. A popular product that the utilities use is the Itron OpenWay wireless communications system which is installed throughout Tucson, Arizona. The manufacturer states:

The Itron OpenWay wireless communication equipment operates in the Industrial, Scientific and Medical (ISM) bands at frequencies from 902 MHz to 928 MHz and from 2,400 MHz to 2,483 MHz. Also, a small number of devices incorporate wireless modems operating at frequencies 824-849 MHz and 1,850-1,910 MHz designated for the cellular operators (Cell Relays constitute about 1% of all the OpenWay wireless devices and can be mounted on poles or as part of a meter).

Tucson utilities appear to be using 0.5 watt Itron 100G transmitting gas meters, 0.1 to 0.3 watt transmitting Itron Centron electric meters and 1 watt transmitting Itron 100W water meters. So each property can have up to 1.8 watts installed at them. The homes are close together in Tucson and in a home like mine where the neighbors utility equipment is near, you essentially can have up to 6 utility meters transmitting approximately 3.6 watts of energy at or very near to your property! Unfortunately some homes may have what is known as the "mesh node" or "repeater" transmitter which may be much higher powered and may transmit much more frequently. The utilities appear not to notify the home owners that have these "mesh node" and "repeater" transmitters at or near to their properties. Some utility meters have multiple transmitter systems in them, so you may get subjected to higher levels of radiation at multiple frequencies from them. The utilities are willfully making many people sick with their biologically toxic transmitting meters.

It has been known for many years that a subset of the population cannot tolerate the radiation emitted by

transmitting utility meters and sickness results in these people. The utilities appear to be engaging in silence regarding this fact and they know that some of their customers develop electromagnetic hypersensitivity that is easily preventable but is commonly misdiagnosed as other conditions that may result in the person being placed onto prescription medication, losing their job, and possibly being placed onto disability. Their children may be the most affected and may not develop correctly.

It is important to note that many transmitters have a minimum distance that you should not get within, otherwise you will put yourself into known biological harm. The radiated transmitter power levels are much higher than stated closer to the transmitter and are of a "near field" exposure. For Itron Centron utility meters: *"RF Exposure (Intentional Radiators Only). In accordance with FCC requirements of human exposure to radiofrequency fields, the radiating element shall be installed such that a minimum separation distance of 20cm is maintained from the general population."*

They also have co-location requirements that specifies a minimum separation distance from adjacent transmitting systems.

Wireless radiation is readily absorbed by the human. The human is 70% to 90% water and the radio waves that are in the environment react with water. In the communications industry this is called "Rain Fade". When it rains, the wireless radiation power levels reduce as the rain drops absorb the energy. The human body does the same thing!

When queried about how wireless radiation affects the human mind and body, the wireless radiation industry will commonly incorrectly state that the "skin effect" protects the human. The skin effect is an observation that high frequency currents will travel down the outside of a conductor and not the center of it. This effect was noticed during the development of high frequency electricity.

The human body is not a conductor, but rather a semiconductor. Different electrical process are taking place

and it is clear today that the human mind and body can be greatly affected by these high frequency man-made exposures. The human skin evolved in a natural electromagnetic radiation environment and is now in a very unnatural man-made one that is making many people sick.

These harmful effects can be shown by growing plants in the electromagnetic fields. Dr. John Nash Ott extensively pioneered the field of electromagnetic radiation plant growth defects and his books on the subject are an interesting read. Like Dr. John Nash Ott, I have been able to deform plants with electromagnetic fields. This is what I have established:

- Found that Smart/AMR/AMI utility transmitting meters can have a toxic effect on the various biological systems that are near to them. The harmful biological effects can occur for at least 76 feet from some of the devices and can kill plants.

- Found that the radiation emissions from ionizing smoke detectors can retard cellular growth and may actually kill certain types of plants.

- Found that wireless radiation puts plants into a dormant state where they follow the changes in the seasons but do not actually grow nor bear fruits. They become sterile and stunted Removing the wireless radiation exposures resurrects them.

- Found that wireless radiation affects the growth and branching structure of some plants. Plants that grow tall may instead grow low to the ground.

- Some vines will not grow into areas of biologically unnatural radiation.

- Found that wireless radiation fields are patchy and unpredictable. Just moving a few inches can be the difference between a plant being healthy or it being stunted and deformed.

- Found that pulsed radiation from wireless weather station sensors and wireless utility meters can really retard and deform plants that are close to them. In some cases they will kill the plants.

- Discovered that certain electromagnetic exposures deform and retard plant growth and when removed, the plant drops all of the previous deformed leaf growth and starts growing normal growth from the tips of electromagnetic exposed part of the plant. The previously exposed part of the plant stays bald.

- Discovered that certain plants in unnatural radiation fields will only grow leaves on their branch tips at the edge of the plant. The interior of the branches of the plant stay bald. This growth pattern rectifies itself when the unnatural radiation field is removed.

- Found that the pomegranate tree will drop all of its leaf growth when the harmful wireless radiation field is removed and put up new growth from its base. The existing branches stay bald. The following year, it will put new leaf growth on both the old and new branches and bear fruit.

- Found that certain plants in biologically unnatural electromagnetic fields will turn their normally patterned leaves into dark green glossy leaves with no patterning.

It appears that when analyzing wireless radiation exposures you should think of them as you would think of a Tesla coil. The Tesla coil was where wireless radiation devices were developed from. A Tesla coil can emit biologically harmful visible sparks over long distances, often exceeding 100 feet. Some electrical, electronic, and wireless devices appear to emit similar biologically harmful "invisible sparks" a comparable distance. I call this: **"The Tesla Coil Model of Biologically Harmful Invisible Electromagnetic Radiation"**

The human mind and body cannot sense these biologically harmful invisible sparks and it slowly gets sick from exposure to them. The longer you are exposed to it, the more toxic you become. The range of these toxic electromagnetic fields varies with each device and is very unpredictable.

The leaf defects that the Dieffenbachia (Dumb Cane) plant displays in unnatural electromagnetic fields are shown in the following picture.

Leaf Deformities

The fully grown leaf deformities are shown. As you can see, a wide range of different size leaves can be generated, depending on the field type and strength that the Dieffenbachia (Dumb Cane) plant is exposed to.

Regarding wireless transmitting devices, I have found after many plant growth experiments:

- **Near exposures to transmitters are the most harmful. The most harmful transmitters that I have found are the lowest power ones that are sold to consumers as harmless wireless products! Devices that continually broadcast pulses of radiation every several seconds are the worst, such as wireless weather station sensors.**

- **Intermediate exposures are those from your neighbors wireless devices and those from Smart/AMR/AMI utility meters. These are the next worst exposures and you should be familiar with the wireless products that your neighbors have at their properties. You should consider installing electromagnetic shielding between the homes if they have harmful wireless products in use.**

- **Far exposures are those that are coming from high powered transmitters that are far away from your property. Examples of these are airport, port, and weather RADAR systems, TV and radio transmitters, government transmitters, cell phone towers, and so on. You should be aware of the locations of these to both your home and workplace. Only after working through the near and intermediate exposures should you start suspecting these as sources of your problems. Distance is your friend in the world of harmful electromagnetic radiation exposures!**

My research is indicating that home wireless devices can produce a biologically toxic field close to them. The size of this harmful field varies from device to device. Some of the harmful fields from home devices can extend at least 76 feet and the field is very patchy. Some areas are fine and others are toxic. Regarding the toxicity of wireless radiation exposure from common devices in the home, a clear classification is now emerging about the level of toxicity of these devices.

119

The most biologically harmful fields appear to be produced by pulsed radiation devices that broadcast regularly. Smart/AMR/AMI utility meters and wireless outdoor temperature sensors are good examples. "Smart" enabled devices that are designed to integrate into your utility "Smart" meter are likely to behave in a similar fashion. Some Wi-Fi devices and smart phones also display this behavior and it may be related to the applications that they have installed on them. Automatic door opening RADAR sensors that are common in large stores may fall into this category.

After this, I have the Wi-Fi router exposure rated as the next most toxic device as it is broadcasting continuously in the home and workplace, make sure you do not sit near to them. You should use your computer on a wired network connection whenever possible and turn off the Wi-Fi. Some cordless home phones may be in this category as they appear to behave like wireless networks. Wireless game controllers and radio controlled toys are in this category.

The cell phone is in the third class of toxic devices and I recommend people to avoid them. They communicate with the cell phone tower every ten minutes or so. Each time they do so, they will fill your home with wireless radiation. If you have multiple phones in the home, then your home will be filled with wireless radiation every few minutes. Some types of cordless home phones may fall into this category.

The fourth class of wireless device appears to be devices that only broadcast a short wireless pulse when they sense an event that triggers them. A garage door open or closed sensor would fall into this category. Most wireless security sensors and wireless door chimes behave in the same way. Some wireless utility meters also can exhibit this behavior.

This is the classification that appears to be emerging for home wireless devices from most toxic to least toxic:

1. **Devices that emit regular pulses of wireless radiation at short intervals of every 60 seconds or less.**

2. **Devices that constantly emit wireless radiation.**

3. **Devices that emit pulses of wireless radiation every several minutes.**

4. **Devices that emit pulses of wireless radiation infrequently.**

If you have several wireless devices close together, then you may have to reassess which category they fall into as it will increase the frequency of wireless pulses and/or wireless energy power being transmitted.

The frequency that a wireless device operates on may increase the toxicity of it. The most toxic device I identified at my home was a wireless outdoor temperature and humidity sensor. It operates for about a year on two AA 1.5 volt batteries. The frequency that it operated at was 433.92 megahertz and it appeared to be deforming a wide range of plants for at least a 45 feet radius from the device.

The gas company later installed an Itron 100G gas meter that surpassed the biological toxicity of that device to the human. Installed 76 feet away from my bedroom, that device induced classic radio wave sickness into me! It is listed as operating at between 908 to 924 megahertz at up to half a watt of transmission power. Half a watt is high powered for a residential application that constantly transmits pulsed radiation every several seconds. It is unfortunate that the highest powered transmitting devices at your home may actually be the utility meters that you cannot switch off!

To sum up, the biological toxicity of a transmitter to a human depends on the following:

- Transmission power.

- Transmitting frequency.

- Modulation of the signal.

- Intermittent, pulsed or continuous transmission.

- Reflections and interference of the transmission.

- Distance from you.

- The fat to muscle ratio of your body.

- Metal implants.

- The amount of metal in your environment.

- The height above the ground that you live.

You should be very wary of where you keep your cellphone and men should avoid keeping it near to their testicles and women should avoid keeping it near to the breasts. You should avoid putting a cellphone in your shirt pocket as it will be irradiating your heart and lungs. You most certainly do not want to sleep with your cellphone under your pillow, but unfortunately, many children do this every night. It is preferable to carry a cellphone in a separate bag away from the body.

It is interesting to note that astronomers have always thought that a mass human radiation extinction would come from a solar flare or a supernova. Pulsars may present the biggest naturally occurring risk to human extinction, as they behave like pulsed wireless transmitters. As we know today, the pulsar radiation emission is far more harmful at much lower power levels than the continuous radiation emissions from the Sun or supernovas. This opens up the range of nearby astronomical objects that can threaten the Earth by orders of magnitude. As such, a human radiation extinction is far more likely to come from a pulsar than any other astronomical object!

When we talk about extinction, we must remember that this will also affect everything on the Earth. Human survival is completely dependent on plants. Plants are affected by many forms of radiation and I have performed numerous tests that show the biologically harmful effects from man-made radiation exposures.

Regarding the toxicity of wireless radiation exposures, this is the official stance currently: *Lyon, France, May 31, 2011: The WHO/International Agency for Research on Cancer (IARC) has classified radio frequency electromagnetic fields as possibly carcinogenic to humans (Group 2B), based on an increased risk*

122

for glioma, a malignant type of brain cancer, associated with wireless phone use.

I have found climbing vines will not grow into areas of harmful wireless radiation and that the Golden Pothos will lose the patterning on its leaves in these fields. This is shown in the following pictures.

Golden Pothos

The Golden Pothos will lose the patterning in its leaves when in harmful wireless radiation fields. They grow dark green.

Climbing Vines

Some climbing vines will not grow into harmful wireless radiation areas. They provide an excellent indicator of the invisible patches of harmful wireless radiation that now exist.

Electrical energy interacts with the natural fields of the Earth. The human is genetically adapted to interact with natural, weak magnetic and electromagnetic fields. The cities represent the opposite of what nature created and today are an alien environment for the modern human. As such, it is reasonable to say that the modern human is an alien having developed in such an alien environment.

The alien human is revealing itself in many ways. We can see it in the dramatic rise in childhood development problems. Autism, attention deficit disorder, hyperactivity, insomnia, depression, fatigue, and accelerated puberty are all problems that are prevalent in modern children. Autism is the most striking and has accelerated from being a rare problem in the 1970's where only 1 in 10,000 children were diagnosed with the condition to a common development issue where 1 in 40 boys have it today!

Autism has been following the rise in wireless communications for the last decade and this is shown in the next graph. The graph was complied from data presented by CTIA-The Wireless Association and Talk About Curing Autism (TACA). It is clearly an electromagnetic radiation disease. The longer the damaging effects of man-made electromagnetic radiation are denied, the more this graph will continue to increase. Unfortunately, the wireless radiation era is not a good time to be born into.

Copyright Steven Magee Books

Year	Autism (ratio * 20000)	Cell Phones (millions)	Cell Towers (thousands)
1996	2	44	30
2001	133.4	128	128
2006	181.8	233	196
2011	333.2	332	283

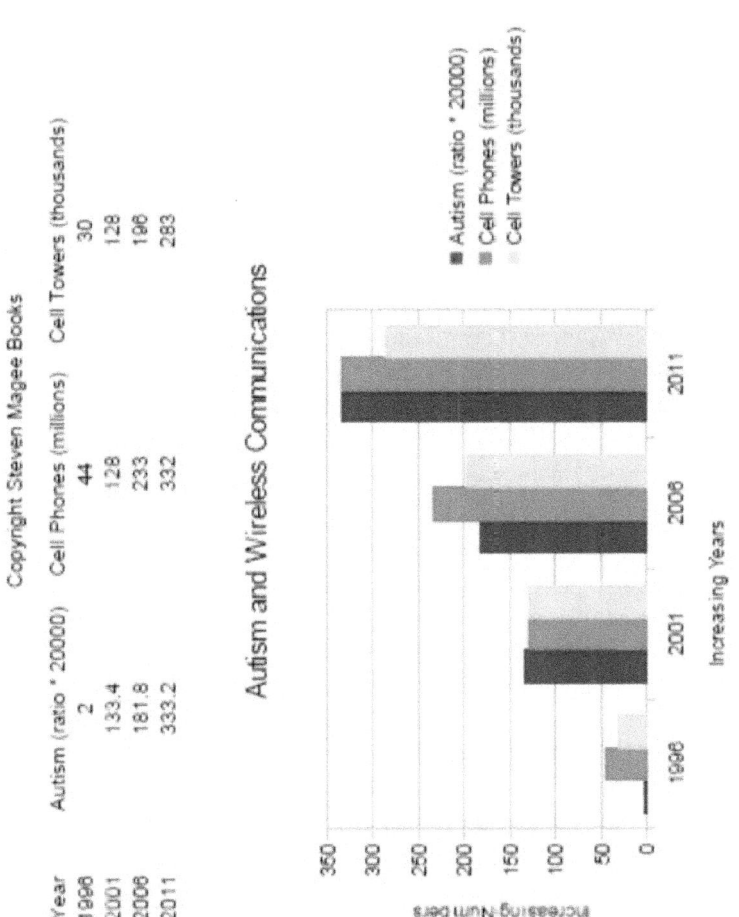

Autism and Wireless Communications

The BioInititaive 2012 report states: *The premise of this review is that although scant attention has been paid to possible links between electromagnetic fields and radiofrequency exposures (EMF/RFR) and Autism Spectrum Disorders (ASDs), such links probably exist. The rationale for this premise is that the physiological impacts of EMF/RFR and a host of increasingly well-documented pathophysiological phenomena in ASDs have remarkable similarities.*

You can find out much information about transmitting systems by obtaining the FCC ID number. This is stamped on all transmitting systems and the presence of it reveals that the device has an intentional radiation transmitting device installed into it. This number can be typed into the FCC website at http://transition.fcc.gov/oet/ea/fccid/ to obtain many items that relate to it. You will commonly find the technical manual and the radio frequency data in amongst the FCC submittals by the manufacturer. It is a very useful resource for obtaining transmitter data. Press the "advanced search" button to be taken to a more advanced search menu with many more options on it.

If you find that you are being biologically damaged by a transmitter, then you can file a complaint to the FCC under rule 15. FCC rule 15 states that no transmitter may cause harmful interference. Simply state in your complaint that you have found harmful biological transmissions from an FCC approved device. List the health conditions and the FCC identification number of the device. Request the FCC to inform the operator of the FCC approved device to be notified to cease biologically harmful transmissions into your environment. You should mail your complaint to: Federal Communications Commission, 445 12th Street SW, Washington, DC 20554

People who typically have high radio frequency exposures are:

- Emergency service workers.

- Radio frequency technicians and engineers.

- Amateur radio operators.

- Utility metering workers.

- Roofers.
- People who live in communities that have Smart/AMR/AMI meters.
- People who work near to transmitter systems.
- People who are issued a radio transmitter in their jobs.
- People who work with RFID devices.
- People who work with wireless scanners.

Some reasonable health precautions are:

- Do not purchase wireless products.
- Shield the area of your home that has the utility meters near to it.
- Plant tall trees near to transmitting utility meters, as they will absorb the signal.
- Have the utilities remove their transmitting meters and replace them with non-transmitting versions.
- Do not live near to an antenna transmission system.
- Do not spend extended periods of time next to a transmitter.
- Avoid trips to scenic mountains that have transmitters on them. Generally these transmitters are the highest powered systems and the energy density will be very high in these locations.
- Avoid taking a job that is located near to a high powered transmitter.
- Avoid taking jobs that issue you with a radio transmitter for communications.
- Change you metal coil mattress to a foam one.
- Change your metal furniture to wooden furniture.

- Avoid being in areas with large numbers of people, as they may all have cellphones and WiFi devices. This increases the energy density.

- Avoid being inside metal structures with transmission devices. They will fill the area with reflected and interference energy.

If you combine the last two, you have an airplane! Frequent travelers are known to be amongst the sickest people in the general population.

You must remember that radiation transmitting antenna systems function by electrifying their environment. The peak energy density in the environment is at the transmitter and it falls off with distance.

There are some systems that actually function as inadvertent transmission antenna systems:

- Electronic products.

- Home wiring.

- Electrical utility wiring.

- Earthing (grounding) systems.

The size of an antenna system is based on the frequency that it transmits at. For very low frequencies you have a very large antenna and for very high frequencies you have a very small antenna.

In the wireless radiation plague that we now find ourselves in, radio frequency (RF) meters have become popular products that people are obtaining to protect themselves. There are a few things that you should be aware of when operating these RF meters. When measuring radio frequency fields, the RF meter manuals typically instruct you to hold the meter at arms length. You should be aware that putting the RF meter near to metal can throw off the reading. That is why you should not put it near to electrical outlets.

Mass market RF meters are typically only accurate in the far field and the far field of residential transmitters can be very large at lower frequencies. Indeed I have a 400 MHz weather station transmitter at my home and you would have to keep the RF meter at least three feet away from that to get an accurate reading. My Tenmars TM-196 RF meter starts reading at 10 MHz which means that you would have to have the meter at least 30 meters away from a 10 MHz transmitting source to get an accurate reading!

Know the frequencies that you are dealing with and keep the minimum measuring distance at least one wavelength away from the transmitting device which is regarded as the near field. When measuring radio frequencies, the RF meters are typically only accurate in the far field which is outside of these distances:

- 1 MHz = 300 meters.

- 10 MHz = 30 meters.

- 50 MHZ = 6.0 meters.

- 100 MHz = 3.0 meters.

- 200 MHz = 1.5 meters.

- 300 MHz = 1.0 meter.

- 400 MHz = 0.75 meters.

- 500 MHz = 0.6 meters.

- 600 MHz = 0.5 meters.

- 700 MHz = 42.9 cm.

- 800 MHz = 37.5 cm.

- 900 MHz = 33.3 cm.

- 1.0 GHz = 30 cm.

- 2.0 GHz = 15 cm.

- 3.0 GHz = 10 cm.

- 4.0 GHz = 7.5 cm.

- 5.0 GHz = 6.0 cm.
- 10 GHz = 3.0 cm.

The health effects of the near field and far field exposures may be different. One is likely to be more toxic than the other. The near field contains far more energy than the far field. Regarding transmitter systems, generally it is the far field exposure that is quoted for the radiant power of the antenna system.

RADAR (RAdio Detection And Ranging) systems should be avoided. They have a very high powered pencil like beam of energy. The power can be in the range of 250,000 watts on the weather systems. RADAR workers have shown numerous health effects from near exposure to the beam. Cataracts are common in RADAR workers. If you live in a large city, you will be subjected to the RADAR from many RADAR systems. RADAR is in common use to open automatic doors on many shops and large buildings and they fill the area inside and outside of the shop with RADAR radiation. Some people may exhibit sickness when in a RADAR field. Dr. John Nash Ott filmed animals reacting to airport RADAR, they would react every time the sweep of the RADAR beam went through his home.

Male impotence is on the rise and so are the sales of impotence curing drugs. The impotence effect was noted to occur in RADAR workers during its development. Cell phones use RADAR frequencies, as does WiFi, and most domestic wireless products. It is likely that these wireless energies are contributing to the emasculation of the modern man.

Humans are acting as antenna systems and that is why you need to keep the RF meter away from you when performing measurements. Humans also act as reflectors and can increase the RF power density near to them.

Regarding electronic products, the operating frequencies have been getting very high due to the increasing computer processor speeds. If the product has not been designed well, then it may well be acting as a transmitter. An example of this is my digital television. It was transmitting energy that was stunting the growth of my outdoor plants over sixty feet away in the garden!

Electrical wiring is a horrendous transmitting device and you should pay attention to your home electrical system due to this. If you install certain products onto your electrical system, then you will turn it into a transmitting device! This effect has been especially noticed with people who use certain types of electronic energy star lighting products.

Electrical utility wiring is an interesting transmitter. The frequency of 60Hz is very low, but the utility transmission and distribution lines are very long, sometimes thousands of miles long! The utility companies may be inadvertently building transmitter systems. The city electrical distribution system may actually be a fractal antenna system! These are much smaller than conventional antenna systems. Harmonics on the utility power lines may make power lines that normally do not function as a transmitter turn into one.

Wikipedia states: *A fractal antenna is an antenna that uses a fractal, self-similar design to maximize the length, or increase the perimeter (on inside sections or the outer structure), of material that can receive or transmit electromagnetic radiation within a given total surface area or volume.*

Because the electrical grounding system is connected to the utility neutral transformer connection, if the neutral conductor has dirty electricity on it, it may turn the entire area around your ground rods into a transmitter. The area for tens to hundreds of feet around your ground rods may turn into a transmission hot zone, even your plants may be acting as transmitters! Anyone in this area may get sick with extended exposure to this.

The AC electrical system operates in a range called the "Schumann Resonances" that are typically between 3 to 60

Hertz. Schumann resonances occur due to the cavity between the surface of the Earth and the conductive ionosphere, it acts as a "closed waveguide". Schumann resonances have distinct peaks at 7.86 Hz (fundamental), 14.3 Hz, 20.8 Hz, 27.3 Hz and 33.8 Hz. It does not surprise me to hear people saying that utility electrical frequencies affect them as it is likely that they are interfering with the natural Schumann resonances.

Due to these problems, I advise people to avoid transmitter systems, turn off the circuits in your home that you do not normally use, and to use minimal electronic products. Use mains filtering products with your electronic systems and also in the fuse board.

Metal should be avoided in the home and workplace because it acts as an absorber and reflector of radio frequencies and may distort the natural magnetic field. Avoid sleeping on metal coil mattresses as they have a wide range of unnatural energies flowing on them, you can easily obtain foam mattresses that do not have these problems. Unfortunately, some people may be developing electromagnetic hypersensitivity as they sleep! Use wooden chairs and wooden furniture as they are healthier.

Regarding wireless radiation exposures, the EMFields Acousticom 2 radio frequency meter manual states:

6 to 3 V/m: Too high for ambient levels.

1-0.3 V/m: Too high for many people.

0.1 to 0.05 V/m: Many people have symptoms.

0.02 to 0.01 V/m: Most people with EHS are okay.

I can recommend the free BioInitiative 2012 report for further reading on the subject of wireless radiation: http://www.bioinitiative.org/

Books that document the known biologically harmful effects of wireless radiation are:

• "Disconnect" by Devra Davis.

- "Public Health SOS: The Shadow Side of the Wireless Revolution" by Magda Havas and Camilla Rees.
- "Cellular Telephone Russian Roulette" by Robert Kane.

The following pages show the side lobe effect and the many types of antenna systems that are commonly found today.

"The evidence for risks from prolonged cell phone and cordless phone use is quite strong when you look at people who have used these devices for 10 years or longer, and when they are used mainly on one side of the head. Recent studies that do not report increased risk of brain tumors and acoustic neuromas have not looked at heavy users, use over ten years or longer, and do not look at the part of the brain which would reasonably have exposure to produce a tumor."

Lennart Hardell, MD, PhD

Side lobe fields are around all directional transmitting antenna systems.

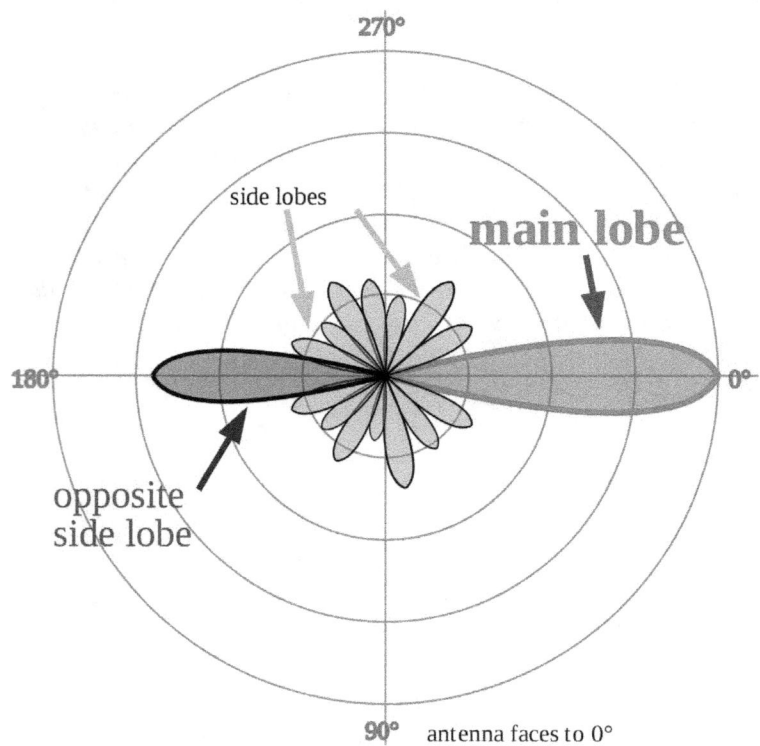

This extremely tall antenna system may be broadcasting very high power levels of electromagnetic radiation. The power poles and buildings give a sense to the height of this antenna system. Across the road is the local school.

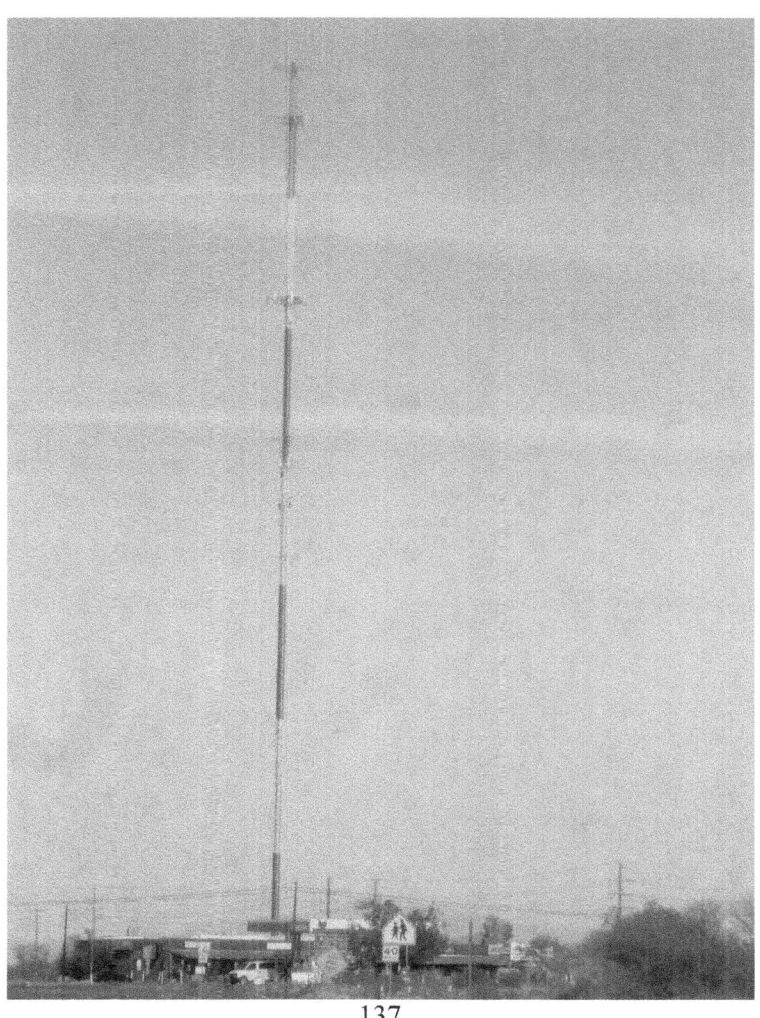

This is a typical dish antenna. Behind the wall is a residential neighborhood.

Here is a combined power distribution pole and antenna system. This was in front of the church in a residential neighborhood. At the back of the church was a playground.

Here is a combined transmission line tower and antenna system. This was in the shopping mall.

Here is a cell phone tower that is inappropriately sited. The wireless energy will be reflected from the electrical transmission lines. Both the transmission lines and the cell phone towers appear to be too close to the homes and the people may be sick in this location.

Here is a communications tower disguised as a palm tree. It was in the center of a residential area. These are called "stealth towers" in the industry.

The police car may be a toxic environment today due to the extensive wireless communications in use, RADAR and LASER systems, the police computer system in the car, the flashing light emissions, and the car electromagnetic radiation emissions.

Satellites

Several decades ago the Earth only had one moon orbiting it. Today it has several thousand! The development of the Space industry has lead to massive amounts of satellites to be put in orbit. However, the Space industry did not do its homework prior to developing this field.

Mankind has known for thousands of years that when the moon eclipses the Sun, many strange behaviors are observed in animals and plants. All of the cycles go off and some plants will open their flowers and others will close them. The animal behaviors show a state of confusion. Some animals will wake up and others will go to sleep. Birds and bees stop flying. It does not matter what time of day the eclipse occurs, animal behavior is affected, so it is not just a change in lighting levels or heat that does this.

What an eclipse of the Sun does is to create a very strange radiation environment on Earth. The animals and plants are reacting to the changed electromagnetic radiation environment. Light and heat is just a small part of that changed environment.

The same effect appears to happen with satellites. The International Space Station is so large now, that it is the biggest thing in Space that can be photographed passing across the surface of the Sun, other than the moon. It is far larger than the sunspots! Every time a satellite passes in front of the Sun, the electromagnetic environment is changed on the ground below. The effects of this are currently unknown.

However, in recent years a disorder in the Bees has shown up called "Bee Colony Collapse" disorder and it may well have a link to man-made satellite eclipses of the Sun that cause interference radiation to occur. Bee colony collapse was noted to significantly increase late in 2006, after the International Space Station had new solar arrays added onto it. The greatly increased its size and its effect when eclipsing the Sun.

The other problem with satellites is that they are continually bombarding the Earth with electromagnetic radiation! No one is quite sure what types of radiation that they are broadcasting as there are so many of them, many of which are secret military satellites. However, it is a fact that it is diverse.

This diverse man-made radiation is an addition of electromagnetic radiation on the surface of the Earth. Today, there is nowhere on the surface of the Earth that is free from it. The Earth has complete man-made satellite coverage.

These effects are shown in the next diagrams.

Satellite Interference

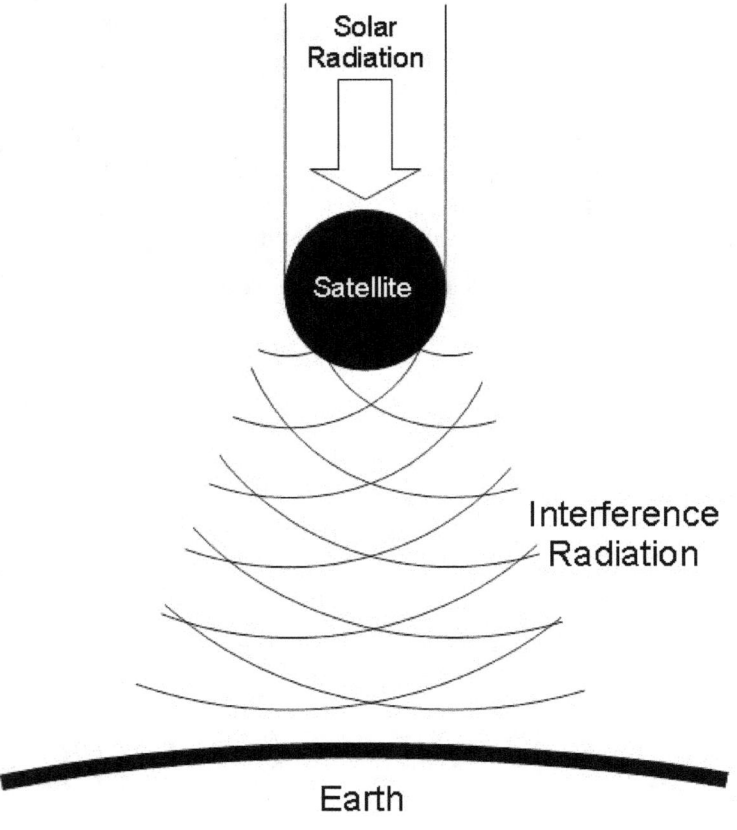

The Earth has complete artificial satellite coverage.

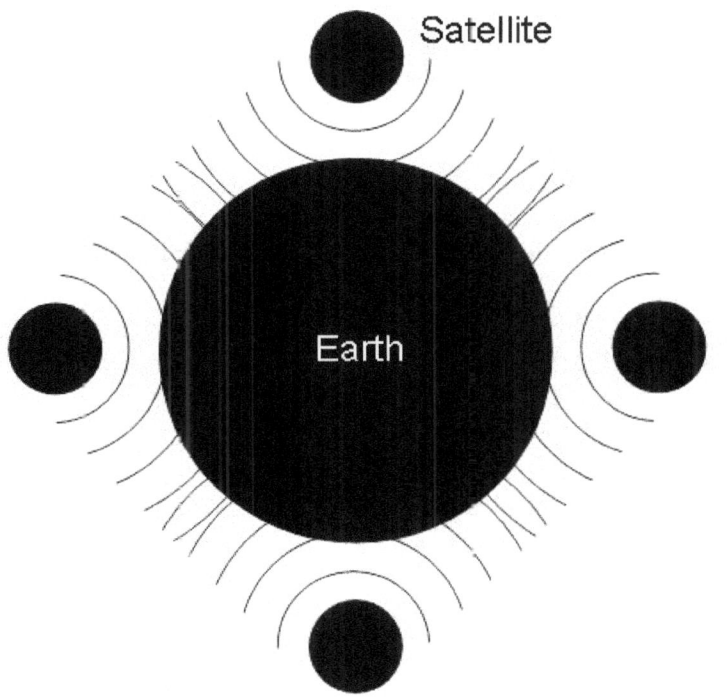

This is somewhat concerning, given the extensive denial about the health effects of electromagnetic interference. There is only one European country that appears to acknowledge it and that is Sweden. In Sweden, over 300,000 people are registered as having electromagnetic hypersensitivity. It clearly is a problem that is not unique to Sweden!

Unfortunately for the modern human, the development of the satellite industry took place without understanding these problems and today, it may actually be one of the biggest problems facing the future of humanity!

A scary thought about satellites is that once a nation has complete global coverage of the Earth, if they were to broadcast the correct types of electromagnetic radiation frequencies to the surface of the Earth, they could feasibly cause massive species extinction. This is called: **Satellite Extinction**

Extinction energy frequencies are already being broadcast and they may be doing extensive harm to both plants and humans. The military has identified frequencies of energy that are harmful to human health and developed them for use in war zones. It is probably a feature that is present on secret military satellites.

I expect to see many countries in the future to be requesting the removal of satellites from their field of view of the sky. Satellites are the latest pollutant to be identified as a potential human health hazard.

"The U.S. spends over $2 trillion dollars on health care each year, of which about 78% is from people with chronic illnesses, without adequately exploring and understanding what factors —including EMF/RF—contribute to imbalances in peoples' bodies' in the first place. After reading The BioInitiative Report, it should come as no surprise to policymakers, given the continually increasing levels of EMF/RF exposures in our environment, that close to 50% of Americans now live with a chronic illness. I grieve for people who needlessly suffer these illnesses and hold out the hope that our government leaders

will become more cognizant of the role electromagnetic factors are playing in disease, health care costs and the erosion of quality of life and productivity in America."

Camilla Rees, MBA

Power Lines

Power lines and poles running through the streets is a bad idea. They have a number of problems that may lead to illness:

- Electrostatic attraction.

- Electrostatic fields.

- Magnetic fields.

- Electric fields.

- Wide band radio wave emissions.

- Plasma emissions.

- Ion emissions.

- Ozone emissions.

- Nitrogen dioxide emissions.

- Reflection and interference of sunlight.

- Reflection and interference of radio and microwaves.

- AC electrification of the ground around them. (Stray voltage/current/frequency).

The utility power lines have setbacks that apply to them and for 13,800 volt AC lines, this setback is typically thirty feet either side of them. Building of homes and offices in these setbacks is generally not allowed due to the high electromagnetic fields that are present within the setback. The larger the voltage, the larger the setbacks become. Power line set backs can be several hundred feet wide on the higher voltage transmission systems.

Power line wide band radio wave emissions may be erratic, occurring only at certain times of the day or during certain weather conditions. They are generally caused by the induction of electrical energy into the surrounding metalwork on the power pole that can cause sparks to jump between the metalwork   A failing or dirty insulator may have a similar effect. When a power line starts to emit radio waves, these may extend beyond the power line set back. The radio waves cannot be heard and a standard AM radio tuned to static (no radio station) can generally be used to detect them. Extended exposure to these wide band radio wave emissions may lead to electromagnetic hypersensitivity.

Power lines that carry harmonic energy may have a wide range of emissions from them. Harmonic energy levels will vary during the day and the seasons. It is important for human health to stay away from power lines that have harmonic energy on them.

While developing the power line section of this book, I spent three hours each night for two nights examining the power poles and power lines in the area of my home. I noticed the following conditions occurring over the following weeks:

- Headaches.
- Insomnia.
- Fatigue.
- Sore throat.
- Irregular heartbeats.
- Intestinal pains.
- General poor health.
- Heightened sexual desire occurred in the first few days after testing was finished, it appeared to be a side effect of electromagnetic interference withdrawal.

You should not spend time directly under power lines, as this will put you into the plasma field. Plasma is the fourth state of matter and under the power poles is an invisible flow of electrons from the power lines into the ground below.

There may be an electrostatic field present and this appears to be the reason why florescent tubes will light there. You can place 8 foot long florescent tubes vertically into the ground and watch them light up at night if the electrostatic field is present! A large piece of aluminum foil can also detect the electrostatic field with an AC voltage meter that has the ground probe electrically grounded. Do not touch the foil, as it may shock you! It may also damage your meter if the voltage on the foil is too large. It is a strange sensation to walk into a high powered electrostatic field as it is this field that makes your hair start to react. Nikola Tesla was trying to develop wireless lighting products using this field. We are fortunate that he never achieved his dream, as he may have made many people sick with his wireless lighting system. Nikola Tesla did end up being regarded as "nutty" and exposures to the electrostatic field may have been one of the things that was affecting him.

During my research into power lines producing AM radio frequencies, I noticed the reflection effect. The cell phone tower wireless energy seems to be interacting with the power lines and may be producing pockets of AM radio frequencies that can be picked up on a standard AM radio tuned to static (no radio station). If you were in one of these pockets for an extended time period, you may develop electromagnetic hypersensitivity.

You will find very high levels of body voltage around high voltage power lines and poles. It is shocking at how high they can get to. I will no longer work with high voltage systems due to the many problems that are around them and the strange behaviors that I have observed in people who work with it.

The following pages demonstrate the various effects of power lines.

Power lines and poles can have many types of large fields around them. "Dirty electricity" effects may cause extensive radio wave fields.

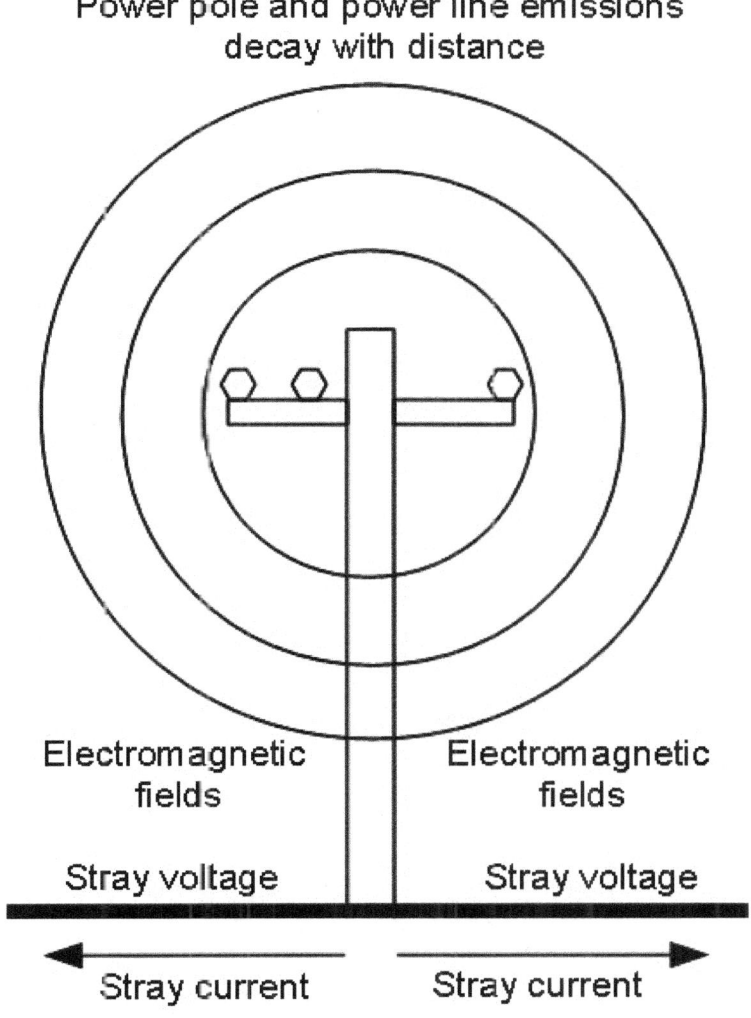

Power pole and power line emissions decay with distance

Electromagnetic fields

Electromagnetic fields

Stray voltage

Stray voltage

Stray current

Stray current

Induction effects in power pole metal work may cause sparks to jump between it which will cause radio wave emissions to occur. Defective insulators, oxidized clamps, defective fuses and damaged lightning arrestors may do the same.

Power lines and poles can emit plasma and ions. The high voltage causes the electrostatic attraction effect. Power lines and poles have fields that extend out from the area that set backs should be applied to, to protect human health.

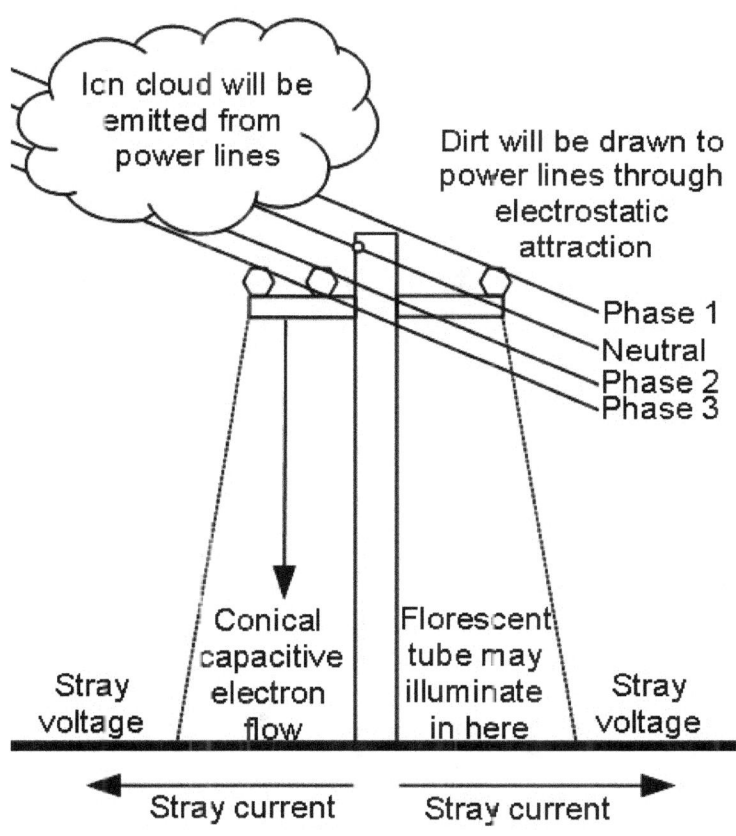

Power lines running down the pole may be the largest source of electromagnetic radiation in the human environment. You should stay away from poles that have conduits running down them.

Power poles have a grounding (earthing) cable running down them. This connects the neutral cable at the top of the pole to the ground (earth) below. The ground in the vicinity of utility power poles is commonly electrified with stray voltage/frequencies and has ground currents in it.

Power Line and Pole Solar Interference

The power poles and lines can interfere with the solar radiation
transmission when in front of the Sun.

Power lines may cause solar, radio and microwave reflections and interference effects to occur.

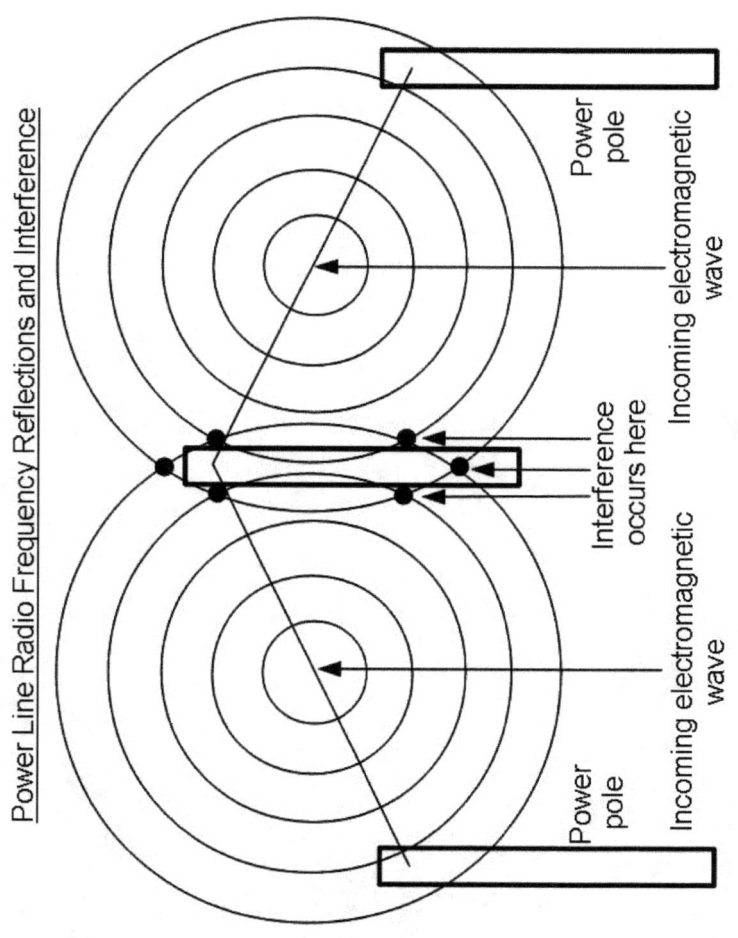

Power Line Radio Frequency Reflections and Interference

Dr. Phillip Stoddard, Professor of Biological Sciences at Florida International University, has done extensive research on power lines. He has found very significant health risks from their presence:

- **The closer you live to a power line, the more likely you are to develop leukemia.**

- **Living in a magnetic field of 3.5 milli-gauss doubles the leukemia risk.**

- **Living within 0-50 meters of a power line doubles the risk of Alzhiemer's Disease and presents a 1.5 increased risk of developing senile dementia.**

- **Burying the power lines brings the magnetic fields closer.**

I do not recommend that you spend significant time underneath high voltage power lines, as you may be getting a free radiation treatment! They really should be fenced to keep people from venturing under them, especially young children. You should not buy a home that is underneath them if you value your health, as many people have become sick in such homes.

People have reported that they feel better in areas that the power lines are routed underground. However, this apparent improvement to health occurs only when the power lines are buried for at least half a mile in radius from the person. This is consistent with observations of lightning strikes preferring to hit tall grounded metallic objects. It is also consistent with the various electromagnetic emissions that power lines may create near to them.

A common problem on buried power lines is the corrosion of the concentric neutral. The concentric neutral is the wire that you see wrapped around the outside of the utility cable that comes down the power pole. If this corrodes, then the neutral starts to become high impedance and this will cause current to increase though the ground. Basically, corrosion of the concentric neutral will electrify the surrounding ground and is clearly a human health hazard. Faulty insulation on the live conductor that causes leakage currents will have a similar effect. Many children have been killed by stepping onto electrified ground during and after rains, when the problem is made much worse by conductive water.

The orientation of power lines with respect to the Earth's magnetic field may be an important factor in how they interact with human health. Power lines are known to interact with electromagnetic fields and this generally occurs during solar flare activity. Solar flares can knock out the electrical grid system if the flare is strong enough by inducing energy into the system. It appears that the electrical utilities may have built an inadvertent antenna system for solar flare energy!

It is not a good idea to live near to electrical equipment. The following locations should be avoided if you value your health:

- Streetlights.
- Power lines.
- Power poles.
- Transformers.
- Substations.
- Switch yards.
- Electrical power generation plants (coal, gas, oil, nuclear, steam, dams).
- Electronic power generation plants (wind, solar, tidal, wave, etc).

The areas in the vicinity of these may have large amounts of stray voltage/current/frequency.

Regarding human health, Wikipedia states: *The UK Department of Health set up the Stakeholder Advisory Group on ELF EMFs (SAGE) to explore the implications and to make recommendations for a precautionary approach to power frequency electric and magnetic fields in light of any evidence of a link between EMF and childhood leukemia. The first interim assessment of this group was released in April 2007, and found that the link between proximity to power lines and childhood leukemia was sufficient to warrant a precautionary recommendation, including an option to* **lay new power lines underground where possible and to prevent the building of new residential buildings within 60 m (197 ft) of existing power lines.** *The latter of these options was not an official recommendation to government as the cost-benefit analysis based on the increased risk for childhood leukemia alone was considered insufficient to warrant it. The option was considered necessary for inclusion as, if found to be real, the weaker association with other health effects would make it worth implementing*

Areas of known electromagnetic radiation hazards should be clearly signposted and preferably fenced to keep people out of harm. This is a particular problem for USA police officers and delivery drivers who spend their day driving around the city next to the power lines.

Areas around power plants may have strange environmental conditions associated with them. When reviewing the *Atmospheric Inversion Layers* article on bookrags.com, we find: ***The mere presence of a city or factory often creates a microclimate of its own, creating a pocket of warm air within the cool ground layer. Smoke from a stack, instead of escaping upward or laterally, will descend to the ground, delivering a direct dose of pollution to residents of the area.***

The following pictures demonstrate some of the problems.

Power plants emit large amounts of pollution, electromagnetic fields, and stray voltage/current/frequency effects. For this reason you should avoid living in areas that are near to power plants like this. The chimney emissions will cause solar radiation transmission problems.

Electrical Forensics © Steven Magee

Utility switch yards should be avoided as there may be very
large electromagnetic fields, electromagnetic reflections and
interference, large ground currents, and stray voltage/frequencies
in these areas.

Electrical Forensics © Steven Magee

The lady in the picture has parked her car in the power line corridor and appears to be unaware of the detrimental health problems that may occur by spending extended time in this location.

The USA commonly runs high voltage power lines along sidewalks and through residential areas. This lady appears unaware of the electromagnetic fields and stray voltage effects that may be present in her environment.

Around transformers you will find large electromagnetic fields and stray voltage/current/frequency at times. You should avoid spending time near transformers.

The sidewalk runs next to this equipment. The area should be fenced to keep people out of the electromagnetic fields. The other side of the wall should not be a human inhabited area to protect the health of the people in the building.

To put the public health system for electrical safety to the test to see what would happen, I reported a known defective utility electronic power plant that was generating high amounts of harmonic energy to these agencies:

- Occupational Safety & Health Administration (OSHA).

- State Public Commission (Utility company regulator).

- Federal Energy Regulatory Commission (FERC).

- North American Electric Reliability Corporation (NERC).

- Federal Communications Commission (FCC).

And this is what happened:

- OSHA said they investigated, found no problems, and shut down the complaint.

- State Public Commission never responded.

- FERC never responded.

- NERC said that it was the FCC's job.

- FCC responded and said that they would not investigate.

What I reported was a utility electronic power plant that was known to be producing extensive harmonics into the utility transmission system and that appeared to be affecting the health of the on site staff due to the excessive electromagnetic fields around the equipment. They were informed that I had developed classic symptoms of radio wave sickness while at the power plant and that I had observed similar symptoms in the on-site staff. They were also informed of extensive technical design mistakes and the dangerous problems that it was showing. This is what the FCC said about it:

Electric power transmission lines are considered "Incidental Radiators" under FCC Rules. See Title 47, Code of Federal Regulations, Section 15.3(n). [47 CFR §15.3(n)].

Incidental Radiators may be operated subject to the condition that no harmful interference is caused. See 47 CFR §15.5(b). **FCC Rules prescribe no specific limits for the electric or magnetic fields radiated by Incidental Radiators.** *The information that you supplied appears to suggest that you believe that interference may occur, but provides no evidence that interference is actually being caused.*

Because the FCC does not specifically limit emission levels from Incidental Radiators, no investigation can be initiated without a bona fide interference complaint. This office is aware of no complaints of harmful interference from the power plant.

The FCC does not regulate emissions or exposures at power line frequencies (typically 60 Hertz), which are classified as extremely low frequency (ELF). While harmonics of 60 Hz may be generated for various reasons, it is our believe that those harmonics exist at significant levels only up to a few kilohertz, and not into the radiofrequency (RF) regime. Some states and local jurisdictions have established their own requirements limiting ELF emissions or exposures in residential areas. I do not know whether any such limits exist in your area, but you may wish to contact the local planning department or state public utilities commission to find out. It is unlikely that such limits, if they exist, would apply to occupational settings however. I see that you have already contacted OSHA, which may have regulations that cover occupational exposure to ELF fields.

"Radio Wave Sickness" appears to be another term for a condition formerly known as Electromagnetic Hypersensitivity, having more recently been named Idiopathic Environmental Intolerance (IEI) attributed to electromagnetic fields. The World Health Organization notes that this "condition" has no agreed-upon diagnostic criteria and there is no consensus within the scientific community that its symptoms are linked to exposure to electromagnetic fields. Some information is available from the World Health

http://www.who.int/mediacentre/factsheets/fs296/en/index.html

The policy of the FCC with respect to environmental radiofrequency (RF) emissions has been developed to ensure that FCC-regulated sources do not expose the public or workers to levels of RF energy that are considered by expert organizations to be potentially harmful. The FCC has adopted guidelines for human exposure to RF electromagnetic fields based on recommendations from the U.S. Environmental Protection Agency (EPA), the Food and Drug Administration (FDA) and other federal health and safety agencies.

As you can see, there is an extensive web of deceit being woven within the governments agencies regarding harmful electrical electromagnetic radiation emissions into the human environment. They are clearly okay with workers health being damaged by dirty electricity and have been so for a very long time!

If you ever make a complaint about a known harmful electrical system, I wish you the best of luck...as you are going to need it!

"Electromagnetic fields are packets of energy that does not have any mass, and visible light is what we know best. X-rays are also electromagnetic fields, but they are more energetic than visible light. Our concern is for those electromagnetic fields that are less energetic than visible light, including those that are associated with electricity and those used for communications and in microwave ovens. The fields associated with electricity are commonly called "extremely low frequency" fields (ELF), while those used in communication and microwave ovens are called "radiofrequency" (RF) fields. Studies of people have shown that both ELF and RF exposures result in an increased risk of cancer, and that this occurs at intensities that are too low to cause tissue heating. Unfortunately, all of our exposure standards are based on the false assumption that there are no hazardous effects at intensities that do not cause tissue heating. Based on the existing science, many public health experts believe it is possible we will face an epidemic of cancers in the future resulting from uncontrolled use of cell phones and increased

172

population exposure to WiFi and other wireless devices. Thus it is important that all of us, and especially children, restrict our use of cell phones, limit exposure to background levels of Wi-Fi, and that government and industry discover ways in which to allow use of wireless devices without such elevated risk of serious disease. We need to educate decision-makers that 'business as usual' is unacceptable. The importance of this public health issue can not be underestimated."

David Carpenter, MD

Home Electrical System

The electrical power system in your home may also affect your health. Around electrical fuse boards there may be very high fields of microwave, radio, magnetic, electric, ion, and so on. The electromagnetic radiation emissions are a function of:

- The quality of the utility electricity.

- The quality of the utility electrical grounding system.

- The electrical equipment that is connected to the fuse board.

- Smart/AMR/AMI transmitting utility meters.

- The type of structure that it is mounted to.

- The quality of the home electrical grounding system.

- The construction of the electrical fuse board.

- The routing of the cables that connect to the equipment.

- The presence of an alternate energy system (such as solar photovoltaic or wind).

- The distance to the utility transformer.

It may be possible that Leukemia in children is linked to the location of the fuse board and the electrical meter on the home. The health of children is a particular concern with the advent of Smart/AMR/AMI utility meters, as they broadcast radio frequencies into their surrounding environment. Babies and children are the ones who are most affected by these effects.

Some fuse boards may need filters installing and line terminators on their radial circuits. These are important in areas that have electrical power quality issues (Dirty electricity).

A simple filtering circuit is shown in the next few pages that can help with reducing dirty electricity. It is simply a selection of different size capacitors that are connected in parallel at the fuse board. The capacitor plates are all different sizes in order to filter different frequencies that may be present on the AC system.

The simple filter should assist with reducing radio frequencies present at the fuse board. It should be mounted in a metal enclosure, as it will be radiating radio frequencies if it is filtering them from the utility network. The filter uses negligible power. If it starts to buzz, then you will likely have a frequency problem that your electrician will need to diagnose.

The location considerations for electrical fuse boards and associated equipment are also shown in the following pictures.

"Sensitivity to electromagnetic radiation is the emerging health problem of the 21st century. It is imperative health practitioners, governments, schools and parents learn more about it. The human health stakes are significant."

William Rea, MD

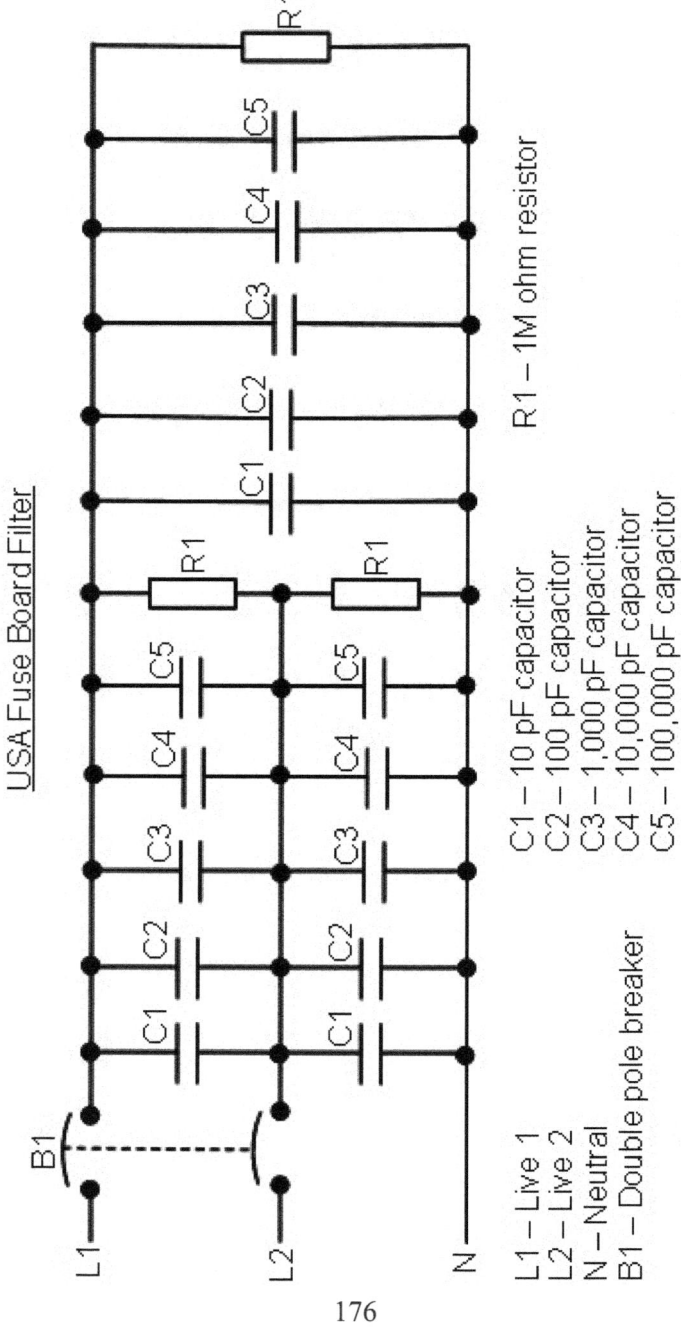

USA Fuse Board Filter

R1 – 1M ohm resistor

C1 – 10 pF capacitor
C2 – 100 pF capacitor
C3 – 1,000 pF capacitor
C4 – 10,000 pF capacitor
C5 – 100,000 pF capacitor

L1 – Live 1
L2 – Live 2
N – Neutral
B1 – Double pole breaker

All components need to be rated for continuous use at 400 volts AC

USA Fuse Board Filter

This is what the USA fuse board filter looks like when it is built.

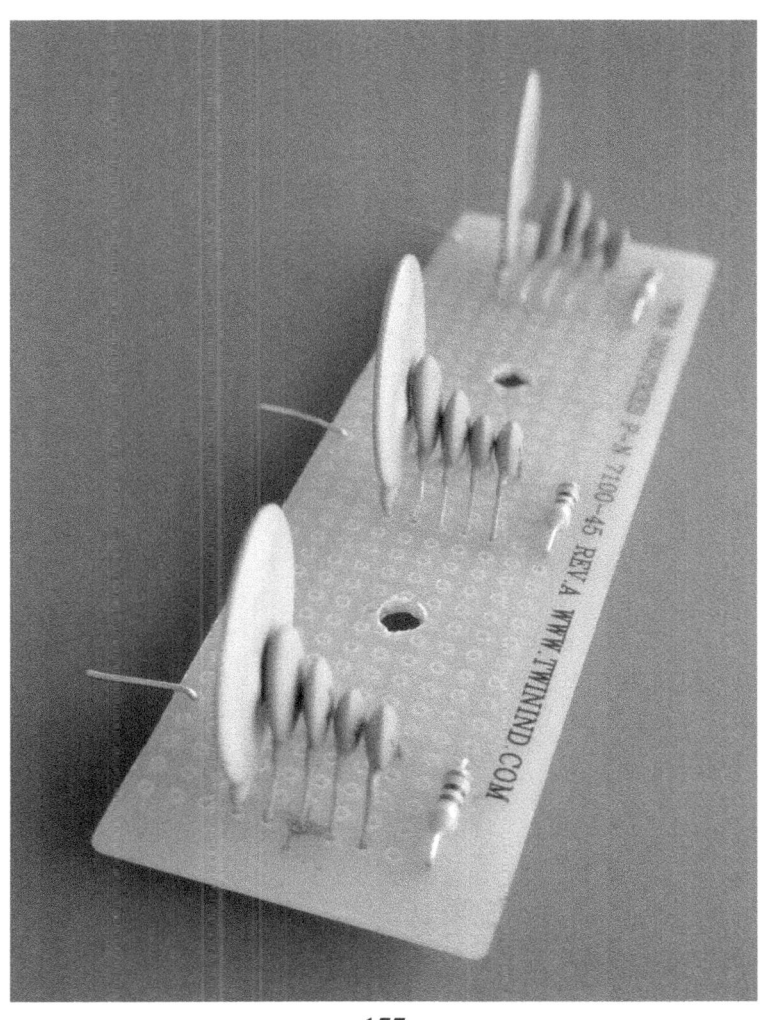

European Fuse Board Filter

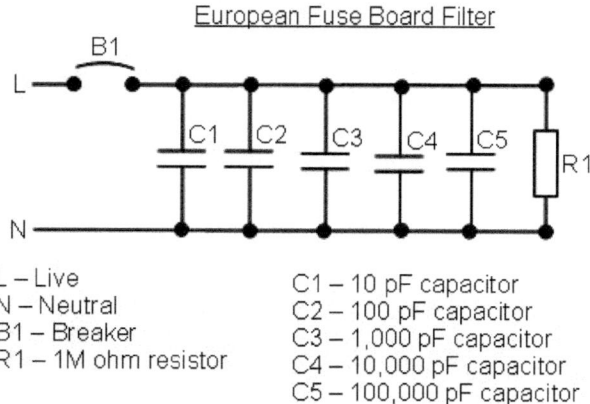

L – Live
N – Neutral
B1 – Breaker
R1 – 1M ohm resistor

C1 – 10 pF capacitor
C2 – 100 pF capacitor
C3 – 1,000 pF capacitor
C4 – 10,000 pF capacitor
C5 – 100,000 pF capacitor

All components need to be rated for continuous use at 400 volts AC

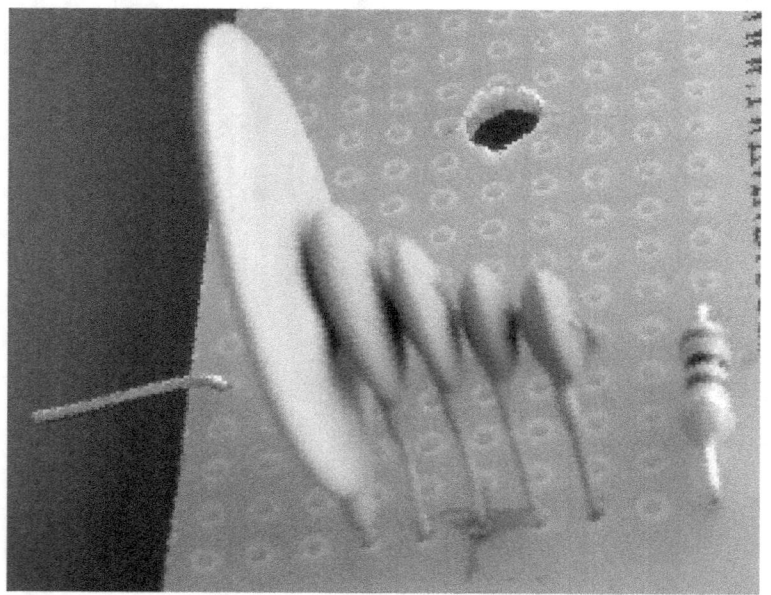

A simple capacitive filter can be made using a resistor in parallel with a capacitor connected to the live and neutral electrical plug connections.

Capacitive Plug

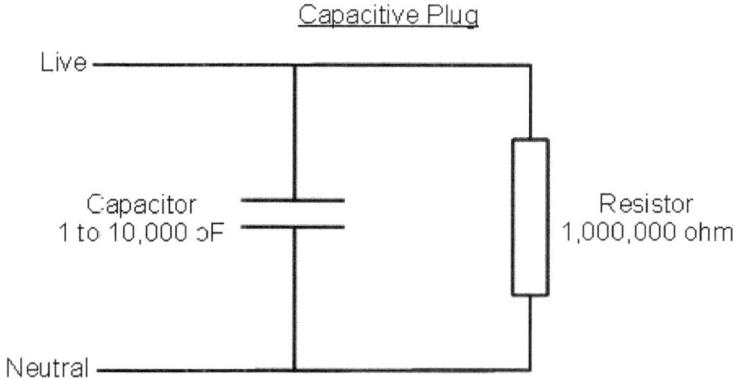

All components are to be rated for continuous use at the electrical system AC voltage. You may need to insert a fuse on the live connection, depending on your electrical system. Reduce the size of the capacitor if it causes interference with other equipment on the circuit. It buzzes when it is filtering high frequencies from the electrical system.

Electrical fuse boards should not be mounted in human habitation areas due to the fields that extend out from them and the possible radio frequency transmissions. An ideal location is on the side of the garage.

Unfortunately, the fuse board in the previous picture was located directly behind the master bed! Electrical fuse boards should not be mounted on human habitations.

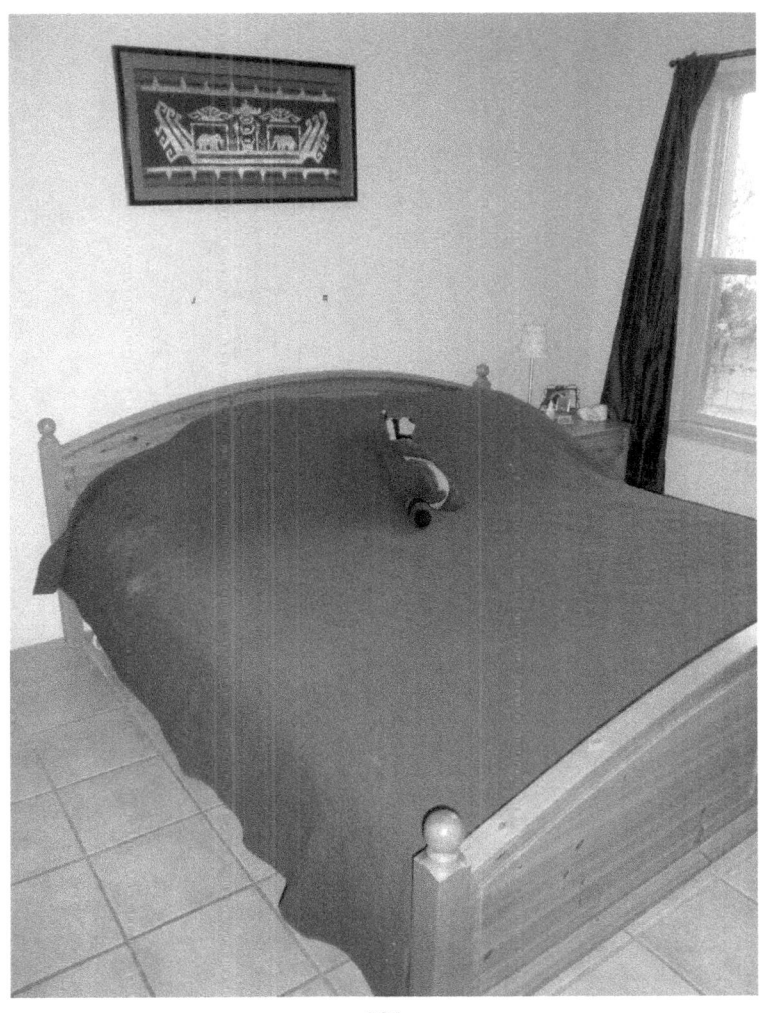

When living in apartments, it is preferable not to live in the apartment that has the electrical meters on the wall. There will be high electromagnetic fields in this area and possibly radio frequency emissions.

The electromagnetic fields around solar photovoltaic systems can vary with the sunlight. You may find the fields entering the human environment below.

Earthing

The utility supplies a combined earth (ground) and neutral connection to your home that splits into the earth (ground) and neutral connection at your fuse board. The ground rods that you see near fuse boards are to effectively connect this combined earth and neutral cable to the ground potential of the property.

The earth and neutral connections will float up and down in proportion to the load on the distribution system in your area if it is not grounded properly by both the utility and the homeowner. The human body cannot sense low AC voltages, currents nor frequencies on the earthing (grounding) system and you may slowly get sick with prolonged exposure to it.

You should remember that the electrical earth (ground) connection in your home or office connects directly to the neutral transformer winding connection that is supplying the electricity. It may be carrying an AC voltage!

This is shown in the next diagram.

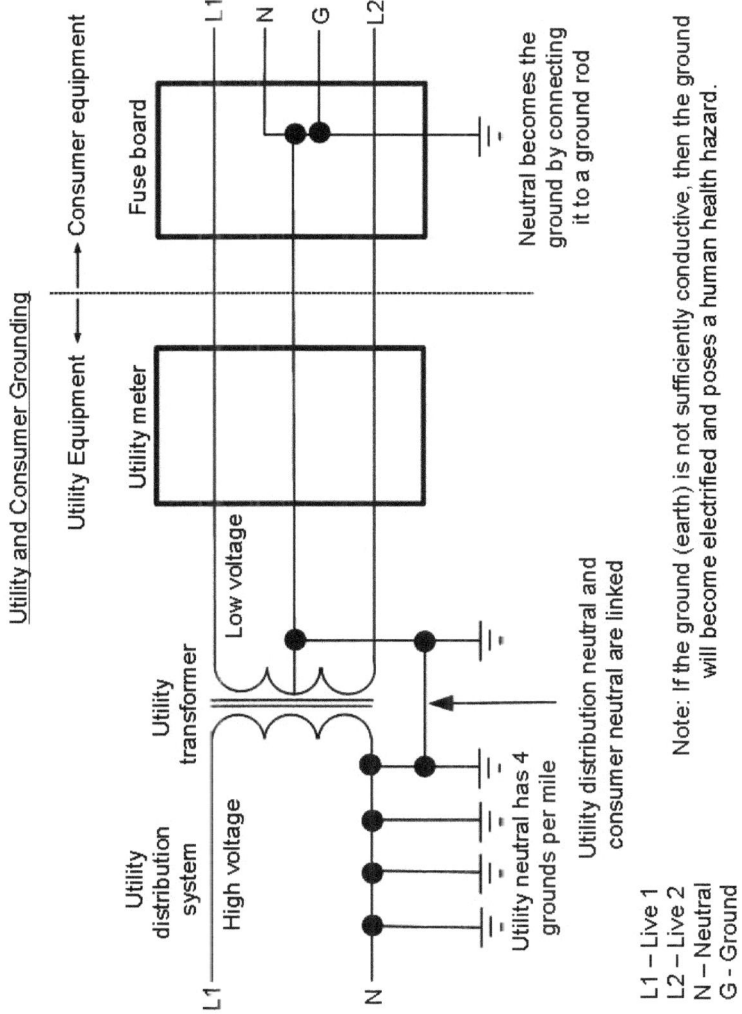

Utility and Consumer Grounding

Note: If the ground (earth) is not sufficiently conductive, then the ground will become electrified and poses a human health hazard.

L1 – Live 1
L2 – Live 2
N – Neutral
G - Ground

During researching electrical grounding systems, it became apparent that many grounding systems are actually acting as antenna systems for wireless energy. The wireless energy is very low at the ground rods, but as you move further away from the ground rods, you start finding increasing wireless energies on the home ground wiring. Indeed, Nikola Tesla documented that antenna systems are more efficient when connected to a ground rod! As such, you should be aware that any cable connected to a ground rod becomes a receiver for wireless energy. The longer that cable is, the more wireless energy that you will find on it.

The concept of grounding is quite interesting. The electrical system was originally designed to be a one wire supply system with an earth return through grounding rods. It was only when people started to get shocked by the electrified earth that a return wire was also installed, which we now call the neutral. However, the ground rods remained and if the neutral is higher in voltage potential than the ground, then it will feed AC voltage and current into the ground. In other words, the ground rods electrify the ground with AC electricity! This is a particular problem anywhere where the ground is a poor conductor of electricity, such as the desert southwest USA.

This is shown in the next diagram.

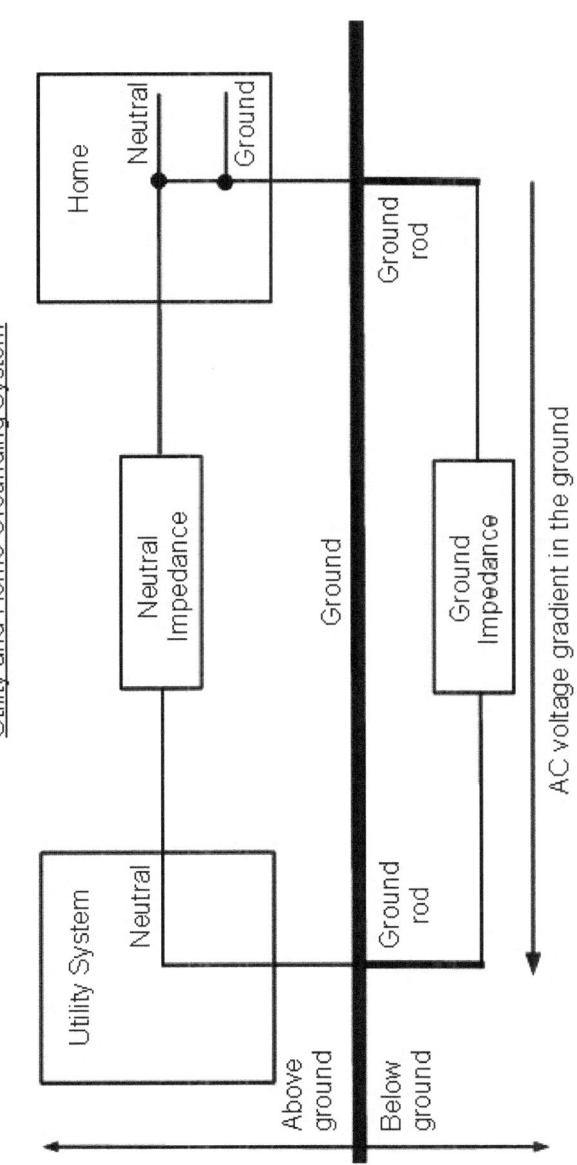

Utility and Home Grounding System

The ratio of the neutral to ground impedance determines the current flowing in the neutral cable and through the ground (earth). If the ground impedance is high, then all current will flow on the neutral cable and raise the voltage on the ground rods. This may create excessive stray voltage that can affect peoples health.

When reviewing the BBC News article *Louis Theroux on dementia: The capital of the forgetful,* we find: *For years Phoenix has been a mecca for America's elderly, who are attracted by the year-round sun and dry desert heat. Now increasingly it is a kind of capital of the forgetful and the confused.*

One has to wonder if stray voltage/current/frequency is causing some of their problems? The dry desert of the southwest USA is one of the poorest conductors of electricity that you will find. Effective grounding systems need water in the ground to increase the conductivity of it. Due to this, grounding systems vary in their effectiveness due to the seasonal water content of the ground.

You should be aware that anywhere that a ground rod is installed, that there may be AC voltage/current/frequency in the vicinity of it. The electrification of the earth may extend several hundred feet from the ground rods. You should keep your shoes on and keep children and pets away from these areas. AC electrification of the earth commonly occurs around streetlights, pad mounted transformers, power poles and lines, and electrical substations too! People who walk their dogs are at particular risk from these energized earth effects.

This is shown in the next diagram.

Electrical Grounding System

Top View

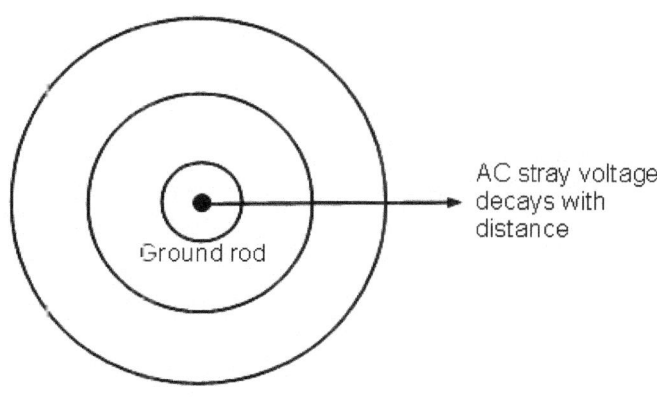

AC stray voltage decays with distance

Ground rod

Side View

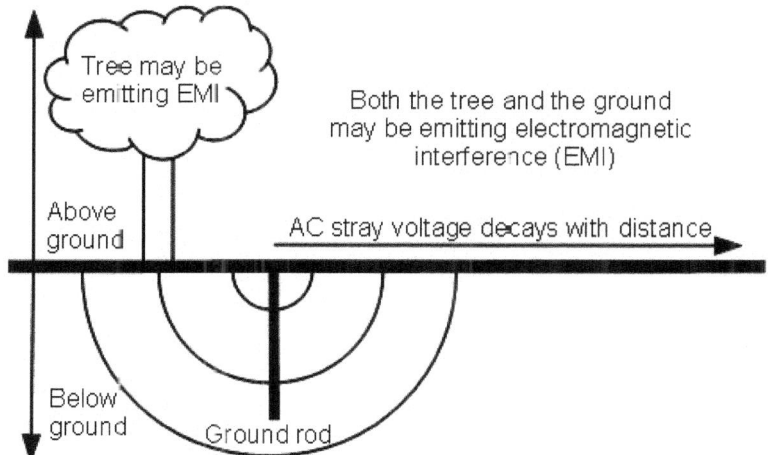

Tree may be emitting EMI

Both the tree and the ground may be emitting electromagnetic interference (EMI)

Above ground

AC stray voltage decays with distance

Below ground

Ground rod

The Ufer ground uses a concrete encased electrode and is a particular problem, as it generally uses the foundation of the building to get the ground connection. This means that the stray voltage peaks near to where it is installed. At my home, this area is the garage floor that is next to my kitchen tiled flooring. As such, there is a significant AC voltage on these floors at certain times of the day!

You should avoid wearing leather soled shoes, as these will connect you into stray voltage sources. Your shoes should have insulated soles in areas that have electricity. Do not walk around barefoot in environments that have electricity installed into them!

A utility electrical substation is shown in the next diagram. The substation relies on an earth (ground) return path for the electricity and as such, the area around electrical substations may have large amounts of electrical ground currents and stray voltage/frequency present.

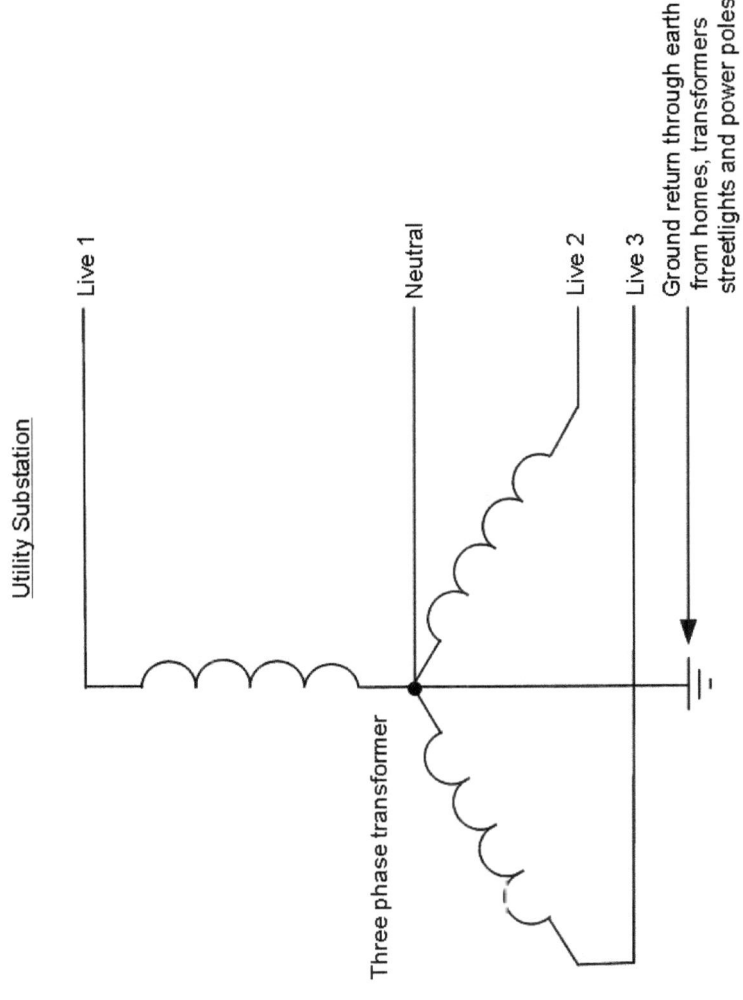

Grounding electrical and plumbing systems at the home can create voltages in the home that are commonly referred to as "stray voltage". Stray voltage is a well known effect in the diary industry and it can wreak havoc on the health of farmers, their families, and their livestock. As one farmer reports: ***"It's a slow, painful tortuous death, is what it is for them," said Siewert, who with his father, Harlan, owns Siewert Holsteins in Zumbro Falls. "It's like watching someone die of AIDS."***

One of the things that has caused stray voltage/current/frequency to become prevalent in the human environment is the widespread adoption of plastic services to houses. In the past, the plumbing was cast iron drains, galvanized steel supply pipes, and copper tubing. All of these were relatively good conductors of electricity and supplied good grounding to the home. This has changed and plumbing is now commonly plastic, which is an insulator to electricity.

You can get a sense to how biologically toxic an electrical grounding system is by grounding the pot of a Dieffenbachia (Dumb Cane) plant to the electrical system ground connection. I have done this and I obtained a "Frankenstien" plant that is very tall and deformed compared to my controls. It takes several months of growth to obtain such a deformed plant. This is shown in the next picture.

My "Frankenstein" electrical utility grounded soil, stray voltage/current/frequency exposed Dieffenbachia plant grew very tall with an unusual double canopy of miniature leaves that are distinctly different from each other. This growth pattern is unique to this plant and it is the tallest Dieffenbachia in my home at 13 inches from the soil surface to the top leaf tip.

The stray voltage effects are shown on the following pages, as measured in the evening at my home during September 2011 in Arizona, USA. The Amprobe 5XP-A meter is logging the minimum and maximum vales of the voltage on the electrical grounding system. The measurements in the garden were also performed with the Amprobe 5XP-A meter. As you can see, there is an AC voltage gradient from the electrical ground rods at the front of the home to the back of the home where the reference ground rod is installed. The reference ground rod is installed well away from the home and electrical systems. There are no electrical connections to it.

The Amprobe 5XP-A multimeter is logging voltage values of the electrical outlet ground pin (Right probe) to the garden ground at the back of the home (Left probe).

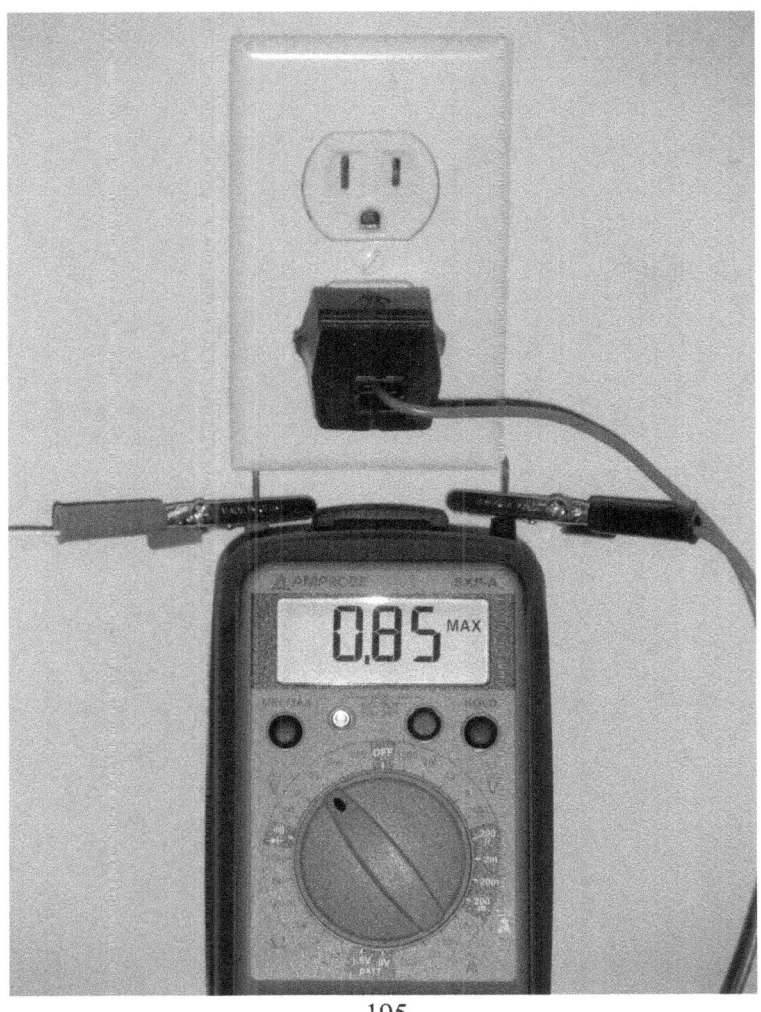

Garden Stray Voltage

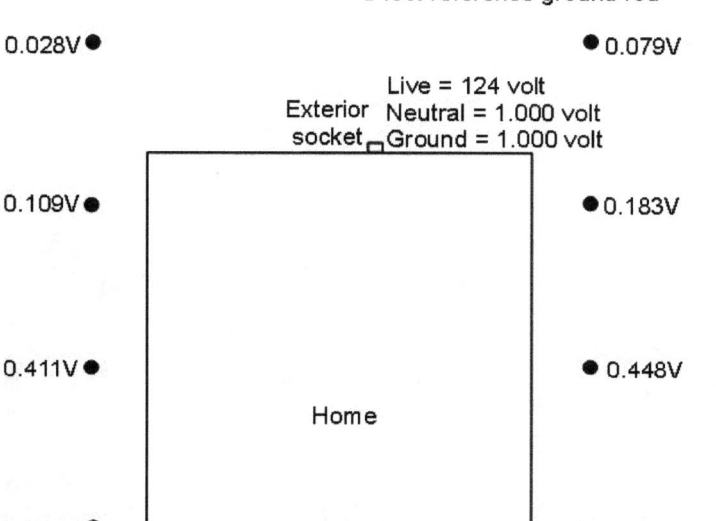

● 8 foot reference ground rod

0.028V ●   ● 0.079V

Live = 124 volt
Exterior Neutral = 1.000 volt
socket ⌐ Ground = 1.000 volt

0.109V ●   ● 0.183V

0.411V ●   ● 0.448V

Home

0.411V ●   ● 0.495V

Fuse board and
ground rods

Stray voltage measurements in the garden using an
Amprobe 5XP-A multimeter. As can be seen, there is a
voltage gradient through the property.

During logging the utility ground to the garden ground for current and voltage in August and September 2011, these are the range of values that I recorded at my home:

- 0.07 to 1.66 volts.
- 2.7 to 55 milli-amps.
- 60 Hertz.
- Low values occurred near sunrise, high values occurred between 16:00 to 20:00 mid-week.
- The electrical distribution system had high loads due to air conditioning loads running in the summer heat.

It is interesting to note that for electrocution to occur in water, the following conditions must exist:

- **Assuming a wet human body impedance of 300 ohms.**
- **Muscle control in the human is lost at between 6 to 30 milli-amps.**
- **1.8 to 9 volts of 60 Hertz AC is needed.**

As we can see, the conditions at my home are very close to those required for a water electrocution. If a surge from an electrical fault or lightning strike on the utility system occurred, then the conditions for a water electrocution may occur. I would be very concerned if I owned a swimming pool!

Plastic plumbing may be hazardous to human health, as it does not ground the water contained within the pipes. As such, any plastic plumbing that is routed with electrical cables may start to couple into the fields of the cables. The result is the water may become electrified. You may well end up with stray voltage/current/frequency at your faucets, basins, showers and bathtubs! Clearly an undesirable effect.

Copper plumbing may have stray voltage/current/frequency on it if your grounding system is bad. You may want to install a dielectric isolator after the

electrical ground in order to prevent the pipes from being electrified within the home with AC stray voltage/current/frequency. Many people have reported that their health significantly improved after doing this. You will need to consult with a qualified electrician about this.

If your walls are conductive, then you may find that your walls are electrified with stray voltage/current/frequency as well as your flooring. This may occur in a brick home or metal framed home. It may also occur when the walls are wet after rain. You may find an AC voltage gradient in them that is similar to what you find around the ground rods. The use of metal back boxes for the electrical sockets and switches may increase this effect.

This is shown in the next diagram.

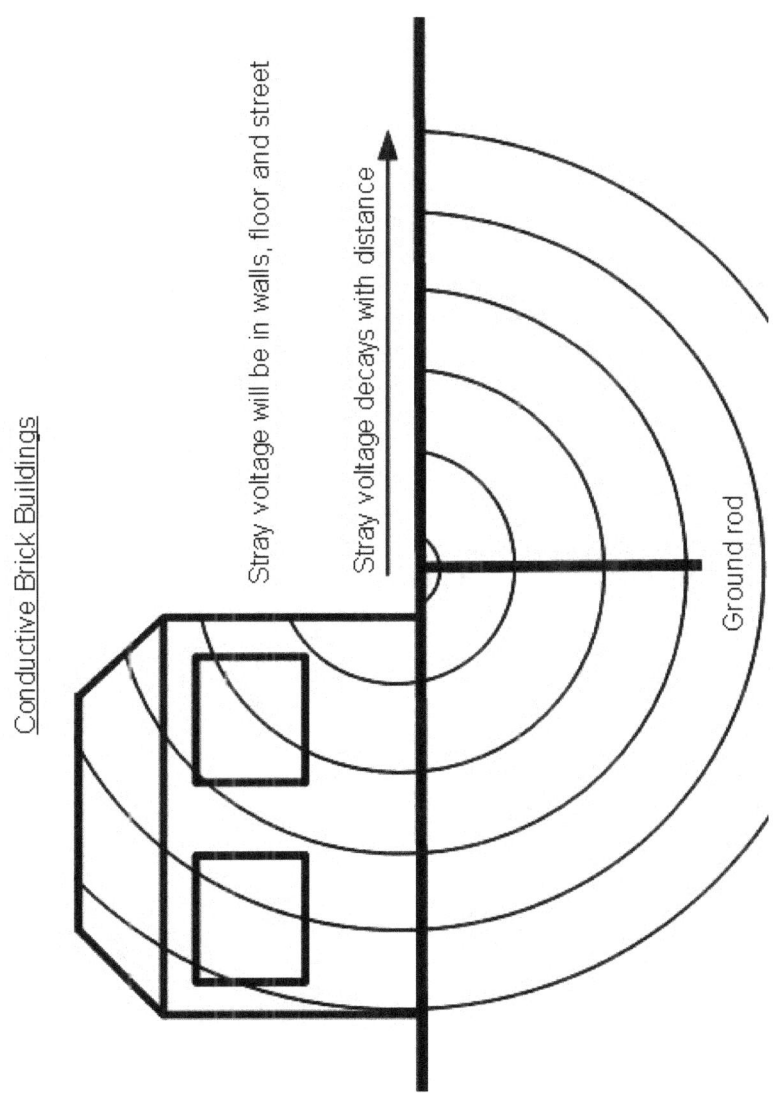

Conductive Brick Buildings

Stray voltage will be in walls, floor and street

Stray voltage decays with distance

Ground rod

Stray voltage/current/frequency in the past was commonly associated with swimming pools and hot tubs, but is now rapidly becoming prevalent in many other areas throughout modern society. Have you ever wondered why competent swimmers drown in their own swimming pools? It may well be stray current that killed them, particularly if an electrical fault or lightning strike occurred in the area. Electricity easily couples into water systems and electrifies the water.

Antistatic devices (ASD) are commonly used in many industries and may present a health hazard to those who work with these. If they are connected into a poor quality grounding system, then they may well cause an AC voltage and many frequencies to appear on the human body. My research into this area is indicating that a direct long term exposure to a low level AC voltage that contains many frequencies may cause the human body to slowly fall into illness and perhaps onto disease. It matches the findings of the diary industry that just 0.5 volt of AC electricity exposure can lead to illness in the human body. The effects that I noticed during two weeks of wearing an antistatic strap that was connected to the electrical utility ground were:

- Headaches.
- Insomnia.
- Fatigue.
- Irregular heartbeats.

It was easily cured by removing the antistatic strap. The symptoms cleared up within a few weeks. When I investigated the grounding system I found 1.5 volts of AC electricity on it when compared to the garden and a wide range of frequencies extending into the megahertz range!

Antistatic equipment is common in the hospital operating room. Dr. William Rae determined that his allergic and neurological symptoms were caused by the electromagnetic fields in the operating room. He subsequently discovered that he was not alone in his electromagnetic hypersensitivity, and that there was a growing population of patients with the same condition. These people are typically told by their physicians that their symptoms are "all in their minds" and that they should seek psychiatric care.

Surgeons have been noticed to be a group of the population that suffer from addictions, depression, and burning out. It appears to be much worse in the female surgeons and this matches the findings that the female body is more sensitive to the effects of AC electricity.

You should avoid using antistatic devices in areas that are known to be electrified. You may find a significant AC voltage waveform appearing on it from time to time!

Whether you use an antistatic device or not, you may find yourself connected into the AC supply through your environment. Walking around in your bare feet or socks on conductive flooring, such as tile or outdoors, may expose you to an AC voltage. Believe it or not, walking the dog may expose you to AC voltage through the dog lead if it is conductive!

Using any device that has a metal case and is electrically grounded through the cable may expose you to an AC voltage. Metal sewing machines, metal mobile homes, metal appliances, and metal electric power tools can be examples of this. Anything that is conductive and electrically grounded that humans come into contact with is a potential health risk. Keeping your shoes on can reduce the risk, as can wearing electrically insulated gloves.

Stray voltage/current/frequency can be on your sewer system and it can come up through the toilet, shower, bath, and sink drains. It is difficult to avoid from these locations and it is recommended that you do not urinate into electrified toilets. Connecting into an electrical source through your urine stream should be expected to lead to long term internal health problems.

Plants can be affected by stray voltage and they may show stunted growth, deformed growth, or go dormant. In extreme cases they may die.

The extensive testing that I have performed showed that a direct contact exposure to the AC electrical system is far more biologically toxic than an indirect exposure through the air. The body appears to have an increased ability to tolerate the air induced exposure that is not present with direct contact with stray voltage/current/frequency from the electrical ground.

Stray voltage/current/frequency varies with the time of the day and can significantly change. Early in the morning it can be very low and during the peak electrical load periods, it can be very high. A multimeter with a minimum and maximum logging feature is ideal to find the range of values of stray voltage and current. I have found the Amprobe 5XP-A multimeter to be ideal for this purpose, as it has a 16 day battery life when using a 9 volt alkaline battery. To get the highest accuracy reading of stray voltage and current, you should be using an oscilloscope, as the voltage and current waveform may be highly distorted. Using a time lapse camera will allow you to record the waveform over long periods of time.

The voltage waveform on the grounding system in my home is shown in the next picture. This was measured at the grounding pin in the home at the electrical outlet. The measurement was taken at 19:30 on a Saturday night after it had just gone dark on April 28th, 2012. It was a warm night and most people were not running their air conditioning units.

You should remember that anything that has a metal case that is grounded will have this voltage on it, such as stainless steel appliances. An antistatic device (ASD) that was plugged into the wall outlet would also have this voltage on it. A similar voltage would also be on electrically conductive tiled and concrete flooring near to the ground rods.

The frequency content of the voltage waveform is shown in the following pictures. You can see that there are a wide range of frequencies on the grounding system.

The distorted voltage waveform on the grounding system of my home. It is almost two volts peak to peak. It is much higher in summertime!

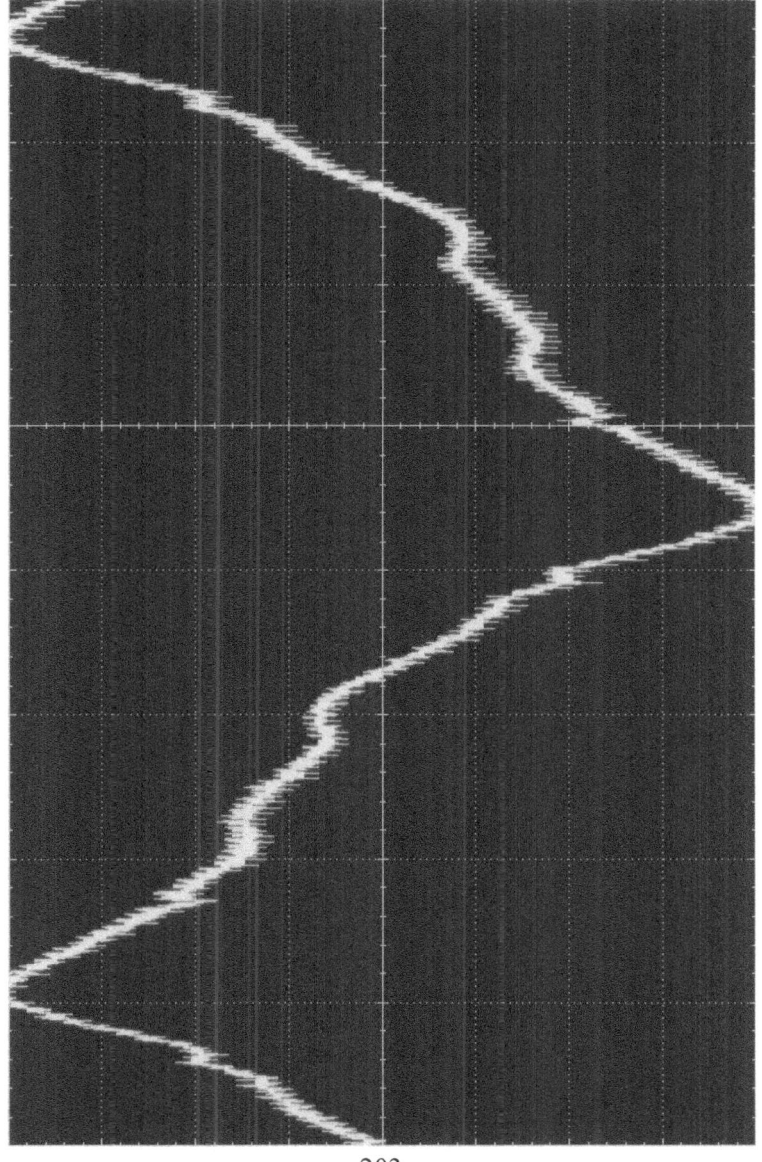

The low frequency content on the grounding system. The repeating 60 Hz harmonics can clearly be seen.

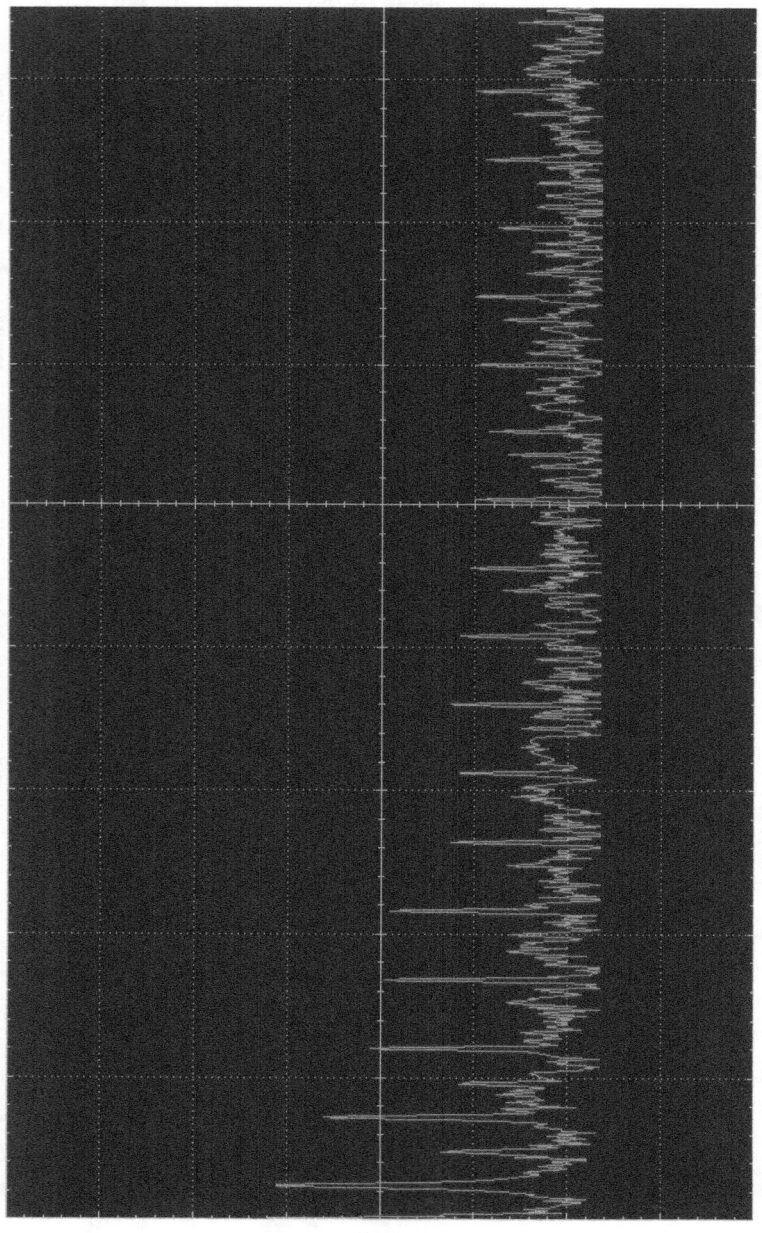

The high frequency content on the grounding system. A peak can clearly be seen centered around 1,250,000 Hz.

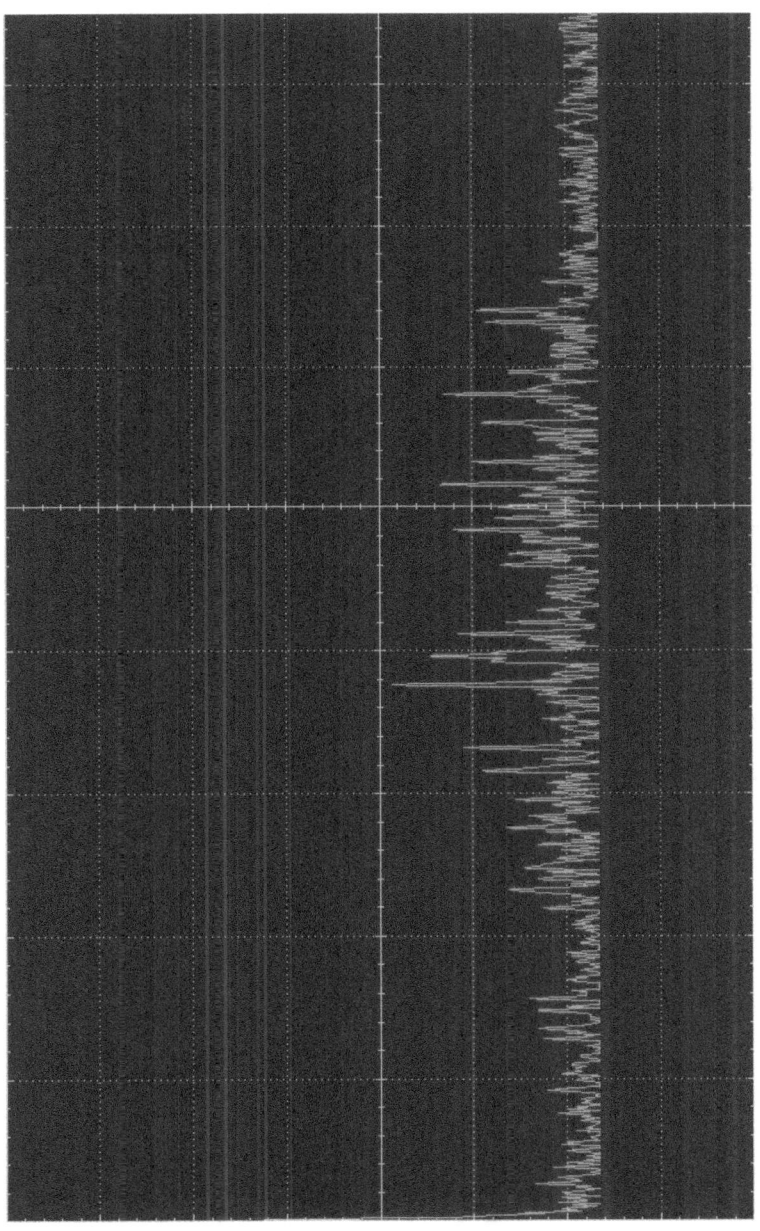

You can sometimes pick up the frequencies coming off grounding systems using a standard AM radio tuned into static (no radio station). If you put the radio near to the grounding system, you may hear it start buzzing. A telephone voice coil used to record telephone calls connected into an amplified speaker can be used to detect the lower frequencies on grounding systems. Radio Shack sells the voice coils, they are called "Recorder Telephone Pickup" Model: 44-533, Catalog #: 44-533.

Communities that have alternate energy systems in them may have large amounts of frequency content on the grounding systems that come from electronic power generation systems that are called "inverters". The next images show the voltage and frequency content of a neighborhood with a large amount of solar photovoltaic generation systems installed into it. The ground voltage measurement is highly distorted and will be producing harmonics. It has approximately 1.2 volts peak to peak and a 60Hz waveform. The ground frequency scale goes from 0Hz at the bottom of the page to 500,000Hz at the top of the page. There are significant frequency spikes present in this range. This will typically change during the day, as it will vary with the sunlight.

Solar PV Powered Neighborhood Ground Voltage

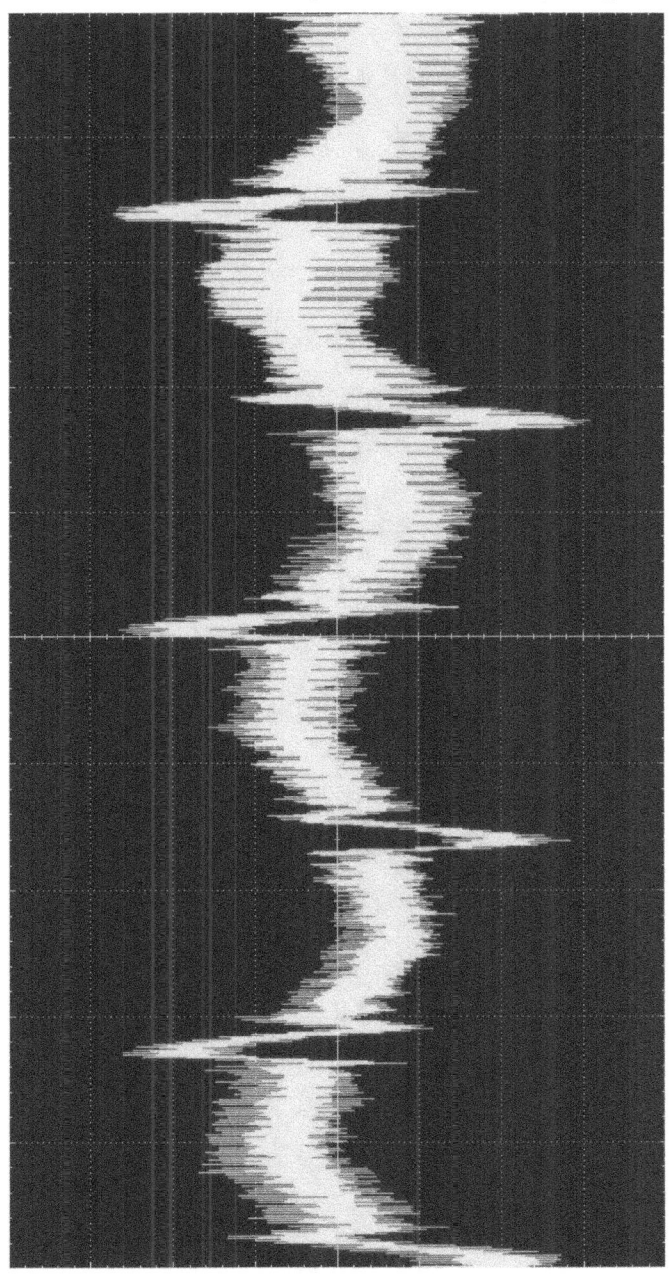

Solar PV Powered Neighborhood Ground Frequency

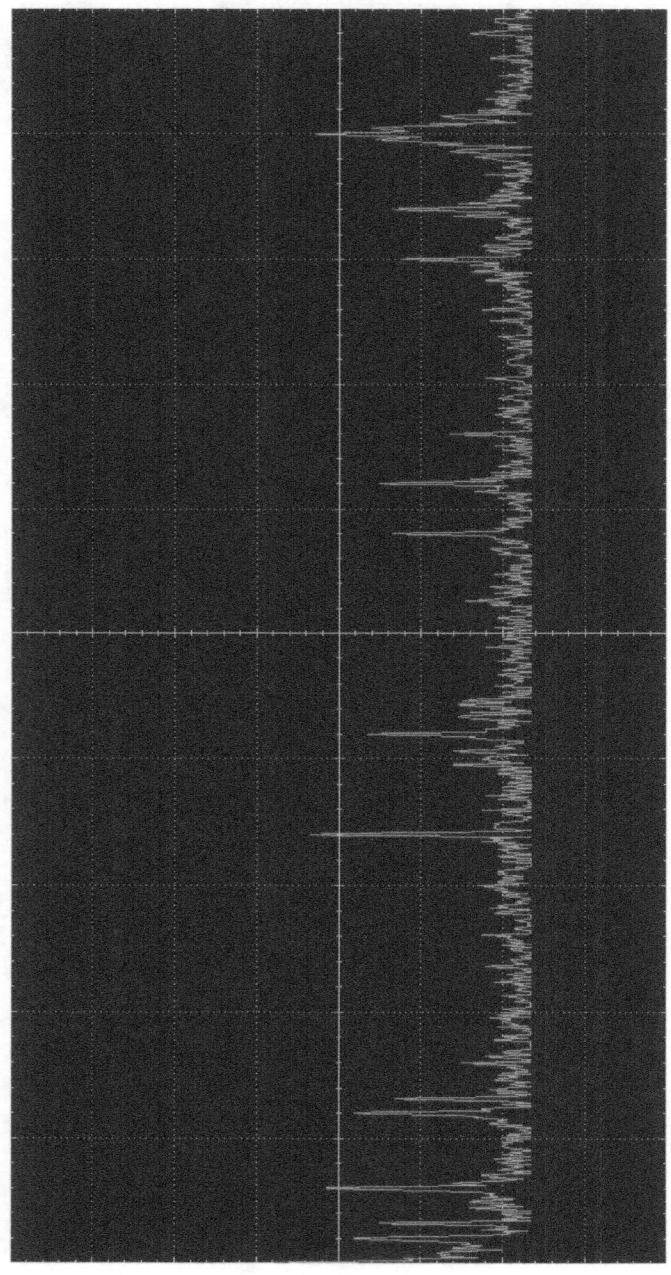

Whether you like it or not, stray voltage/current/frequency is present within your own body. The body will couple into electromagnetic fields and this can be detected with a digital multimeter or an oscilloscope. The alternating current voltage of the human body can get quite high, often exceeding fifteen volts when next to an AC cable. Just 0.5 volt of stray AC voltage is known to affect animals and just 2 volts of AC voltage is known to kill them with long term exposure! The farming industry has set an upper limit on stray voltage of 0.5 volt AC due to the effects that have been observed in the animals.

The electrical grounding system on my home in August and September 2011 regularly exceeded this value by three times the allowable animal contact value! I have noticed sore knees and aching bones occurring every year in summertime at my current home which I now have linked to this stray voltage/current/frequency effect. I no longer walk around the home in bare feet, I wear insulated slippers now.

Ground loops can be a particular problem. They occur where there are multiple ground (earth) paths for the electricity to take. It is commonly seen to occur on metal pipework. You may find very high magnetic fields around such pipework from the current flow through it. It can be prevented by having a licensed contractor install dielectric isolators into the pipework.

Ground loops can also occur from appliances that have metal feet. The metal feet provide a current path through the conductive floor to the ground (earth). It can be prevented by having insulated plastic feet on the appliances. If you encounter this, simply put insulated plastic spacers under the metal appliance feet to break the ground loop. Many people have found that their health problems subside by taking this simple action.

High magnetic fields may occur on electrical wiring when the neutrals from multiple electrical circuits have been inadvertently connected together in the home. They can also occur if the neutral has short circuited to the ground. Instead of the neutral current flowing down the same cable as the live current, it takes an alternate path that creates a current imbalance in the electrical cables that creates high magnetic field emissions.

The characteristics that are observed in animals that have been exposed to stray voltage/current/frequency are:

- Reduced feed and water intakes.

- Increased defecation in the milking parlor.

- Increased incidences of mastitis.

- Elevated somatic cell counts (white blood cells in the milk).

- Increased still births.

- Calves born crippled.

- Calves born blind.

- Sickly newborn calves.

- Calves dying within several days of birth.

- Crippled cows.

- Joint problems.

- Behavioral changes.

- Anxiety.

- Nervousness.

- Fatigue.

- Depression.

- Poor hair coats.

- Poor reproductive performance.

- Increased aborted pregnancies.

- Reduction in milk output.

- Depressed immune systems.

- Increased death rates.

In the human, the effects appear to be similar:

- Changed personality.
- Degrading mental health.
- Forgetfulness.
- Anger.
- Irritability.
- Anxiety.
- Fatigue.
- Eye problems.
- Nerve tingling.
- Itchy skin.
- Joint problems, especially the hips, knees and ankles.
- Arthritis symptoms.
- Aching bones.
- Sexual problems.
- Suicide.
- The problems may appear to be seasonal or related to the time of day.
- Cancer, Fibromyalgia, and Chronic Fatigue Syndrome are suspected to be linked to it.

So how do you prevent stray voltage/current/frequency from occurring? Here are some suggestions:

- Install your ground rods well away from your home and use insulated cable ran inside plastic conduit to connect them to your fuse board.

- Landscape the area that your ground rods are located in to prevent people from walking and sitting on the ground in that area.

- Get the utility to install a stray voltage isolator onto the transformer that feeds your property.

- Have the utility install larger neutral cables to your property.

- Have the utility provide you with a separate ground cable from the transformer.

- Have a licensed contractor install dielectric unions in areas that have ground loops occurring.

Ultimately, the electrical utility system should never have connected energized conductors into the ground. It was just a really bad decision that was made before the stray voltage/current/frequency problem was discovered in the 1970's. Instead of doing the right thing when the utility industry became aware of it, it has been in constant denial by them ever since. They know that this effect is ruining peoples lives and they are okay with that. Willfully polluting the ground with AC electricity is just another aspect of how the electrical utility companies will be remembered by the next generation.

This quote by Russ Allen, author of "Electrocution of America", sums up how stray voltage has been allowed to become the problem that it is today:

"Utilities are rarely fined for their wrongdoings. What's more, they have nobody inspecting their distribution systems—they regulate themselves. Utility companies have polluted our water, our air and the soil we walk on. The effect on farms and livestock alone is enough to warrant mass concern, but factor in what it does to people, and you have a huge crisis on your hands."

Russ Allen

Stray Voltage, Stray Current and Stray Frequency

The earth around electrical equipment is commonly electrified by ground rods. You should avoid coming into contact with electrified earth, as it is a human health hazard. You should keep children away from these areas.

DC & AC

The direct current (DC) system is either positive or negative polarity and does not use the sine waves and frequency of the alternating current (AC) system. It simply supplies a fixed voltage all of the time. Batteries are a form of DC electricity and most people associate them with the DC system.

It is clear why the alternating current (AC) system was chosen over the direct current (DC) system. One word sums it up:

Fire

The DC system suffers from arcing and fires. We know this due to the recent adoption of DC solar power systems for power generation. As they are aging, people are finding that they are failing through arcing, and in some cases, going on fire. Once DC has started to arc, things start to melt very quickly. The arcing generally is not enough to blow the fuse, but is enough to start melting equipment and to possibly start a fire.

The arcing effect would have been apparent when unplugging appliances from the wall without first turning them off. There would have been a significant arc during this process. It may have actually been quite scary to see it!

The AC system does not, in general, suffer from this problem and it is rare to see it. This is due to the AC system having many zero crossings of current and voltage every second. This difference between the two systems would have been noticed by the electrical engineers during the time that both the AC and DC utility systems were in general use, before the decision to standardize on AC was made.

The AC system facilitates the efficient changing of voltages through the use of transformers. Transmitting electricity at high AC voltages was desirable as it uses small cables and saves money. AC motors are much simpler and more reliable.

The DC system would have been emitting large amounts of electromagnetic interference due to the use of brush motors. Brush motors create sparks and increase the risk of fires. It is likely that many people were getting sick around the DC systems due to the dirty electricity on the system.

We see this in some models of cars and motorbikes. Car sickness has a link to the effects of electromagnetic interference on the human body. Most transportation uses DC electrical systems.

The AC system suffers from dirty electricity problems, but was generally cleaner than the DC system until the widespread adoption of electronic systems.

Electric lights do not suffer from flicker on DC systems and the DC system was more desirable for this application.

High powered AC electricity cannot be found in nature and one has to wonder why that is?

"Throughout space there is energy. Is this energy static or kinetic? If static our hopes are in vain; if kinetic - and this we know it is, for certain -then it is a mere question of time when men will succeed in attaching their machinery to the very wheelwork of nature."

Nikola Tesla

50Hz & 60Hz

The world has standardized on two forms of AC electricity. Europe has the 50 Hz frequency and America has 60 Hz frequency. There is a mixture of the two systems around the rest of the world.

One has to wonder why there are two frequencies of electrical systems? The frequency was always a trade off between safety and efficiency. The higher the frequency, then the smaller the motors and transformers become. However, increasing frequencies also increase the biological coupling effects and system losses through capacitance and inductance effects.

Believe it or not, the low frequency was chosen to be high enough to prevent the visual perception of flickering electrical lighting products. Electrical lighting was the primary application of the mass market electricity during the early years. Clearly, flickering lighting products would have killed off any consumer markets for the product!

So high enough to prevent visibly flickering lights and low enough to prevent significant coupling effects. It is still unclear as to why two different frequency systems are in use throughout the world and this probably reflects Europe and America being separated in their development of the AC electrical system.

"If there is any one secret of success, it lies in the ability to get the other person's point of view and see things from that person's angle as well as from your own."

Henry Ford

Dirty Electricity

"Dirty Electricity" is the name given to any effects that are on the utility system that are not related to the fundamental system frequency. These effects comprise of:

- Transients.

- Voltage swings.

- Brownouts.

- Surges.

- Lightning.

- Faults.

- Arcing.

- Noise.

- Harmonics.

Transients are generally caused by switching products on or off. Every time a product does this, a transient is generated. It is simply a spike in voltage and current on the system.

Voltage swings occur whenever you turn on or off an appliance on the electrical system. You may see this as the brightness of your lights changing when you use a high powered appliance. What happened was that the voltage changed slightly on the system. This is normal and is simply an effect of the electrical current flowing through the wiring which causes the voltage to change slightly on the electrical system. You may see this frequently in areas with a large amount of solar photovoltaic power generation installed into them. The power feeding in from the solar power systems may cause the voltage to fluctuate, especially on a day with broken clouds.

Brownouts (voltage sag) are caused by high powered items that take much more current than normal to start up.

Electrical motors are an example of this. Another example is the utility system switching on a transformer in the area. You may see brownouts whenever these large devices are connected to the electrical system or if the utility is having power supply issues.

Voltage surges are the opposite to brown outs. Large loads being removed from the system may cause the voltage to rise on the system.

Lightning strikes in the area can cause surges and raise the voltage on the grounding system. It is a good reason not to use a swimming pool during a storm.

Faults on the utility system can cause high and low voltages to appear on the system. They will also cause transients.

Arcing of components on the system may cause radio wave emissions to occur. These will travel down the cables and may turn the electrical cables into a radio transmitter.

Noise has many sources to it and comprises of all of the above. The electrical system absorbs energy from its surroundings and there may be frequencies of energy that have got onto it from antenna transmission systems. This is likely to occur in areas closest to the antenna system. Most of the noise is generally low level noise and this can be seen as a wide range of frequencies riding on the utility system voltage sine wave and the combined utility ground (earth) and neutral connections. The main source of noise on the utility system is from harmonics that are generated by equipment that is connected to it and from electronic power generation systems. We will look into this in the next chapter.

"In summary, I believe that there is ample evidence that EMF exposure is associated with increased cancer in humans."

Dr. Sam Milham

Harmonics

Harmonics occur when the current draw from the electrical system is not following the voltage sine wave. Linear loads have a constant impedance and do not create harmonics, and the filament light bulb is a good example of this. The current and voltage waveforms for a filament light bulb is shown in the next picture and you will notice that they both have the smooth sine wave shape. The voltage is the larger sine wave.

When the current draw is not linear (non-sinusoidal), then harmonics occur on the system. Harmonics are higher multiples of frequencies of the electrical system frequency. For 60Hz system, you would get increasing frequencies on the system of 120Hz, 180Hz, 240Hz, 300Hz, 360Hz, 420Hz, and so on. They continue on indefinitely and generally start to diminish their magnitude as the frequencies get higher.

Harmonics are important in understanding the difference between the toxicity of the two different electrical frequency standards of 50Hz and 60Hz. So let us take a look at the 10th, 100th, 1000th and 10,000th harmonic on each system:

50Hz: 500Hz, 5,000Hz, 50,000Hz, 500,000Hz.

60Hz: 600Hz, 6,000Hz, 60,000Hz, 600,000Hz.

Voltage and Current Waveform of a Filament Light Bulb

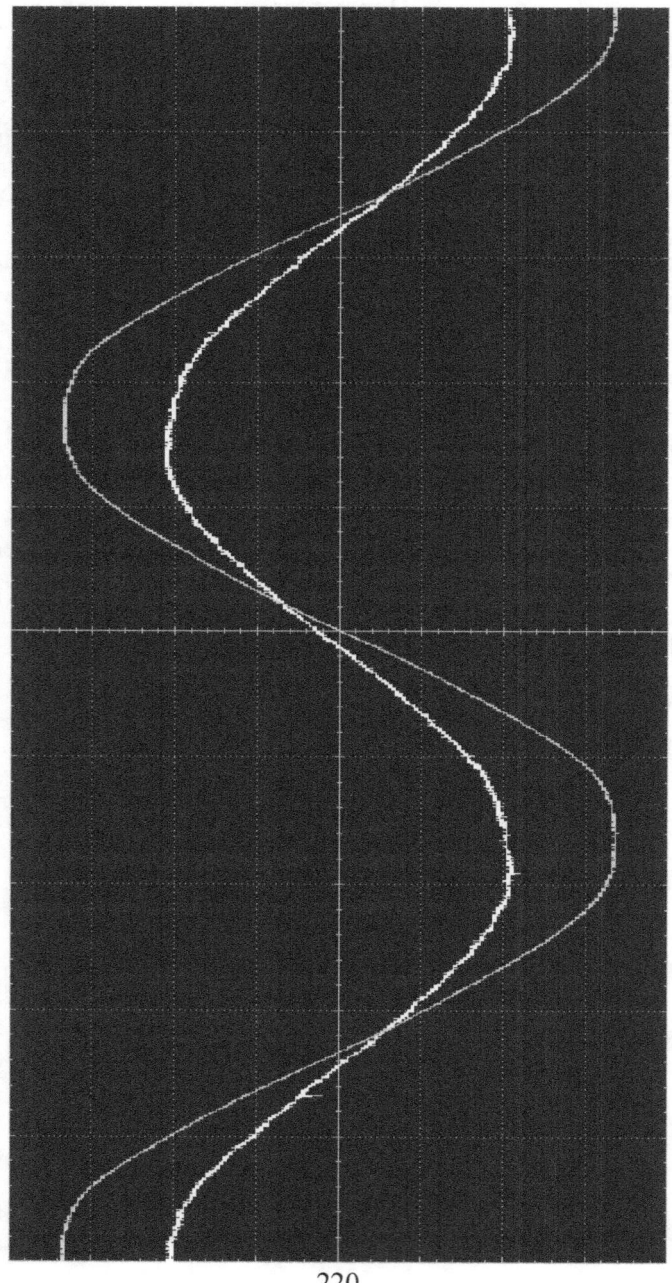

As we can see, the harmonic frequencies are 20% higher on the 60Hz system when compared to the 50Hz system. This matches an observation that I have made that American power engineers appear to be sicker than their British counterparts. It is likely that there is a link to exposure to higher frequency harmonic energy content from the American power system.

Harmonic energy can occur in two ways:

- A non-linear (non-sinusoidal) draw on electrical current that is characteristic of electronic products, street lights, and electronic lighting products.

- A large load on the utility system that deforms the voltage waveform.

You will see the current harmonics long before you see the voltage harmonics.

All electronic products will produce some level of distortion on the current waveform. Some are worse than others. Certain combinations of electronic products on the system may create severe distortions on it. You should be concerned about these distortions as it changes the characteristics of the electrical system emissions into the human environment.

If you are seeing distortion of the voltage sine wave and large amounts of harmonics, you should be really concerned! When troubleshooting a problem like this, you should limit your time in the area, as you may get sick from excessive electromagnetic interference exposure.

If you look at the waveform in the next image you will see that it is a 60Hz voltage sine wave.

If you look at the same waveform that is on the utility system with an oscilloscope with a fast Fourier transform (FFT) you will see that it looks like the image on the following page. It is normal to see the odd harmonics as they are a feature of all electronic power generation and electronic loads in general. In the image from bottom to top you can see the 60Hz (fundamental), 180Hz (3rd), 300Hz (5th), 420Hz (7th), and

540Hz (9th) harmonics as spikes. The even harmonics generally cancel out on a utility system.

If you have really severe harmonics on the system you will need to start troubleshooting it. Your utility voltage sine wave should never look like the last picture! A waveform like this may make the wiring on the utility system radiate radio waves, magnetic fields, electric fields, and many other forms of electromagnetic radiation!

Utility 60 Hz Voltage Sine Wave

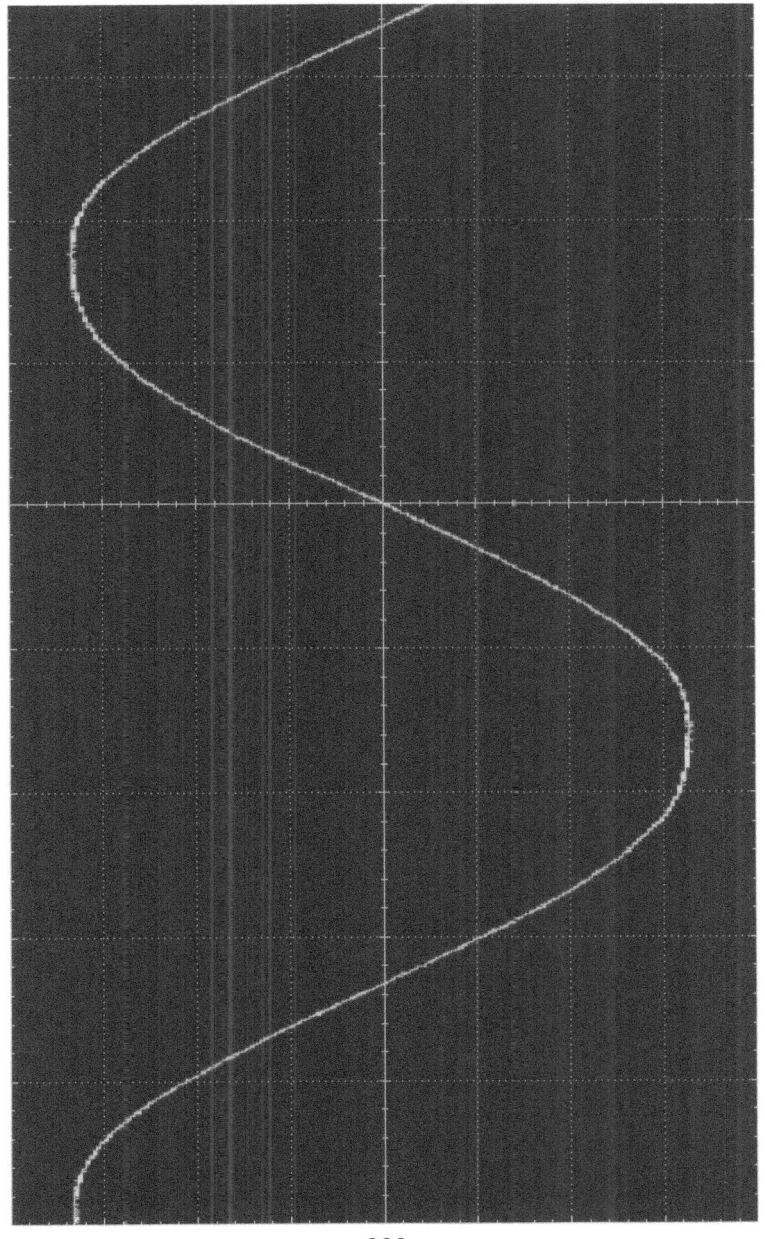

Utility Voltage Harmonics

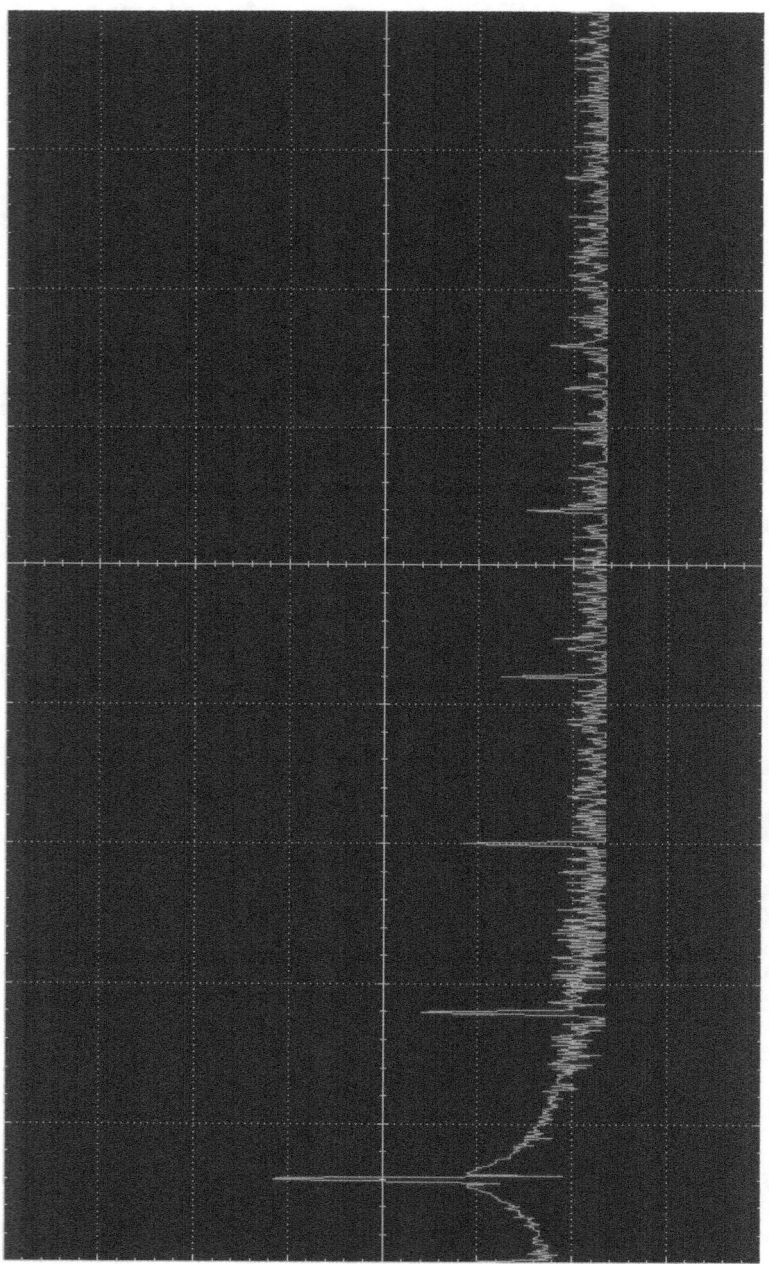

Severe Harmonic Distortion Sine Wave

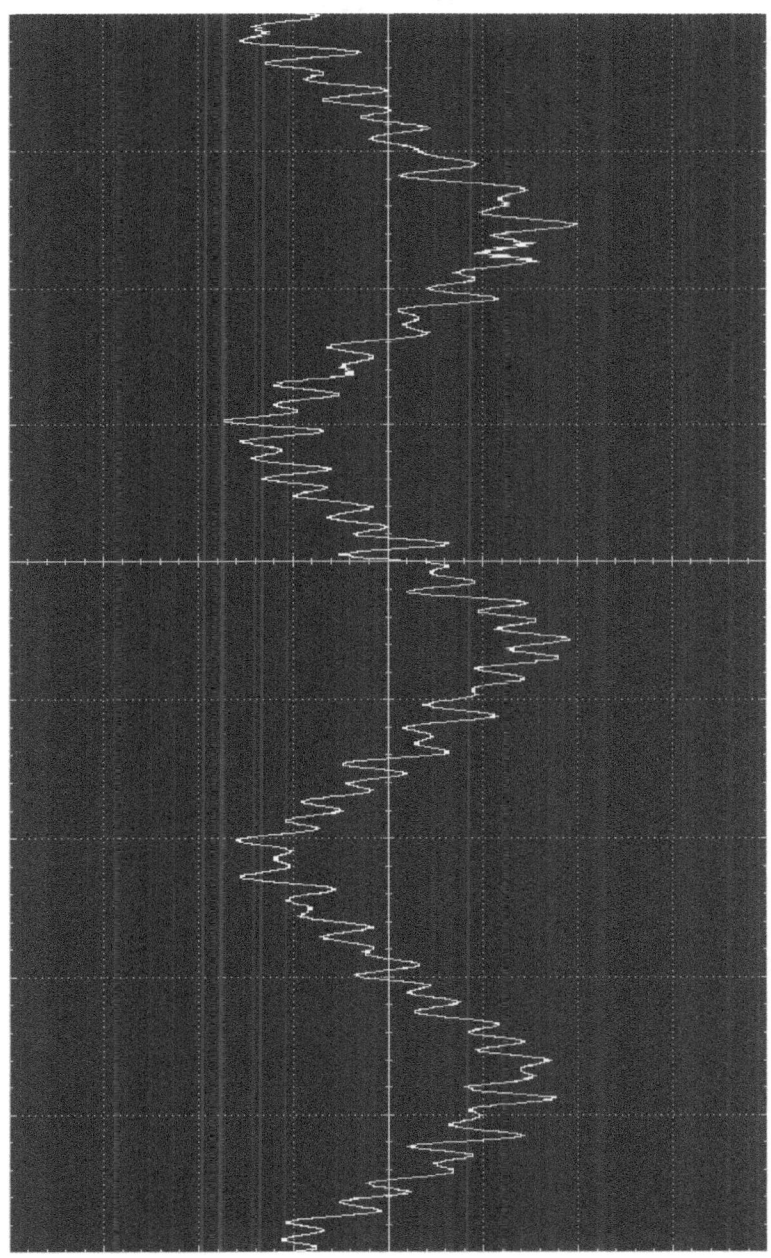

When you put harmonic energy onto an electrical cable, you generally see the following effects occur on cables and equipment:

- Very large electric fields.

- Very large magnetic fields.

- Very large wide band radio wave fields.

- Very large electrostatic fields on high voltage cables.

- Very large ion fields.

- Overloading and overheating.

- Tripping of breakers and blown fuses.

- Exploding fuses.

- Fires.

As you can see, harmonics changes the characteristics of the electrical system considerably and you should avoid using products that generate them.

Individual products that appear to generate low amounts of harmonics may actually start to generate large amounts of harmonics when used in conjunction with other products on your electrical system. The electrical system is always changing with the different times of day, the seasons, and the different loads on the system.

When measuring electrical system harmonics you should do it with a direct connection to the electrical wire. You should avoid using current or voltage transformers to do it as these filter out some of the harmonics. Clamp-on ammeters are relatively useless for accurately reading the system harmonics. You generally will lose all of the high frequency content.

If you cannot use a direct connection to the cable, then you can get an assessment of the harmonics by using a simple AM radio that is tuned to static (no radio station) and using a TriField 100XE meter to read the magnetic and electric field emissions.

I have noticed in the solar photovoltaic industry that usually the best harmonic value is listed on the data sheet and that it does not state if it is the current harmonic or the voltage harmonic that it refers to. To accurately quote electronic inverter harmonic values they should be listed as a low and high range for the current harmonics, and a low and high range for the voltage harmonics as they do vary with the power. A chart showing both values over the power range of the inverter is also useful.

When connecting multiple power generation inverter systems together, this may lead to excessively high harmonics on the electrical system with correspondingly high electromagnetic interference emissions. When assessing inverter systems, the manufacturer should also state the harmonics for the inverter system when there are many utility power generation inverter systems connected to the system. This is called "High Penetration" in the electrical utility industry.

If you want to understand harmonics better, then I can recommend building a harmonic generator. A harmonic generator can easily and cheaply be built using electronic lamp dimmers. The more electronic lamp dimmers and light bulbs that you use, the more extensive the harmonics will be that it generates. You can also install CFL and LED light bulbs that are rated for use with electronic lamp dimmers to increase the harmonic content. Be careful about spending too much time near the harmonic generator, as it may make you sick!

Using a standard AM radio tuned to static (no radio station) and a TriField 100XE meter, you will find some very interesting electromagnetic fields around it. You will be able to see the harmonics by using an oscilloscope with a fast Fourier transform function (FFT). The most extensive harmonics will be found on the neutral current waveform. When using conventional filament light bulbs you will notice that you get very high magnetic fields at low lighting levels and very high electric fields at high lighting levels. The wide band radio wave fields vary with the dimming settings.

The diagram of a harmonic generator test system is shown in the next image and the following picture shows the voltage waveform created by the electronic lamp dimmers.

Harmonic Generator

Harmonic Generator Current Waveform.

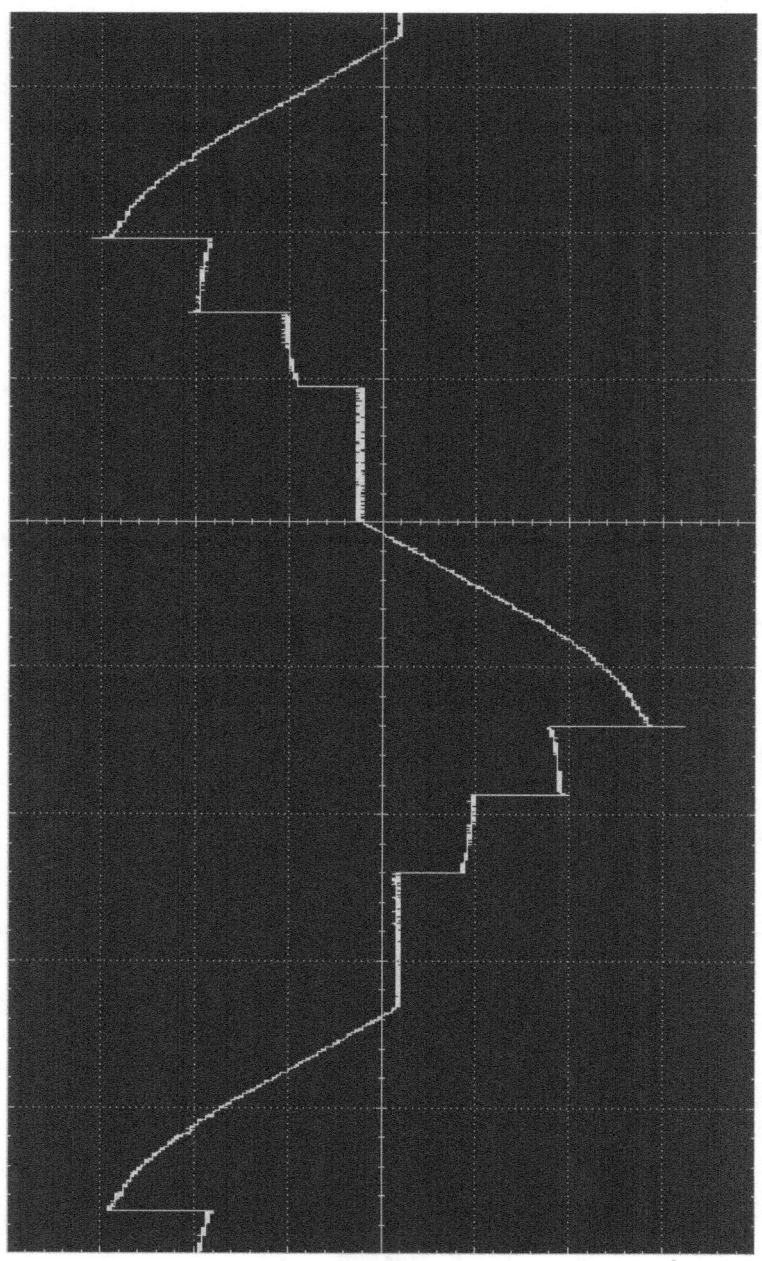

When you test the harmonic generator for magnetic and electric fields, you will find that the peaks for each type of field are in different dimming settings. The peak magnetic field is found by triggering the dimmers before the peak of the voltage waveform and the peak electric field is found by triggering the lamp dimmers after the peak of the voltage waveform.

The following graph shows the current waveform for peak magnetic field overlaid with the peak electric field current waveform.

Peak Electric and Magnetic Field Current Waveforms

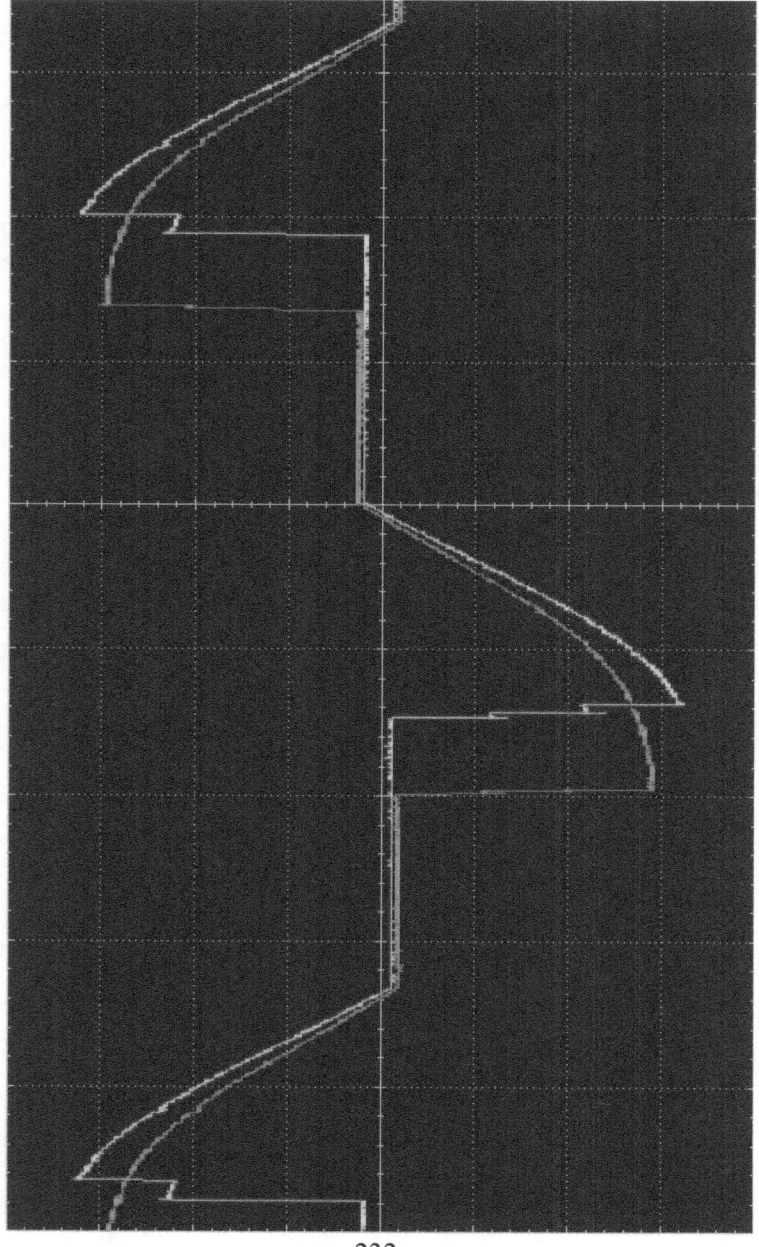

12 volt DC to 120 volt AC inverters used for cars, camping and off grid homes are also good harmonic generators. The cheaper units are called modified sine wave inverters and use square waves to produce the AC power.

I lived in an off grid home for a couple of years and the longer I lived there, the sicker I got! The phone line always buzzed there and this appeared to be an effect of dirty electricity exposure. Off grid homes generally have the poorest power quality and it will vary with the electrical products on the system. I was seeing problems in the two other people that I knew well that lived in off grid homes. One was showing habitual passive aggressiveness and the other was extremely forgetful! Extended dirty electricity exposure may have an intoxication effect that is similar to being on drugs.

The modified sine wave inverter waveform and frequency content can be seen in the next two pictures. The following two pictures show the waveform and frequency content for the more expensive and much better sine wave inverter, note the slightly distorted waveform that causes harmonics to occur. Both types of inverters cause harmonics and the cheaper modified sine wave inverter is horrendous for doing so. I do not recommend extended exposure to these modified sine wave inverter systems, as you may develop some strange health issues.

Modified Sine Wave Inverter Waveform

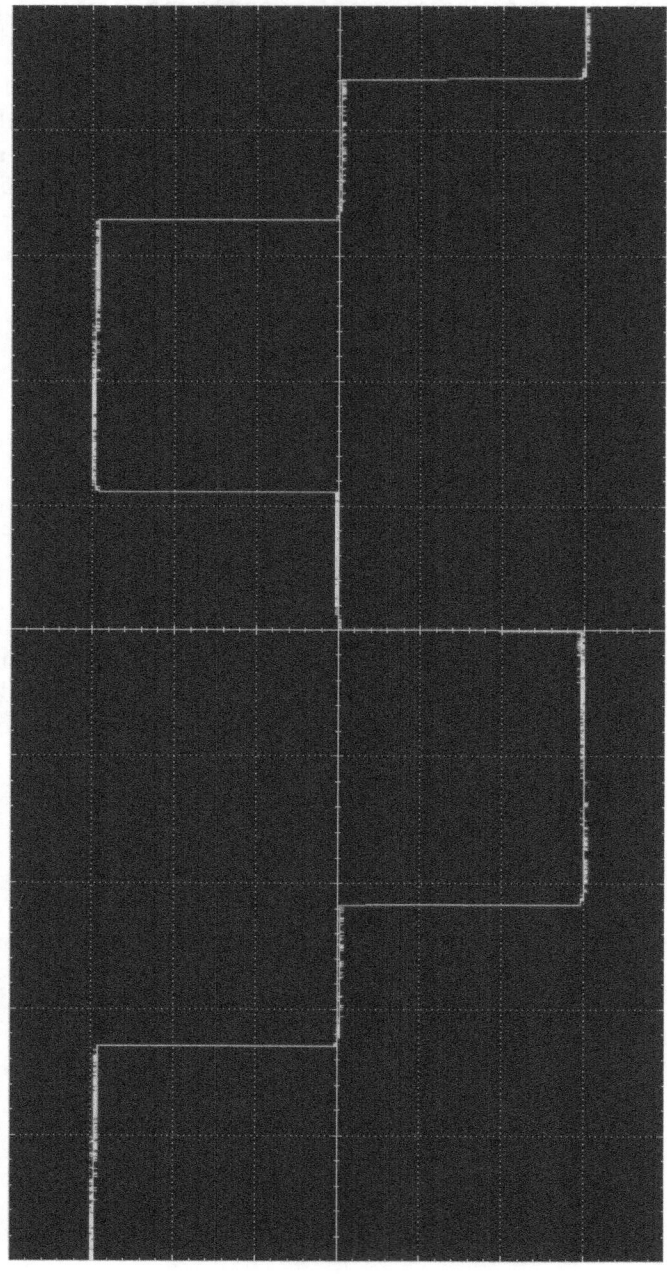

Modified Sine Wave Inverter Frequency Content

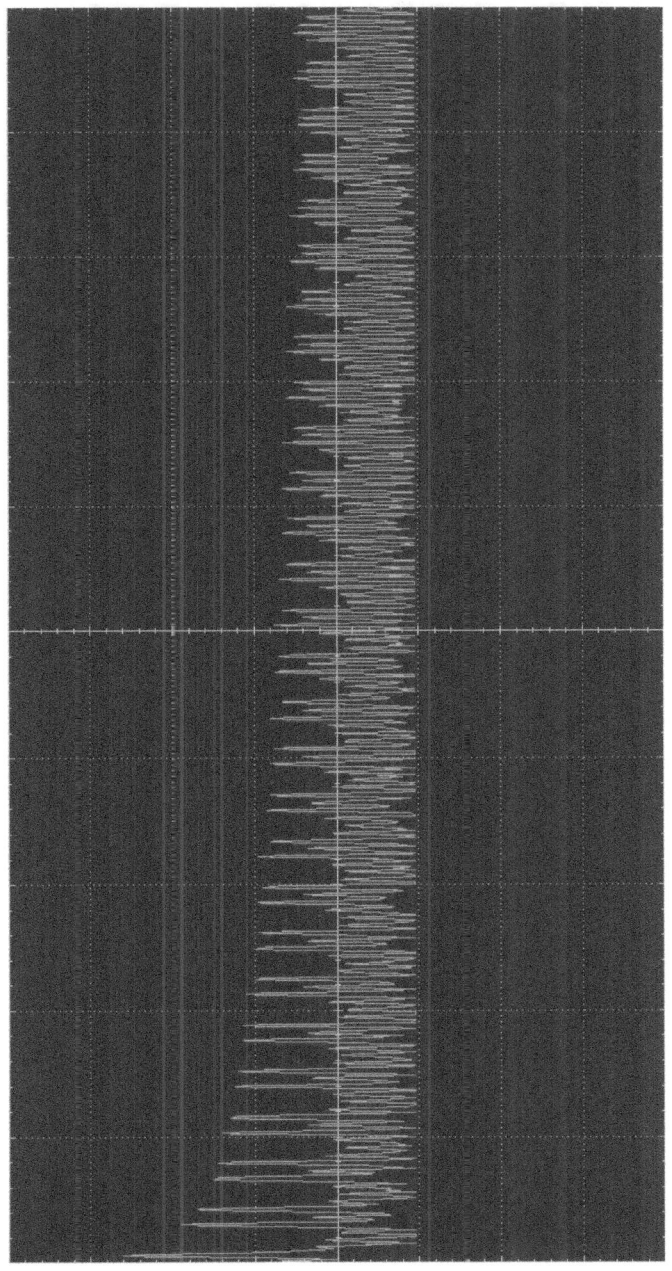

Sine Wave Inverter Waveform

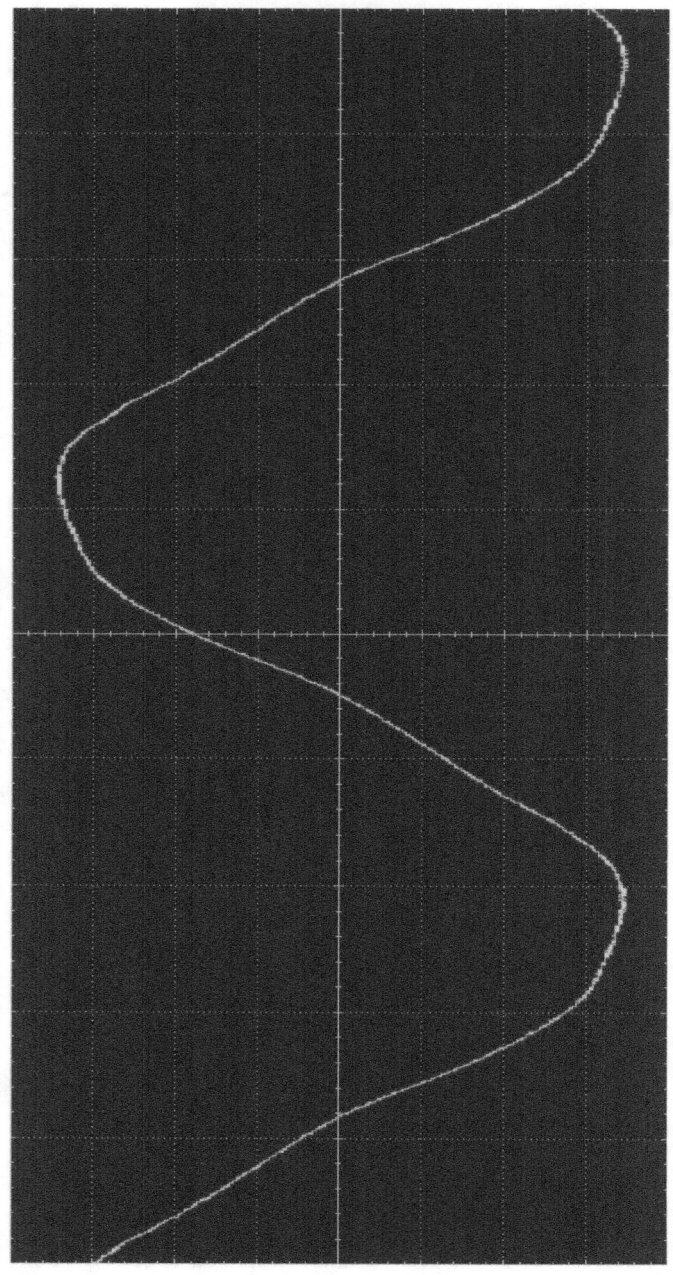

Sine Wave Inverter Frequency Content

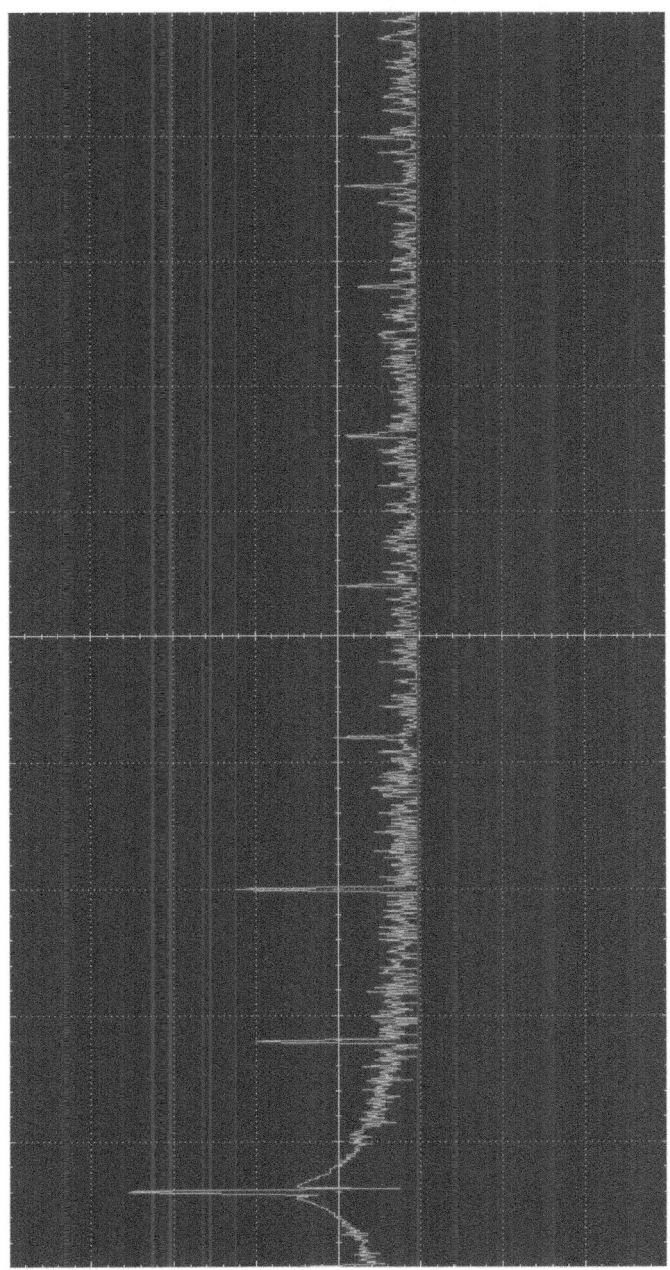

For those with an eye on developing the next hot consumer product, here are a few suggestions:

- Household "Dirty electricity" monitor.

- Household electromagnetic radiation meters.

- Baby room safety scanner for harmful electromagnetic radiation emissions.

- Household "Stray voltage/current/frequency" testers.

To sum up harmonics, I want you to understand that a non -linear current draw is a really bad idea on both AC and DC electrical systems. The more non-linear the current on your electrical system is, then the more toxic your electrical system will become. The cable that supplies the non-linear load may start acting like a radio transmitter! Once there are radio frequencies on the system, then the electrical system may turn everything into a radio transmitter, including the ground that you walk on! Clearly a really bad idea.

"Harmonics are the cancer of the electrical system."

Steven Magee

Direct Electrical Exposure

Direct electrical exposure is the human body coming directly into contact with the electrical system. There appears to be three types of exposure:

- Electrocution.
- Shocks.
- Stray voltage/current/frequency.

We all know that electricity can kill us if we come into contact with the electrical conductors (cables) of the system. The conductors that are energized above earth (ground) potential are called the "Live" conductors and these are the ones that present the risk of electrocution.

Most circuits in the home in the USA are 15 amp circuits. But how much AC current is needed to kill a human? It is a tiny amount of this value. Just 0.02 amp of AC electrical current may kill a human! It is a little lower in the female. A human coming into contact with a live electrical conductor would never blow the fuse.

You need much more DC current than AC current to electrocute a human. For this reason, contact with DC electricity is considered safer than AC.

Most human deaths from electrocution are from these exposures:

- Contact with high voltage.
- Contact with voltage where they are unable to let go.
- Burns from electrical current exposure.
- Arc flash.
- Heart attack.

The human body varies in its risk of electrocution. A very dry body needs a much higher amount of voltage to cause electrocution, whereas a wet body needs a much lower level for electrocution. A dry person may be electrocuted on 120 volts AC and a wet person may be electrocuted on just a few volts.

It is for this reason that you see wet areas of homes being protected by ground fault circuit interrupters (GFCI). These sense very low current leakage in the circuit conductors and will trip the circuit if you come into contact with it. If you are working outdoors in the garden with electrical items, you should ensure that your cables are protected by one of these devices.

Most people in the home are electrocuted through not being able to let go of the live conductor that they are in contact with. It causes a grip reaction to occur and paralyzes the human body. Unless you can get yourself off the conductor, you may die from electrical burns or a heart attack. I have experienced this and it is a very strange sensation to lose control of your body. I eventually realized that I could control my legs and kicked my way off the electrical system. I had very deep skin burns on my hands at the entry and exit points of contact with the electrical system.

If you are ever confronted with a person in the process of being electrocuted, do not go near them or touch them. Find the circuit breaker and turn it off. If you do not know where it is, find a dry wooden pole and push them off the electrical system. If they are in a wet area, you should not enter the area. If you do not know where the circuit breaker is located and it is not accessible, you should consider shorting the circuit to trip the breaker. Do not short high powered circuits as you may get arc flash issues. You will need to act quickly to save the persons life, but do not act in a way that could endanger your own life. If you cannot get them off the electrical system, call the emergency services. A person who has had a severe shock should be sent to the hospital for evaluation, as they may have internal damage that may show up later.

Arc flash is not electrocution, but it can kill a person. It happens around high energy equipment failures and it is a radiation exposure. The radiation emitted by arcing electricity irradiates the human body, causing extensive radiation burns. It is the burns that kill the person. This is a particular problem in the utility industry.

Electrical welders have a similar problem to arc flash. In welders, it generally causes a sunburn reaction, as the arc is not high powered. "Arc Eye"(Photokeratitis) is a condition associated with welders and is the reason why you see them using face shields. You should never watch a welder working, otherwise you may develop arc eye. Welders are a group of people who get extensive exposure to stray voltage/current/frequency and electromagnetic radiation emissions.

Shocks are caused by coming into contact with electrical currents that are high enough to be sensed by the human body but are low enough not to kill it. So how much current is needed to sense electricity in the human? Dr. William B. Kouwenhoven, a professor of electrical engineering at John Hopkins university, found that it is about 0.003 amp of AC current. 0.006 amp AC causes a painful shock in the female and 0.009 amp AC is needed for pain in the male. It is important to note that the female is more vulnerable than the male to electrical exposures.

DC shocks can be far worse than AC shocks. One of the worst electrical shocks that I have ever had was from a 330 volt DC circuit It was so bad that I had a headache for a week afterwords! The difference between AC and DC is noticeable when you are in contact with it. The AC shock sends pulses of electricity through the human body that can be felt. The DC shock is just continuous.

Stray voltage/current/frequency is the most serious form of exposure. Electrocution kills very few people per year. Stray voltage/current/frequency exposure is suspected to be making people sick in the millions!

It is quite possible that tens of thousands of deaths per year in the USA have stray voltage/current/frequency at their root cause. The problem with stray voltage/current/frequency exposure is that the symptoms vary with the voltage, current and frequencies of the electricity that the person is exposed to. No two people will have the same exposures. Around stray voltage/current/frequency the persons exposure will vary according to their lifestyle. Things that will increase stray voltage/current/frequency exposure are:

- Copper plumbing.
- Cast iron drains.
- Swimming.
- Hot tub.
- Location of grounding rods.
- Conductive tiled floors.
- Conductive concrete floors.
- Conductive counters.
- Conductive brick home.
- Conductive metal home.
- Conductive shoes.
- Walking a dog.
- Sitting or laying on conductive flooring.
- Their career.
- Their electrical utility company.
- Their electrical and electronic products.
- Dirty electricity.
- The presence of an alternate energy system in the area.

As you can see, there are a lot of variables that feed into your exposure to stray voltage/current/frequency. You should assume that wherever electricity is installed, that there is a risk of stray voltage/current/frequency exposure.

You will not be able to feel it, you will just notice that your health is mysteriously deteriorating.

Stray voltage/current/frequency is poorly understood and is one of the biggest threats to long term human health around electrical systems

"Someone confronted with an electrocution, for example, usually stands there helplessly."

Susanne Woelk

Lightning

Lightning is nature's electricity. Our knowledge of electricity was developed from it. Wikipedia states: *Lightning is an atmospheric electrical discharge (spark) accompanied by thunder, usually associated and produced by cumulonimbus clouds, but also occurring during volcanic eruptions or in dust storms. From this discharge of atmospheric electricity, a leader of a bolt of lightning can travel at speeds of 220,000 km/h (140,000 mph), and can reach temperatures approaching 30,000 °C (54,000 °F), hot enough to fuse silica sand into glass channels known as fulgurites, which are normally hollow and can extend as much as several meters into the ground. There are some 16 million lightning storms in the world every year. Lightning causes ionization in the air through which it travels, leading to the formation of nitric oxide and ultimately, nitric acid, of benefit to plant life below.*

Lightning is high voltage, high current DC electricity and can have positive or negative polarity. When a lightning strike occurs it generates an electromagnetic field. This can be heard on a standard AM radio that is tuned into static (no radio station). If there is a lot of lightning in the area then you will hear a lot of noise on the AM radio.

The lightning strike occurs when the electrical breakdown of air is reached, typically at one million volts per meter. When the lightning passes through the air it heats it to three times hotter than the surface of the Sun! The strongest electromagnetic radiation produced appears to be below 300,000 Hertz. This is called the low frequency (LF) and very low frequency (VLF) ranges. Lightning also has a significant amount of energy in the high frequency range (HF) up to 30,000,000Hz.

There are two wave types associated with lightning. The ground wave is the direct line of sight electromagnetic radiation from the storm. The sky wave is the reflected electromagnetic radiation from the ionosphere part of the atmosphere.

244

Lightning produces wide band radio waves by pulsing the DC current. These pulsing DC currents cause a wide range of frequencies to be generated. It can be compared to dirty electricity. One of the reasons that dirty electricity is so harmful to the human is that it is not seasonal, it is continually in the modern human environment. The human is designed to only have short exposures annually to lightning storms.

When listening to the lightning storms in your area on a standard AM radio, you will hear a sound like bacon frying and this is the electromagnetic energy that the storm is generating. Plants react to this energy and may show vigorous growth during lightning seasons.

It is quite possible that crime is tied to the electromagnetic emissions from lightning. The high amount of electromagnetic energy in the area may affect human mental health and trigger a crime spree. This may be especially the case in areas that are prone to large amounts of lightning like Florida, USA.

For human health purposes, you may want to avoid living in areas that are prone to high levels of lightning. Certain parts of Florida may actually have too much lightning in them for it to be considered safe for humans to inhabit long term. Too much lightning may bring about the symptoms of radio wave sickness and electromagnetic hypersensitivity. Fatigue is the top reported symptom and you may see it appear during periods of seasonal lightning storms and disappear outside of these times of year. If you live in a high lightning area and are seeing seasonal fatigue occurring, you should consider moving away from the area.

There are no doubts that electromagnetic radiation exposure can trigger the human mating cycle and it is quite possible that birth rates may be tied to lightning!

Lightning strike rates increase in areas that the man-made structures exceed the height of trees. The higher the structure is, the greater the increase in lightning strikes in the area. It increases by approximately the square of the height of the structure. Lightning travels relatively slowly through the air but increases to the speed of light when it travels through a metal conductor to the ground below. This causes increased radiation emissions from the lightning strike which may affect people in the surrounding area.

Downtown areas will be more prone to lightning due to their tall buildings and people who live near to these areas may actually find that there are too many lightning strikes taking place at close proximity to them. They may actually get overloaded on electromagnetic exposure from the lightning strikes! You should avoid living in areas that have tall structures that short circuit the atmospheric layers as the long term health problems are currently unknown.

Lightning rods on tall structures short circuit the atmospheric layers. This can be seen when studying lightning strikes. The lightning will come down through the atmosphere as normal, but when it hits the short circuited atmospheric layer it will travel horizontally to the lightning rod where it discharges down the lightning conductor to the ground. As it does so, it fills that area with electromagnetic radiation emissions that are distinctly different from what the storm naturally produces. This is shown in the next diagram.

Lightning & Short Circuited Atmospheric Layers

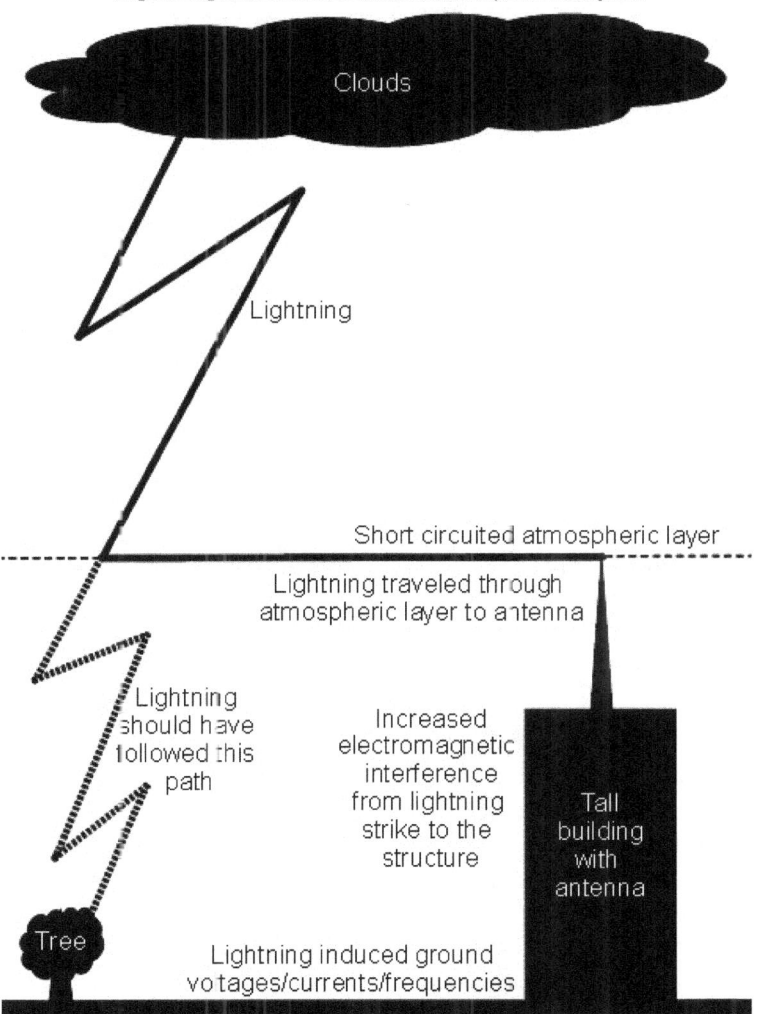

Lightning will tend to hit the tallest structure in the area. Trees, towers and power lines all have the same probability of being hit if they are at the same height. However, the frequency emissions appear to be different between the man-made objects and those of nature.

Lightning is well known for its ability to damage electrical and electronic products. A close lightning strike raises the voltage on the utility electrical system and can destroy electrical and electronic products. Another effect of nearby lighting strikes is that they produce significant levels of radio frequencies. These will be induced into anything that is acting as an antenna system and may create damage to the system. Some solar photovoltaic power systems are known to be affected by this, as the solar modules and electrical wiring create a large antenna system.

Airplane pilots are at risk of lightning exposure and may get intoxicated from it when flying through an electrical storm. The electrical activity will envelop the airplane in St. Elmo's Fire and create very high electromagnetic radiation levels inside the airplane. The pilots may display poor brain functioning, aggression, poor senses, human senses may be reporting information that is not true, human actions may not reflect thoughts, and confusion. This appears to be what happened in the Air France flight 447 crash.

The problem with subjecting the human to man-made electromagnetic interference fields is that the human exposure to EMI is seasonal. Subjecting the human to daily EMI from electrical, electronic and wireless products is comparable to constantly sitting in the middle of a high intensity lighting storm! Clearly an unnatural activity.

Accompanying lightning is a shock wave. This is what we hear as thunder. It is a supersonic wave that is created by the rapid expansion of the heated air. The shock wave is likely to have an affect on the human as well. Supersonic shock waves are associated with heart problems.

One of the problems with climate change, global warming and global air pollution is that it may change the

frequency and intensity of electrical storm activity. Too much lightning activity may cause excessive mating, aggression, fatigue, illness and disease to occur. Too little may turn off the animal and plant breeding cycles.

We know that static ceases to occur at above 30% relative humidity. As the Earth's atmosphere heats up, the humidity will fall and may turn on major static electrical activity in the atmosphere. The falling humidity levels may also turn off the lightning storms! With no clouds, there will be no electrical storms.

"Electricity is really just organized lightning."

George Carlin

Static

Static is an electrical charge that forms on dissimilar materials and objects due to the differences of movement between them.

When an object is charged up with static, the fibers repel from each other. This also happens to the human and the body hair will stand up. Synthetic materials generate this effect when in contact with the human body. You need to be careful with clothes that generate static, as they may have you walking around in a static generated electromagnetic field! You can hear this effect with an AM radio tuned to static (no radio station). Every time you see a spark, you will hear it on the radio.

High humidity kills static. This is why sometimes you may see it and other times not. If the clothes are humid you will not see the effect. Having plants inside your home humidifies your home and helps to prevent static from occurring.

In the past people used to wear leather soled shoes and these were good for keeping the person electrically grounded to the side walk. They provide a discharge path for the static. Today, you should be wearing insulated shoes, due to the presence of electrified ground near to electrical grounding systems. With insulated shoes, you should ensure that you are wearing natural clothing in order not to generate the static. Insulated shoes that generate static should be avoided, as they may make you sick!

It is quite possible that some people's illnesses are tied to the static discharges that are occurring in their environment. The radio wave fields that it generates may cause electromagnetic hypersensitivity to occur and this is why it is important to wear natural clothing.

Static is generally very high voltage and very low current. We are lucky that the current is low, otherwise we would all be dying from electrocution!

"We tested his clothes with a static electricity field meter and measured a current of 40,000 volts, which is one step shy of spontaneous combustion, where his clothes would have self-ignited."

Henry Barton

Direct Current (DC)

Most people associate direct current (DC) with batteries. It has a constant voltage that does not change over time. In nature you find DC electricity in areas such as:

- Swamps.
- Bogs.
- Marshes.
- Moors.
- The tree canopy.
- The atmosphere.

Atmospheric energy has direct current in it and it has a voltage gradient that is negative for the first couple of miles above the ground and that then changes to positive polarity as you go higher into the atmosphere. Close to the ground the voltage increase is between 1 to 19 volts per foot. Flying kites with conductive strings will expose you to this atmospheric voltage, as will helium balloons with long conductive strings. Higher up in the atmosphere, the voltage increases by approximately 30 volts per foot.

All living organisms that stand tall on the ground are subjected to this DC voltage and this is evidenced in the following pictures.

The Dieffenbachia grows well regardless of if the voltage is positive or negative 1.5 volts on its stem relative to the roots. It indicates that the atmospheric DC voltage polarity may reverse in nature over time. I can only get the Dieffenbachia to grow normally at my home by using a 1.5 volt battery which indicates that the atmospheric DC voltage in my area has changed, which is very concerning!

If the DC voltage gets too high, then the Dieffenbachia plant starts to show stress. 9 volts positive polarity on the stem appears to cause growth defects (shown) and seems more harmful than 9 volts negative stem polarity that seems to stunt growth and corrodes the metal alligator clip.

My plants are grown in high radiation fields that appear to come from radio frequency transmitting utility meters and three cell phone towers that are between 600-700 meters from my home. The Dieffenbachia's all deform at my home regardless of where they are grown at on my property. The only ones that grow normally have 1.5 DC volts on them! As we can see in the plants, we can restore the normal growth patterns by applying a DC voltage to them. The voltage has to be kept to the correct level, otherwise stresses will show up if too high or too low. Applying a DC voltage between the soles of the feet of the human and the upper body may have applications in the field of human health. This is shown in the next diagram.

I am currently experimenting with putting the human mind and body into a DC electric field during sleep. I have a large sheet of conductive aluminum foil attached to the 10' high ceiling above the bed and a large sheet of conductive aluminum foil on the floor under the bed to effect this. The upper sheet is connected to the negative terminal of a battery and the lower sheet is connected to the positive terminal. This can be seen in the following photograph.

The upper sheet is akin to the tree canopy which is known to have a DC voltage on it. A company called Voltree Power (www.voltreepower.com) is developing the use of tree voltage to power electronic systems and has extensively researched the DC voltage of trees.

The feet are connected together through being in contact with the conductive ground and are earthed (grounded). The mind and body are walking around in a DC voltage field. That DC voltage will energize the mind and body and the lack of it may make the human sick.

Human Electrical Model

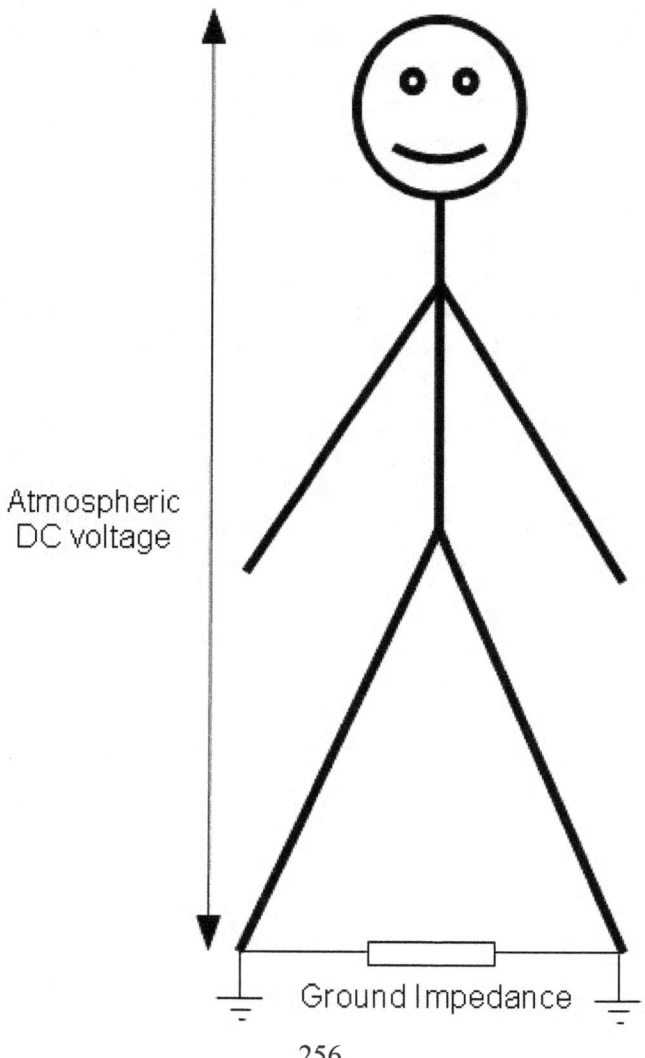

Atmospheric
DC voltage

Ground Impedance

The upper and lower sheets of aluminum foil are the same size as the bed. The DC voltage on the conductive sheets will set up a DC voltage field between them with a small flow of electrons that should pass through the human sleeping in the bed. This is currently an unproven experimental health technique that may have unknown side effects. I call this technique: "Electromagnetic Sandwich"

I started testing the electromagnetic sandwich with a 9 volt battery which should give approximately 2 volts of a negative atmospheric voltage exposure to my mind and body during sleep. The atmospheric voltage gradient between the floor sheet and the ceiling negative sheet is 0.9 volt DC per foot. I could definitely feel the difference when I was sleeping and headaches and muscle weakness showed up after about a week of testing. I changed the battery to 1.5 volt DC and found that this was much more agreeable to human health and the health problems cleared up. 1.5 volts DC appears to be more comparable to what you find on the tree canopy. I may adjust the DC voltage later, depending on what I find with long term testing.

It is interesting that the human health difference in the DC voltage exposures matches what I saw in the Dieffenbachia plants. Exposure to a very low DC voltage that is comparable a single DC battery cell appears healthy for biological systems and 9 volts DC stresses them.

My initial assessment of the electromagnetic sandwich health technique is that the occasional daytime fatigue that I was experiencing has been significantly reduced. I find this very concerning, as it indicates that a DC atmospheric voltage is missing at my home that is required for both good plant health and good human health. It appears that people who suffer from electromagnetic hypersensitivity may be reacting to this loss of atmospheric DC voltage. They appear to be the electromagnetic radiation equivalent of the "Coalminers canary" and it is very foolish to ignore the health symptoms that these many people are reporting. They are very clearly reacting to unnatural man-made electromagnetic radiation conditions.

I have further developed the electromagnetic sandwich technique for daytime use. It is easily implemented using an anti-static wrist strap and an anti-static mat. This is shown in the next picture. For those of you on the go, you can wear an anti-static heel strap and an anti-static wrist strap and just put the 1.5 volt DC battery in your pocket. Keep the cables as short as possible and it is preferable to use straight cables as opposed to the coiled cables shown in the picture. Long cables and cable coils act as antenna systems and will put strange frequencies onto the DC voltage that may lead to electromagnetic hypersensitivity.

These health techniques are experimental and have unknown side effects at the time of writing. The DC voltages may require adjusting to higher or lower levels and will be person dependent due to the impedance of the fat to muscle ratio. They may need to only be applied for short periods rather than continuous use. This is a developing area of research that is very new and there are a lot of unknowns currently.

If you choose to implement them, you should be under qualified and competent medical supervision and discontinue the techniques if adverse health symptoms show up. You would be assuming any and all risks using these health techniques.

During the daytime I am now experimenting with wearing an anti-static strap on my wrist that is connected to the negative terminal of a 1.5 volt DC battery. The positive terminal is connected to an anti-static mat that my bare feet rest on. This creates a DC voltage gradient across my body that is similar to what nature does. Both the mat and the wrist strap have 1,000,000 ohm resistors built into them.

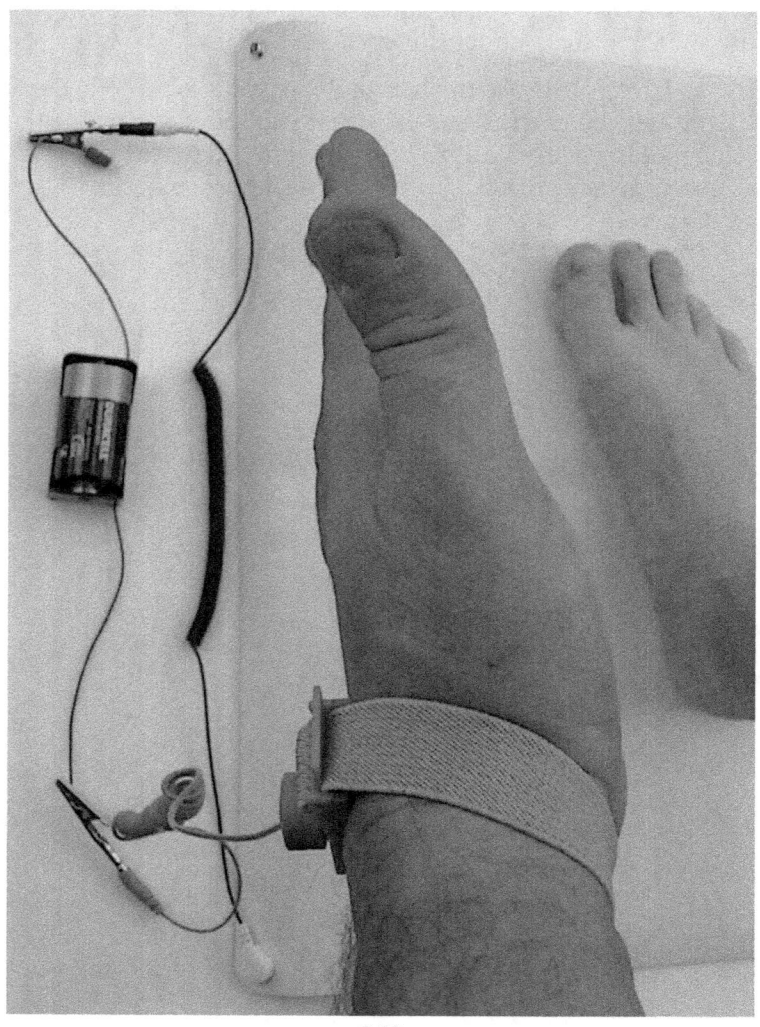

High powered DC batteries are used for industrial applications and are commonly found in vehicles and battery powered systems. I have found fields around these batteries, so you should be careful with exposure to them. People that I have met who work full time with high powered batteries tend to have strange personalities and is likely due to daily exposure to them.

Batteries tend to be low voltage and each battery cell is about 1 to 2 volts, depending on the technology used. Higher voltage batteries are simply a collection of many battery cells connected together in series. You need to be careful with such high voltage batteries and a DC shock can be more severe than an AC shock. Both can kill you.

"We cannot hope to either understand or to manage the carbon in the atmosphere unless we understand and manage the trees and the soil too."

Freeman Dyson

Faraday Cages & Screening

Faraday cages have been around for hundreds of years. First reports of them were by Benjamin Franklin and Micheal Faraday documented the use of these cages for protection from electricity sources. They have been known as Faraday cages ever since.

David Blaine recently demonstrated the phenomenon in his October 2012 "Electrified" show. Standing for three days and three nights surrounded by numerous million volt Tesla coils, he was repeatedly hit by high voltage sparks. He was wearing a metal "Faraday cage" suit and an open wire frame helmet. He did appear to get shocked during the show and he was reporting that his skin was tingling during practice. It was clear that the suit was not fully protective of the energies that he was exposed to.

I did try and contact David Blaine to get feedback on the health symptoms that showed up before, during and after the show, but no reply was ever received. I have never seen a public statement issued by him regarding this subject either. I am curious to know what health symptoms showed up and if there were any lasting effects from the exposures that he received from the "Electrified" show. If you know what happened, I would like to hear from you.

David Blaine demonstrated one of the myths surrounding Faraday cages and that is if you are inside a Faraday cage, that you are fully protected from the energies that are outside of it. This is not true. Faraday cages are simply attenuators for energy transmission through the surrounding atmosphere. They reduce some energies more than others. The energy reduction effect is frequency dependent and a Faraday cage may significantly reduce some frequencies and may only slightly reduce others. Many energies will pass into the Faraday cage, generally with attenuation.

Tesla coil performers generally report a feeling of euphoria and it probably comes from the intense flashes of light, the electromagnetic exposures and the gasses that they breath during the show. The Telsa coil performer should be wearing ultraviolet blocking glasses during the show due to the ultraviolet emissions from the sparks. Muscle soreness may be reported afterwords. The electromagnetic exposures for a Tesla coil performer are increased if they are in contact with the Faraday cage. High frequency electromagnetic exposure is known for its effects on the brain and is linked to increased rates of brain tumors. Tesla coil performers should be aware of the symptoms of electromagnetic hypersensitivity in case they start to develop it. The audience is also at risk of developing some of the above problems.

Faraday cages are commonly grounded to discharge the energy. While energy discharge is needed around high powered equipment, we know today that sometimes it is actually healthier to leave the Faraday cage ungrounded. It is one of the myths that is around that they only function effectively against high frequency radiation sources when they are grounded. I have done extensive testing of Faraday cages around AM and FM radio receivers and 2.4 gigahertz Wi-Fi transmitters and have found no noticeable performance gain in the electromagnetic shielding properties of these Faraday cages when grounded. It is quite the opposite. If you connect a Faraday cage into a source of stray voltage/frequency/current, then you may turn it into a transmitter!

Regarding electromagnetic hypersensitivity, people have been using the principles of Faraday cages to protect themselves from radio frequency sources. They have noticed that grounding them sometimes increases their symptoms and they use their Faraday cages ungrounded.

Plants do not grow correctly inside Faraday cages and may show abnormal branching, leaf size, stalky growth patterns and unusual growth rates. Dr. John Nash Ott noted the natural cycles were interrupted in plants that he took to the bottom of a coal mine. This is in line with work that has been done in the past that shows that when the human is

263

disconnected from surface radiation effects that the biological cycles become affected. The experts on this subject are the manned Space programs. Spaceships and space stations are nothing more than Faraday cages that are in extremely unnatural environments. Astronauts show many health problems when living in Space and typically only spend several months there. I find it very concerning that people who are suffering from electromagnetic hypersensitivity are now resorting to living in Faraday cages! This may cause radiation deficiency conditions in the long term.

The growth effects of a Dieffenbachia plant that was grown in an ungrounded aluminum window mesh Faraday cage is shown in the next photograph.

This Dieffenbachia has spent eleven months living inside an ungrounded Faraday cage. It is showing extensive growth problems that include very small leaves, loss of patterning and abnormal branching structure.

Similar to the Faraday cage is electromagnetic shielding. People who have electromagnetic hypersensitivity are known to install shielding where there are sources of radio frequencies. They have noticed that grounding these electromagnetic shields sometimes makes their symptoms worse and they will disconnect the ground for improved health. The shield becomes a transmitter of radio frequencies when connected to dirty electrical grounding systems. It is also well documented in the field of antenna systems that grounding antennas increases the radio frequency content and energy on them.

Electromagnetic shielding fabric is sold and many people with electromagnetic hypersensitivity use it. It tends to have conductive threads woven into it. Some people have noticed that when it is in contact with their skin, it can make them sicker. If they have the shielding fabric with an air gap between it and their skin, then they get the benefits of reduced radio frequency exposure. It appears that these shielding fabrics can act as antenna systems and couple the radio frequencies on them into the human when they are in contact with it.

Installing shielding onto a single wall can create an electromagnetic reflector. Electromagnetic waves that hit it at the correct angle may cause what is known as an interference pattern to occur near to it. Interference causes zones of much higher levels of radiation to occur. Many people are reporting that they install shielding and it makes them sick. It is likely that a radio frequency interference pattern is set up in the shielded room.

There is a difference between the shielding materials in general use for radio frequency protection and they are listed in the order of my recommendation:

1. Radio frequency (RF) absorbing paint: This is the most expensive shielding material and is the preference to use due to it absorbing the radio frequency signal rather than reflecting it. However, it is very difficult to remove later.

2. Aluminum foil: This has the best radio frequency signal blocking properties but is reflective to them and may create interference patterns.

3. Aluminum window screening mesh: This is effective at blocking most radio frequency signals, but will let through some very high frequencies. It is reflective to radio frequencies and may create interference patterns.

4. Space blankets (Mylar film): The quality of space blankets varies and it tends to be the worst performing electromagnetic shield. It is available in large sheets and many people have used it successfully to reduce radio frequency levels. It is reflective to radio frequencies and may create interference patterns.

It is preferable to have shields that have a distorted surface to them. This is so that they will reflect the radio frequency signal from them as a scattered signal. This will reduce the chances of setting up high powered interference patterns near to them. If using space blankets or aluminum foil, simply crumple it up before installing it. Loosely install it so that the surface stays distorted.

Regarding mesh shields, these typically perform better the smaller the holes are within the mesh. Mesh shields are regarded as needing the holes to be smaller than 1/10 of a wavelength of the highest frequency that you are shielding from.

When connecting your electromagnetic shield to ground, then you should make your ground cable to be exactly a multiple of half the wavelength that you are trying to shield against. Cable impedance to high frequencies is high at quarter wavelengths and low at half wavelengths. It is desirable to have low impedance grounding with shielding.

Some people who have electromagnetic hypersensitivity sleep inside of conductive bed canopies that look similar to mosquito nets. The bed canopy shielding has mixed reports and it works for some and not for others. The technique may be modified by the insertion of an appropriate voltage battery and resistor between the non-electrified ground rod and the bed canopy. The resistor should be sized to keep the current limited to one milliamp for safety. For a 1.5 volt battery, you would use a 1,500 ohm resistor in series with it. So the bed canopy would have a low level DC voltage on it relative to the ground below.

You need to be careful with creating Faraday cages and electromagnetic shielding for human health purposes. You may create electromagnetic deficiencies in the human that are similar to what is observed in the astronauts on the International Space Station. If you choose to use electromagnetic shielding techniques, you should be monitoring your long term health and discontinue the techniques if health issues start to show up.

People are inadvertently living in excessively electromagnetically shielded homes and this may occur from the use of radiant foil barriers, the use of insulation that has electromagnetic shielding properties, metal roofs, metal siding, windows that have electromagnetic shielding properties, and so on.

"The Hum" is a steady droning sound that can only be heard by a small group of people and they report headaches, nausea, dizziness, nosebleeds and sleep disturbances. These match closely to the conditions reported for electromagnetic hypersensitivity. Someone contacted me about "The Hum" and they said it started when they installed aluminum foil radiant barrier attic insulation in their home and it cleared up when they moved home. They essentially had a lot of ungrounded aluminum foil in their attic in close proximity to their electrical cables for the lighting circuits! They had created a very unnatural electromagnetic radiation environment which they appeared to be reacting to.

Electromagnetic shielding is a tricky subject and you should not be engaging in the practice unless you understand the biological consequences. You should be using an RF meter to enable you to confirm effective shielding from a known biologically harmful source. The only area of my home that has shielding in it is the garage where the transmitting utility meters are located.

"Every great advance in science has issued from a new audacity of imagination."

John Dewey

RWS & EHS

Radio Wave Sickness (RWS) and Electromagnetic Hypersensitivity (EHS) are rapidly accelerating plagues in modern society. Sweden appears to be the only country that currently recognizes the conditions. In Sweden approximately 300,000 people are registered as having EHS. Sweden has a population of 9,555,893 as reported in the 2012 census. This equates to 3.12 percent of the population, or 1 in 32 people, that is aware that it is being affected by unnatural radiation exposures which include electrical, electronic and wireless systems. Elizabeth Kelley, electromagneticsafety.org, reports that:

Since the early 1990s, health practitioners world-wide have seen a rapid increase in the number of people who report a cluster of neurological symptoms that is called electromagnetic hypersensitivity. EHS symptoms commonly include headache, sleep problems, poor memory and concentration, depression, anxiety, changes in heart rate and, skin burning sensations. These symptoms are being reported mainly by people who live in the developed world where there has been rapid human adaptation to wireless digital technologies over the past two decades.

In 2005, the World Health Organization published Fact Sheet No 296 entitled Electromagnetic Hypersensitivity: "Well controlled and conducted double-blind studies have shown that symptoms were not correlated with EMF exposure... The symptoms are certainly real and can vary widely in their severity... Further, EHS is not a medical diagnosis, nor is it clear that it represents a single medical problem."

Dr. Olle Johannsson, a Swedish neuroscientist, reports that in Sweden electrohypersensitivity (EHS) is an officially fully recognized functional impairment and those who have this condition are eligible for government services and accommodations. Recent studies show that over 5% of Swedish men and women report a variety of symptoms when exposed to electromagnetic field (EMF) sources.

Dr. Magda Havas, a professor of environmental science at Trent University in Ontario Canada, states that EHS studies with negative results can have major biases. "The researchers assumed that reactions to EMFs are immediate, while there is often a delay between exposure and response. People are not switches that can be turned on and off. These studies incorrectly insinuate that, if you can't feel anything, it can't harm you. We know very well that we can't detect the taste of arsenic, lead, DDT nor asbestos, but they are all toxic."

European medical doctors are estimating that, by 2017, 50% of the world's population will be affected by mild to severe EHS symptoms.

The problem with RWS and EHS in the USA is that it is commonly misdiagnosed as another condition. The USA has become addicted to wireless communications technologies and electrical and electronic products, so the rates are likely comparable to Sweden. The recent adoption of Smart/AMR/AMI radiation transmitting utility meters in many USA cities has probably significantly increased the number of people who have RWS and EHS, but are currently incorrectly diagnosed.

This is unfortunate, as it is well known today that RWS and EHS is easily preventable. All you have to do is remove the sources of man-made electromagnetic interference. I find it very concerning that the USA government simply ignores people who are trying to restore their environment back to natural radiation levels in an effort to clear up their RWS and EHS symptoms. It appears to be rare for the Federal Communications Commission (FCC) to enforce rule 15 that relates to harmful electromagnetic interference. Indeed, I recently put rule 15 to the test and notified the FCC that the gas company was causing biologically harmful interference at my home. They simply ignored my request for them to notify the gas company to remove their biologically harmful transmitting meters from the area around my home.

The FCC have established one of the most lax electromagnetic radiation standards in the world. At 61 volts per meter (V/m) for 1800 MHz public exposure, the

permissible radiation emissions are higher than most other countries in the world. For contrast, 0.06 V/m is the recommendation in Salzburg, Austria, which makes the USA standard 1017 times higher! The reason for this ridiculously high standard in the USA is obvious when you look at the military. The most technologically advanced military in the world has been developing wireless warfare for decades. If the FCC was to lower the standards, then they would effectively render some parts of the military arsenal as obsolete.

This same military force who became aware of what RWS and EHS was during the development of RADAR in the 1930's and 1940's appears to have been denying the condition exists from the 1950's onwards! Instead, the opposite happened and electrical, electronic and wireless products were heavily marketed to the masses, while the military who were supposed to protect them from biological harm simply stayed silent.

When you look into how electrical, electronic and wireless products are approved for sale in the USA, you find that no laboratory animals are used to assess their safety. Instead, electronic meters make measurements and something that resembles Jello is used to assess if the devices can heat it. If the meter readings are within specification and the Jello is not substantially heated, then the product is approved for sale.

The reality is that if these devices were tested on animals and plants, then many of them would fail the tests! As Dr. John Nash Ott discovered in his research that he conducted from the 1950's to the 1980's, many electrical and electronic products change the behaviors of animals and can make them sick, and some of them go on to die premature deaths. He also found that if you subjected an animal to biologically harmful electromagnetic radiation and made it sick, that you could return it to a healthy state simply by removing the harmful exposures. This is exactly what people are reporting who have RWS and EHS!

Dr. John Nash Ott performed many plant experiments with electromagnetic radiation and he found that plants would react to many common electrical and electronic products.

Growth deformities were observed in many of his experiments. I have been able to reproduce much of his work regarding plants and I can tell you that his findings are easily repeatable.

Many government agencies are aware of not only Dr. John Nash Ott's work, but also of the work done by many other researchers. Indeed, I have mailed many dozens of copies of my books to government agencies. It is rare to get a response and when I do get one, it is typically an acknowledgment that they received the book. It is a similar story at the universities.

People are now reporting curing Autism by electromagnetically shielding the child's bedroom. This is consistent with Autism being an electromagnetic disease and may indeed be easily preventable. The Autism rates have been closely following the rise in cell phone towers and cell phones in the USA over the past decade. Transmitting Smart/AMR/AMI utility meters should be expected to increase the Autism rates, as they create a high powered antenna park at the home that is constantly transmitting pulsed radiation for approximately one mile in residential areas. Pulsed radiation is the most biologically harmful form of radiation transmission.

Electromagnetic shielding is a common response to the problem of electromagnetic radiation. You need to be very careful with shielding, as you can make the problem worse. I have been growing plants in Faraday cages and I have seen extensive growth problems occurring. Some people are inadvertently living in electromagnetically shielded homes and this may occur through the use of metal roofs, metal siding, foil radiant barriers, and insulation and windows that have electromagnetic shielding properties. Long term sickness may occur when living in such a home that may be accompanied by childhood development problems. You should not electromagnetically shield homes and workplaces as you may create radiation deficiency conditions in the inhabitants.

It is one of the dilemmas with RWS and EHS, to get sick from living in an unnaturally high radiation environment, or to get sick from an electromagnetically screened radiation deficient environment. Either way, many humans will eventually get sick! Even pregnant mothers are electromagnetically shielding their unborn babies with a product called "Belly Armor". This action may eventually make them sick from radiation deficiency problems, similar to what astronauts show that live on the International Space Station for many months. The only known effective solution to RWS and EHS is to return your radiation environment back to natural levels.

The human environment is no longer natural and this increasing of the radiation environment should be expected to rapidly accelerate human evolution into an electromagnetically hardened animal. Unfortunately, many humans will die after many years of easily preventable illness and disease during this period that we are currently in.

The precursor to disease are strange health conditions showing up. Radio Wave Sickness is well categorized today and the top reported radio wave sickness symptoms in order of frequency are:

1. *Fatigue.*
2. *Sleep disturbance.*
3. *Headaches.*
4. *Feeling of discomfort.*
5. *Difficulty in concentrating.*
6. *Depression.*
7. *Memory loss.*
8. *Visual disruptions.*
9. *Irritability.*
10. *Hearing disruptions.*
11. *Skin problems.*
12. *Cardiovascular.*
13. *Dizziness.*
14. *Loss of appetite.*

15. Movement difficulties

16. Nausea.

Source: Symptoms experiences by people in the vicinity of cellular phone base station, Santini 2001, La Presse Medical.

Indeed, it is well known today that the sickness rates increase within a quarter mile of a cell phone tower. The closer you are to it, the more likely it is for you to be sick. The utilities installing Smart/AMR/AMI meters at your home and in your neighborhood is comparable to turning your home into an antenna park.

When looking back in history we can find documented illnesses that are comparable to RWS and EHS:

- 1829 - Neurasthenia (Also called Americanitis or Nervosism): As a psychopathological term, neurasthenia was used by George Miller Beard in 1869 to denote a condition with symptoms of fatigue, anxiety, headache, neuralgia and depressed mood. This condition showed up in the population during the construction of the railroads and the telegraph that shorted out the semiconductor properties of the natural ground and created man-made electromagnetic interference. It was associated with upper class people and with professionals working in sedentary occupations.

- Mid 1800's - Female Hysteria: Women considered to be suffering from it exhibited a wide array of symptoms including faintness, nervousness, sexual desire, insomnia, fluid retention, heaviness in abdomen, muscle spasm, shortness of breath, irritability, loss of appetite for food or sex, and "a tendency to cause trouble". The women at the time were wearing steel hoop skirts and steel crinolines that would have been acting as antenna systems and electromagnetic shields to electromagetic energy.

- Early 1900's - Shenjing Shuairuo: Chinese equivalent of Neurasthenia. The condition is associated with a

275

collection of symptoms including amnesia, dizziness, fatigue, gastrointestinal disorders, headaches, pain in joints and muscles, poor concentration and sexual dysfunction. This appears to match with the adoption of electricity into the cities.

Full Size Female Hysteria Metal Skirt Experiment

The Palo Verde tree is wearing a steel hoop skirt to see if it will show abnormal growth patterns. The rings are currently insulated from each other and will be connected together the following year with steel wire to turn it into a crinoline.

If you are currently experiencing the symptoms of RWS and EHS, I would recommend that you work on changing the electrical characteristics of your body. Changing the electrical characteristics of the human body can help to alleviate the symptoms of RWS and EHS. There are several proven ways to do this:

- Change your fluid intake.

- Change your diet.

- Exercise.

- Sweat.

- Go into a hot or cold environment.

- Build up muscle mass in every part of the body.

- Reduce or increase your weight.

- Submerge the body in water, such as a bath or swimming pool.

- Have no metal near to nor in contact with the body.

- Have no electrical nor electronic products near to nor in contact with the body.

- Do not wear a battery powered watch.

- Wear clothes made out of natural materials.

- Make sure that you are not wearing shoes that create static.

- Wear conductive shoes or walk barefoot in areas that have no stray voltage problems.

- Sleep on the ground on a thin insulated mat to couple into it through capacitance. Make sure that there are no electrical cables in the ground.

- Sleep directly in contact with the ground in areas that do not have stray voltage/current/frequency problems.

- **Remove metal from the body, such as dental fillings, dental implants and dental bridges.**

Regarding removing implants from the body, you should regard this as a last resort. There are many steps that you can take that may alleviate your symptoms and they are far easier than having implants removed. While metal implants are known for their ability to induce RWS and EHS into the human, you may be able to clear up the conditions without having to remove these. Of course, if you do not have metal implants, then you should ensure that you do not get them in the future.

You should also pay attention to your pets. Looks for signs of RWS and EHS in them, as they can be an early warning sign that your environmental conditions are unnatural. I remember my grandfathers male dog always being sexually excited and aggressive. It would occasionally go crazy and run at full speed around the home for no reason. I suspect that he was walking the dog in areas that had stray voltage, stray currents and stray frequencies in them. My grandfather went on to die of Dementia which is associated with stray voltage, stray current and stray frequency exposure. He was probably being exposed to the same energies as the dog through the conductive dog leash and his leather soled shoes.

I have every expectation that in time, Dr. John Nash Ott will be recognized as the man who could have prevented the Autism epidemic and many other conditions as well! Dr. John Nash Ott was working in areas of "Inconvenient Truths" and the people who he was trying to inform about his valuable work simply ignored him, as it would have greatly affected their business model to acknowledge his work. Simply profits before people.

The modern human is derelict in its duty to the next generation who cannot protect themselves from harm. This madness must be stopped. The modern human is displaying an apathy in the above areas that is leading to great levels of easily preventable sickness occurring in the current adult generations and retardation appearing in large numbers in the next generation. Indeed, experts in the field of Autism are indicating that at the currently accelerating levels, in fifteen years every USA child will have an Autism diagnosis!

"Radio Wave Sickness and Electromagnetic Hypersensitivity are easily preventable and one can only wonder how much longer the insanity of modern governments is going to be allowed to continue in this area."

Steven Magee

Summary

I find it unfortunate that I have worked with a number of professional electrical engineers in the USA that I can only describe their conduct as extremely unprofessional and blatantly illegal. Working with them alerted me to wonder what exactly it was that they were trying to hide.

When you see a large number of utility workers disregarding the laws of the USA and demonstrating a willful lack of caring for the health and safety of the people that they are responsible for, you do start to wonder why they do this? The development of this book revealed what they were up to.

The adoption of electricity led to the regular unnatural exposure of electromagnetic interference in the human mind and body. This corresponded to an increase in illness, disease, cancer, and mental health issues. New illnesses and diseases were born with the progression of electricity.

The reason why I was able to write this book is because I have inadvertently taken the human mind and body through almost the entire range of electromagnetic exposures that are possible without dying or becoming diseased. There are no doubts that dirty electricity has toxic effects on both the human mind and body. The most toxic exposures that I have had are from transmitter systems, stray voltage/current/frequency and electromagnetic fields.

This is consistent with health problems that were documented in Nikola Tesla. Nikola Tesla had many health problems during his life and he appeared to die of dementia. He had occurrences of amnesia and numerous mental breakdowns during his life. He was known for his phobias and his love of pigeons. However, no love interest was ever documented in his life. The book "Tesla: Man Out of Time" by Margaret Cheney extensively discusses his health problems and is an interesting read.

Sick kids? You should take a good look at their electromagnetic environment. It is likely that it is having a significant affect on their health. Children who are inadvertently sitting in fields of unnatural electromagnetic interference may not develop correctly. The same is true for children who do not get the correct daily outdoor exposure to sunlight in a green environment.

Insomnia? Take a look at your lighting products. Avoid the energy star lighting products and use filament light bulbs instead. Keep nighttime lighting low and just sufficient for the application. Reduce your television and computer time. Make sure that you are not inadvertently sitting in electromagnetic fields. Wireless transmitter systems can cause insomnia and you should turn them off.

Fatigue? Your home and office wiring may be radiating radio waves, magnetic fields, and electric fields into your environment. Simply switch off your electrical circuits to reduce your exposure to these. Avoid living and working near to transmitter systems and go back to wired products instead of cordless. Wear slippers inside your home to prevent contact with electrically conductive flooring. Wear insulated shoes when outside of the home to prevent contact with stray voltage/current/frequency.

Random aches and pains? You may need to hibernate for 40 days and nights to detoxify from the radiation sources that you have been exposed to over the years. Avoid sitting near to electrical cables and limit your time on laptop computers and cellphones. Avoid sitting next to windows that have a direct view of the Sun.

Low vitamin D and B12? You will need to increase your daily outdoor sunlight exposure in a green natural environment. Remember not to wear glasses nor sunglasses, no contact lenses, no sunscreen, no lipstick and no make-up. It is a good idea to go for a daily walk in a park or the countryside in order to obtain this exposure.

Sexual addiction? Certain types of electromagnetic field exposures trigger the human mating cycle. You should turn off your electrical and electronic products and install filament light bulbs to see if it clears up. If it does, you will know that one of your products is triggering it. It may be your electrical system at work, so take a camping vacation in the forest in the National Park and see if it clears up. If it does, you will know that it is environmental. You may be walking or driving past power poles that have high electromagnetic interference emissions, so change your route. It may also be coming from the transportation systems that you use.

Irregular heartbeats? You may be in electromagnetic fields that are interfering with the electrical system of the heart. Reduce your electromagnetic radiation exposure and avoid walking near power lines. Stray voltage/current/frequency exposure and radio frequency fields can cause arrhythmia and you should avoid them. Sonic booms and infra-sound are known to interfere with the heart and you should avoid these exposures.

Mental health issues, relationship problems or anxiety? The human mind is constantly adapting to the environmental conditions that it is placed into. When in an unnatural environment, then the thinking will also be unnatural. Unnatural thoughts and behaviors will take over and they will seem normal to you. Ensure your environmental conditions are correct for clear thinking.

Aggression or headaches? Over exposure to electromagnetic radiation causes this. Simply reduce your exposure to fix it.

Eye problems? Artificial lighting sources can cause this. Sit facing shady windows with natural views to prevent it. Radio frequency exposures can cause cataracts and you should examine if your environment is inadvertently exposing you to transmitting systems.

Hot skin, facial pains or blotchy skin? Electromagnetic fields cause a reaction in the skin that can make it exhibit a hot sensation and pins and needles pains. Remove yourself from the electromagnetic fields. Cell phones are known to cause the blotchy skin effect where they are kept against the body. Carry your cell phone in a bag away from the body. Man-made ultraviolet light emissions from lighting products are known to cause skin problems and they may be reduced or eliminated by changing to a different lighting product.

Hearing things? You may have electromagnetic hearing that is documented as a high pitched noise or a low frequency hum. Change your electromagnetic environment.

The modern electrical system presents a high risk of toxic exposures to the human. Some electrical systems are relatively clean, while others present the health risks of high levels of electromagnetic interference exposure. Many products have been made that are unintentional radio and microwave transmitters. Some electrical products test fine when new, but may degrade with age into toxic products.

Electrical wiring and products in the home and office should be minimal. You should consider only having it in the areas that need it, such as the kitchen, bathroom and an entertainment room. Limit wiring in other areas to lighting and one socket in each room. Each room should be on its own circuit breaker and the fuse board should have a filter installed into it. The wiring should not be run close to where people are sleeping.

We appear to be witnessing the development of the next generation of nature. It is the electromagnetically hardened version. The humans that survive this era of rapid genetic change across all species will most likely go on to found the future generation of humans.

Unfortunately, we will witness extensive development problems, sickness, disease, and premature death in the humans that are not destined for this future. That is where we are today and it is comparable to ethnic cleansing of the global population. Personally, I find this situation unacceptable because it is clearly avoidable.

I have every expectation that in the future, electricity will be regarded in the same way that asbestos and smoking are viewed today. The electrification of the ground that we walk on can only be described as the actions of an insane race of people. Stray voltage/current/frequency effects, biological field coupling, toxic electric lighting products, willingly electrifying the environment with radio and microwaves, and developing radioactive energy sources will be documented by future historians as the peak of human insanity.

Energy fields define who we are as humans. If you are in environments that are creating positive energy, then you will have excellent mental and physical health. If you are in environments where the energy levels are negative, then you will fall into poor mental and physical health. Unfortunately, modern society has created far more negative energy fields and finding good mental and physical health is becoming increasingly difficult.

The majority of human illness and disease appears to have its root cause in:

- Unnatural radiation exposures.

- Nutritionally deficient foods.

- Drinking mineral deficient water.

- Toxic exposures from medications and supplements.

- Toxic air exposures.

Feng Shui is the study of positive energy in the human environment. It literally means wind and water. The people who developed Feng Shui understood that human emotions and health were governed by their environments. If you are feeling ill or having emotional issues, you should apply the science of Feng Shui to your environment as it will probably help a lot. You cannot go wrong by having an environment that has the science of Feng Shui applied to it.

I feel that John Lennon's quote is appropriate for what I found when I researched this book:

Our society is run by insane people for insane objectives. I think we're being run by maniacs for maniacal ends and I think I'm liable to be put away as insane for expressing that. That's what's insane about it.

John Lennon

One has to wonder if the time has come to implement the Declaration of Independence to put a stop to the fraudulent corporate and government behaviors that are stealing the future from the children?

Life, Liberty and the pursuit of Happiness.--That to secure these rights, Governments are instituted among Men, deriving their just powers from the consent of the governed, --That whenever any Form of Government becomes destructive of these ends, it is the Right of the People to alter or to abolish it, and to institute new Government, laying its foundation on such principles and organizing its powers in such form, as to them shall seem most likely to effect their Safety and Happiness.

USA Declaration of Independence

For more information on light, I can recommend the book "Toxic Light". Human health is an extensive field and we have only covered one small aspect of it here. As such, I can recommend the book "Toxic Health" to people who want to understand the many aspects that go into being healthy.

I hope that you enjoyed the book and I wish you the very best of health.

"Wisdom and money can get you almost anything, but only wisdom can save your life."

Ecclesiastes 7:12

References

- AARP: http://www.aarp.org/
- Amateur Radio Wiki: http://www.amateur-radio-wiki.net/
- Ansel Adams
- AntennaSearch.com: http://www.antennasearch.com/
- Arizona Daily Star: http://azstarnet.com/
- BBC News: http://www.bbc.co.uk/news/
- Berenson-Allen Center for Noninvasive Brain Stimulation: http://tmslab.org/
- Breastcancer.org: http://www.breastcancer.org/
- Camilla Rees, MBA
- "Challenging the Chip: Labor Rights and Environmental Justice in the Global Electronics Industry." book by Ted Smith, David A. Sonnenfeld, David Naguib Pellow, and Jim Hightower.
- "Color and Light: Their Effects on Plants, Animals and People." book by Dr. John Nash Ott
- "Cross Currents: The Perils of Electropollution" book by Dr. Robert O. Becker.
- Debbie Rubin: http://microwavechasm.org/
- Dick Cavett
- "Dirty Electricity: Electrification and the Diseases of Civilization." book by Samuel Milham MD MPH
- "Do Trees Strengthen Urban Communities, Reduce Domestic Violence?" paper by By W. C. Sullivan, Ph.D. & Frances E. Kuo, Ph.D.: http://lhhl.illinois.edu/

- Dr. Dan Batcheldor
- Dr. David Carpenter
- Dr. George Crile
- Dr. Lennart Hardell
- Dr. Jacqueline McGlade
- Dr. Jim Burch: http://cpcp.sph.sc.edu/fs/burch.htm
- Dr. John Nash Ott: http://www.biolightgroup.com/Ott.html
- Dr. Magda Havas: http://www.magdahavas.com/
- Dr. Philip Stoddard: http://www2.fiu.edu/~stoddard/
- Dr. William B. Kouwenhoven
- Dr. William Rae: http://www.ecopolitan.com/dr-william-rae
- "Earthing: The Most Important Health Discovery Ever?" book by Clinton Ober, Stephen T. Sinatra MD, and Martin Zucker.
- "Electrocution of America: Is Your Utility Company Out to Kill You?" book by Russ Allen
- "Electromagnetic Fields: A Consumer's Guide to the Issue and How to Protect Ourselves" book by B. Blake Levitt.
- Elizabeth Kelly: http://electromagneticsafety.org/
- EMFields: http://www.emfields.org/
- EMFnews.org: http://www.emfnews.org/
- "Exploring the Spectrum: The Effects of Natural and Artificial Light on Living Organisms." film by Dr. John Nash Ott.
- "Gasland" and "Gasland Part 2" films by Josh Fox. http://www.gaslandthemovie.com/
- George Carin

- Google Maps: http://maps.google.com
- "Health and Light: The Extraordinary Study That Shows How Light Affects Your Health and Emotional Well Being." book by Dr. John Nash Ott.
- Henry Barton
- Henry Ford
- Hertel
- International Agency for Research on Cancer (IARC): http://www.iarc.fr/
- Isaac Asimov
- John Cameron
- Leon Byerley: http://www.strikingimages.com/
- "Light, Radiation, and You: How to Stay Healthy." book by Dr. John Nash Ott.
- LIVESTRONG.COM: http://www.livestrong.com/
- Los Angeles Times: http://www.latimes.com/
- "Motorcycle Cancer" book by Randall Dale Chipkar.
- MSNBC: msnbc.com
- "My Ivory Cellar; [the story of time-lapse photography]." book by Dr. John Nash Ott.
- NASA: http://www.nasa.gov/
- Nation of Change: http://www.nationofchange.org/
- Nikola Tesla
- NPR: http://www.npr.org/
- Ornette Coleman
- Popular Science: http://www.popsci.com/science/article/2010-02/disconnected

- Ralph Waldo Emerson
- Robert L. Park
- Scientific American: http://www.scientificamerican.com/
- Shane Gregory: http://smartmeterhealthalert.org/
- Spark Burmaster: http://www.environmental-options.info/
- "Sparking a Worldwide Energy Revolution: Social Struggles in the Transition to a Post-Petrol World" book by Kolya Abramsky
- Stetzer Electric: http://www.stetzerelectric.com/
- Suzanne Woelk
- The Stranger: http://www.thestranger.com/
- UNC Terrorism Research: http://www.unc.edu/spotlight/terrorism_research
- University of Arizona.
- Voltree Power (www.voltreepower.com)
- Wikipedia: http://www.wikipedia.org/
- World Research Foundation: http://www.wrf.org/
- Yahoo News: http://www.yahoo.com/

"None of us is as smart as all of us."
Eric Schmidt.

Useful Links

When researching electromagnetic radiation, I find the following sources to be very useful in developing the information:

The Center for Electrosmog Prevention has excellent information on wireless radiation health effects:

http://www.electrosmogprevention.org/

Two web sites that contain a collection of useful information about dirty electricity:

http://dirtyelectricity.ca/

http://www.dirtyelectricity.org/

Dr. Nina Pierpont is developing the health effects of wind turbines and infrasound:

http://www.windturbinesyndrome.com/

Dr. Magda Havas has a comprehensive EMI web site at:

http://www.magdahavas.com/

Dr. Samuel Milham authored "Dirty Electricity" and has a list of research papers at:

http://www.sammilham.com/

Elizabeth Kelly, Director of the Electromagnetic Safety Alliance, is tracking electromagnetic interference developments in Arizona, USA:

http://electromagneticsafety.org/

EMFacts Consultancy, founded in 1994 by Don Maisch, has produced a wide range of reports and papers dealing with various health issues related to human exposure to electromagnetic radiation.

http://www.emfacts.com/

EMFs.Info has a good listing of research papers on it:
http://www.emfs.info/

EMF News has a good listing of articles:
http://www.emfnews.org/

The Environmental Health Center-Dallas, Texas medically tests and treats human health problems including sensitivities to pollens, molds, dust, foods, chemicals, air (indoor/outdoor), water, electromagnetic sensitivity (EMF), and many more health problems as they relate to our environment.

http://www.ehcd.com/

FEB - The Swedish Association for the ElectroHyperSensitive:

http://www.feb.se/index_int.htm

Less EMF are a leading supplier in the USA of electromagnetic radiation products:

http://www.lessemf.com/

Lloyd Burrell, Author of "Beating Electrical Sensitivity – The Path to Tread", has an excellent website on electromagnetic radiation exposures:

http://www.electricsense.com/

Mast-Victims.org - A international community website for people suffering adverse health effects from mobile phone masts in the vicinity of their homes

http://www.mast-victims.org/

Powerwatch is a small non-profit independent organisation with a central role in the UK Electromagnetic Field and Microwave Radiation health debate:

http://www.powerwatch.org.uk/

Radiation Answers has numerous sources of radiation information:

http://www.radiationanswers.org/

These websites are tracking problems with radio frequency identification (RFID) systems that are now in common use:

http://chipfreeschools.com/

http://rfidinschools.com/

Safe in School is documenting electromagnetic hypersensitivity in children:

http://www.safeinschool.org/

Stetzer Electric have a list of research papers at:

http://www.stetzerelectric.com/

Many websites are documenting the rise in people who are reporting sickness around transmitting Smart/AMR/AMI utility meters and some of these are:

http://eon3emfblog.net/

http://marylandsmartmeterawareness.org/

http://michiganstopsmartmeters.com/

http://microwavechasm.org/

http://www.napervillesmartmeterawareness.org/

http://www.smartmeterdangers.org/

http://smartmeterhealthalert.org/

http://stopsmartmeters.com.au/

http://stopsmartmeters.org/

http://www.weepinitiative.org/

The World Health Organization (WHO) have an interesting EMF web site at:

http://www.who.int/peh-emf/en/

"The Internet is becoming the town square for the global village of tomorrow."

Bill Gates

Acknowledgments

This book was influenced by:

- Claudia Sandoval M.S.W. for her wisdom on how trees and nature interact with human social behaviors.

- My neighbors for their understanding and assistance with my biological experiments.

- Dr. John Nash Ott for his extensive research into health, light, and radiation. His lasting legacy of publications was a wonderful gift to the next generation:

  - My Ivory Cellar; [the story of time-lapse photography].

  - Health and Light: The Extraordinary Study That Shows How Light Affects Your Health and Emotional Well Being.

  - Light, Radiation, and You: How to Stay Healthy.

  - Color and Light: Their Effects on Plants, Animals and People.

  - Exploring the Spectrum: The Effects of Natural and Artificial Light on Living Organisms.

- The numerous people and companies who are referenced in this book that have worked diligently to bring the important science of environmental health to the masses.

"Help others achieve their dreams and you will achieve yours."
Les Brown

About the Author

Steven started his career at one of the largest university research and teaching hospitals in Europe. Working in the electrical engineering group, he obtained a Bachelors with Honors in Electrical and Electronic Engineering. Human health was a strong draw and he moved into the biomedical team, serving the regions hospitals. During this time he developed a fascination for human illness and disease and the causes of it, many of which were not understood.

He joined the Isaac Newton Group of Telescopes in 1999 and went to live in La Palma. La Palma is part of the Canary Islands, governed by Spain. During this time he worked with the leading European astronomers and developed his astronomical and optics skills. He became fluent in Spanish and their culture.

In 2001 he became a Chartered Electrical Engineer and joined the W. M. Keck Observatory in Hawaii. This was the world's leading astronomical facility and home to the world's two largest segmented mirror telescopes. Steven developed segmented optics and interferometry skills while working alongside world leading astronomers. During this time Steven constructed his own off-grid solar and wind powered home in the last of the traditional Hawaiian fishing villages in Miloli'i, Hawaii. He learned Hawaiian Pidgin English and the Hawaiian culture during his time there.

In 2006, Steven became the Director of the MDM Observatory in Sells, Arizona, USA. Working for Columbia University and later, Dartmouth College, he developed the facility to modern standards. He learned an appreciation of the native Americans and their culture from the Tohono O'odham Nation.

In 2008, Steven joined the solar power revolution that was sweeping the USA and commissioned the largest CIGS thin film solar photovoltaic installation in the world.

A year later he commissioned the largest solar photovoltaic power plant in the USA. The system rated power was quoted as 25MW AC with over 90,500 solar modules that were mounted to 158 single-axis tracker systems in three hundred acres of land.

He went on to develop the solar photovoltaic team for a large international company.

In 2010 he started to research radiation and publish the leading books on the subject.

"All truths are easy to understand once they are discovered; the point is to discover them."

Galileo Galilei

Author Contact

I hope that you found the book informative and please let me know about any questions or comments about the book. I can be contacted through the StevenMageeBooks channel on www.youtube.com.

I am a consultant in the areas that I research and please feel free to contact me for any help or assistance.

You may find my other books useful:

Solar Photovoltaic

- **Complete Solar Photovoltaics for Residential, Commercial, and Utility Systems:** Steven Magee has combined his three top selling books on solar power systems into one edition. Complete Solar Photovoltaics will train you on solar photovoltaics and show you how to design grid connected solar photovoltaic power systems. Operations and maintenance is detailed to enable you to have a complete understanding of solar photovoltaics from start to finish.

- **Solar Photovoltaics for Consumers, Utilities, and Investors:** This book details solar photovoltaic systems for consumers, utilities and investors. This would encompass residential, commercial and utility systems that are connected to the utility grid. There is a discussion of the different technologies available for the consumer and their advantages and disadvantages. For the utilities, there is invaluable advice on planning and constructing large projects. For the investor, forward looking statements try to predict the future of solar photovoltaics.

- **Solar Photovoltaic Training for Residential, Commercial, and Utility Systems:** This book details solar photovoltaic training for those who are interested in this area and also for those who are already working in the field. This would encompass residential, commercial, and utility systems that are connected to the utility grid. It is a comprehensive overview of a rapidly growing world of solar photovoltaic power generation technology.

- **Solar Photovoltaic Design for Residential, Commercial, and Utility Systems:** This book details how to design reliable solar photovoltaic power generation systems from a residential system, progressing to a commercial system, and finishing at the largest utility power generation systems. By following the guidelines in this book and your local solar photovoltaic electrical codes, you will be able to design trouble free solar power systems that give many years of reliable operation. When designed well, solar photovoltaic power generation is an excellent source of electrical power that results in much lower electricity bills, the power company will even refund you for the excess energy generated by your system if it is large enough. Building a grid tied solar power system is a relatively easy task. Given the large amount of government and electrical utility financial incentives that are available, it is a great time to join in the solar power revolution that is taking place in the world today.

- **Solar Photovoltaic Operation and Maintenance for Residential, Commercial, and Utility Systems:** This book details how to operate and maintain residential, commercial, and utility solar photovoltaic systems that are connected to the utility grid. By following the guidelines in this book you will be able to operate and maintain solar power systems that should give many years of reliable operation. Invaluable trouble shooting advice will aid in returning your system to full operation in the event of a problem.

- **Solar Photovoltaic DC Calculations for Residential, Commercial, and Utility Systems:** This book details how to run calculations for the DC circuit of solar photovoltaic systems. This would encompass residential, commercial, and utility systems that are connected to the utility grid. It covers the range of conditions that solar photovoltaic modules are exposed to throughout the year and shows how to incorporate these into an effective DC circuit that is well designed and reliable.

- **Solar Photovoltaic Resource for Residential, Commercial, and Utility Systems:** This book is a resource of information that is used in the solar photovoltaic field. This would encompass residential, commercial, and utility systems that are connected to the utility grid. It is a comprehensive collection of notes, diagrams, pictures and charts for a rapidly growing world of solar photovoltaic power generation technology. This book is illustrated in color.

Solar

- **Solar Irradiance and Insolation for Power Systems:** This book is a resource of information that is used in the solar power generation field. This would encompass residential, commercial, and utility systems that are connected to the utility grid. It is a comprehensive collection of notes, diagrams, pictures, and charts for a rapidly growing world of solar photovoltaic power generation technology. This book is illustrated in color.

- **Solar Site Selection for Power Systems:** This book is a comprehensive collection of images, diagrams, and notes that document the effects of light and heat in the solar power generation field. This would encompass residential, commercial, and utility systems that are connected to the utility grid. This is essential information for a rapidly growing world of solar power generation technology. This book is illustrated in color.

Architecture

- **Solar Reflections for Architects, Engineers, and Human Health:** This book is a comprehensive collection of images, diagrams, and notes that document the effects of sunlight in architecture. This is essential information for architects, engineers, and the medical profession. The discovery of the "Multiple-Sun" effect in architecture is detailed and this book is illustrated in color.

Human Health

- **Solar Radiation – A Cause of Illness and Cancer?** Illness and cancers have become part of our modern culture. It has been discovered that extremely high levels of man-made solar radiation exist in modern society. Could this be the one of the causes of illness and cancers? This book examines the increase in solar radiation and applies it to human health.

- **Solar Radiation, Global Warming, and Human Disease:** This book examines the modern development of the Earth and the potential impacts on global warming and human disease. The destruction of the forests for modern agricultural use appears to have effects that are not fully understood and these are explored. Radiation deficiency and radiation overloading are investigated to see if they are factors in many illnesses and diseases.

- **Toxic Light:** Toxic Light takes a look at the light pollution that may be in your local environment and relates it to the health problems that it may cause. Light in the human environment is only just starting to be understood and something as innocent as your sunglasses may be able to make you ill! There are many examples of commonplace items in your environment that may have the ability to affect your health. Get ready for enlightenment about the most important human nutrient of light!

- **Toxic Health:** Toxic Health takes a look at the pollution that may be in your local environment and relates it to the health problems that it can cause.

Pollution in the human environment is only just starting to be understood and something as innocent as light may be able to make you really ill! There are many examples of commonplace items in your environment that may have the ability to affect your health. In particular, we will investigate if modern city life is the most toxic thing of all to the modern human!

- **Toxic Electricity:** Random aches and pains? Fatigue? Headaches? Insomnia? Facial pains? Sore eyes? Irregular heartbeats? Sick kids? Relationship problems? Blotchy skin? Hot skin? Anxiety? Toxic electricity takes a look at the electrical system and asks the question: Is this one of the most toxic endeavors that humanity has ever engaged in?

- **Electrical Forensics:** Electrical Forensics examines the many aspects of electricity, electronics and wireless communications that may lead to unusual behaviors to occur in humans. Electromagnetic interference is well known for its ability to affect mental functioning and human health. Electrical Forensics demonstrates how to identify toxic electromagnetic environments that may be the root cause of accidents and crimes.

Religion

- **Solar Radiation, the Book of Revelations, and the Era of Light – Part 1:** Welcome to the Era of Light! Light has long been known to be essential nourishment for the human body. We will explore the different types of light that are present on Earth and relate it to human health and nature. Light is discussed extensively in the Bible and we will see if we can associate our findings to it. Finally, we will investigate if the Industrial Revolution has created the ultimate toxin of poisonous sunlight!

Professional

- **Engineering Science and Education Journal Volume: 11, Issue: 4, Active Control Systems for Large Segmented Optical Mirrors:** A new generation of optical telescopes is on the drawing board. These will be true giants with primary mirrors having a diameter of up to 100 meters. The technology that will enable this revolution to take place was developed at the W. M. Keck Observatory in Hawaii, where the world's largest segmented mirrors are in daily use. This article looks at how the W. M. Keck Observatory proved the mirror technology that will be behind this new generation of telescopes.

You can search "Steven Magee Books" for the very latest publications.

www.youtube.com videos supporting the ideas in the books can be found by searching: StevenMageeBooks

"Life-transforming ideas have always come to me through books."

Bell Hooks

www.ingramcontent.com/pod-product-compliance
Lightning Source LLC
Chambersburg PA
CBHW051346170526
45166CB00002B/975